PARTIES IN TRANSITION

PARTIES IN TRANSITION
A Longitudinal Study of Party Elites and Party Supporters

Warren E. Miller and M. Kent Jennings

in association with
Barbara G. Farah

RUSSELL SAGE FOUNDATION
New York

The Russell Sage Foundation

The Russell Sage Foundation, one of the oldest of America's general purpose foundations, was established in 1907 by Mrs. Margaret Olivia Sage for "the improvement of social and living conditions in the United States." The Foundation seeks to fulfill this mandate by fostering the development and dissemination of knowledge about the political, social, and economic problems of America. It conducts research in the social sciences and public policy, and publishes books and pamphlets that derive from this research.

The Board of Trustees is responsible for oversight and the general policies of the Foundation, while administrative direction of the program and staff is vested in the President, assisted by the officers and staff. The President bears final responsibility for the decision to publish a manuscript as a Russell Sage Foundation book. In reaching a judgment on the competence, accuracy, and objectivity of each study, the President is advised by the staff and selected expert readers. The conclusions and interpretations in Russell Sage Foundation publications are those of the authors and not of the Foundation, its Trustees, or its Staff. Publication by the Foundation, therefore, does not imply endorsement of the contents of the study.

Library of Congress Cataloging-in-Publication Data

Miller, Warren E. (Warren Edward), 1924–
   Parties in transition.

   Includes index.
   1. Presidents—United States—Elections. 2. Political parties—United States. I. Jennings, M. Kent.
II. Title.
JK528.M526 1986   324.973   86-6771
ISBN 0-87154-602-7

Cover and text design: Huguette Franco

Dedicated to David B. Truman

Contents

PART I
The Structure and Mechanics of Elite Circulation
and Candidate Preference

PART II
Changes Within the Parties

Contents

PART III
Systemic Consequences

APPENDICES

Contents

List of Tables

List of Figures

Preface

This book is a testament to the persistent duality of stability and change in American national politics. For instance, the book rests in substantial part on data collected in 1972, following two years of planning for a study on the evolving role of women in presidential politics. However, Jeane Kirkpatrick's massive contribution to our understanding of American political elites, based entirely on the 1972 study, documented, in passing, the seeming absence of either political or analytic significance attached to the increased number of women engaged in presidential politics in that year. We, in turn, repeatedly note that institutional stability often prevails in the face of reformers' efforts to introduce change. In keeping with a general reading of such persistence in many attributes of the American political process, we conclude this volume with the view that the enduring sequence of struggles for personal leadership, or for the representation of political positions, produces a continuity in political action that promises to overcome all but the most cataclysmic efforts to introduce institutional change.

On the other hand, change lies at the heart of our tale. Alternating victory and defeat in the quest for leadership, turnover in the composition of party elites, and political conversion among individual members of the party elite may combine to create a truly dynamic process of change. Much of the book emphasizes changes within each of the major parties and changes in the relationships between them. The national Democratic and Republican parties are clearly not impervious to change, but perhaps their very ability to adapt to change makes them one of the foundations on which the continuity of American politics rests.

The data on which this book is based come from two major data collections. The first was inspired by a concern with the emerging importance of women as major participants in American national politics. However, given the essentially comparative thrust of any analysis anticipating gender differences, a broad range of data was collected in 1972 depicting, for men and women alike, career patterns, motives for participation in presidential campaigns, commitments to alternatives on major questions of public policy, and a variety of other attributes thought relevant to political leadership beyond the purely local levels of politics and short of the central roles occupied by presidential candidates.

The specification of data collected in the first instance was guided by the conviction that the study of the changes being sought, or taking place, in the presidential selection process would necessarily be a study of change through time. Our plans as we designed the 1972 data collections carried the vision of repeated collections in 1976, 1980, and beyond.

Through a variety of accidental circumstances, the 1972 data collection, made possible by funding from the Russell Sage Foundation and the Twentieth Century Fund, was not repeated in 1976. This was true even though 1976 saw the publication of Jeane Kirkpatrick's signal contribution to American politics and American political science, *The New Presidential Elite*. In 1980, thanks to the efforts of David B. Truman, then president of the Russell Sage Foundation, the aspirations of the early 1970s were given new life with funding for the second major data collection on which this volume rests. The Russell Sage Foundation provided support not only for renewed contact with the participants in our 1972 study, but also with the individuals who had become visible as participants in presidential politics through their selection as delegates to the major party nominating conventions in 1976 and 1980.

The dedication of this volume to David Truman is only in part a recognition of his initiative in sponsoring the 1980 data collection and analysis on which this book is crucially dependent. The dedication in larger part is intended to be a small recognition of the continuing leadership that he has provided for political science over the last four decades.

First, as a scholar, through the publication of numerous articles and the remarkably important book, *The Governmental Process*, and later, as a member of various organizations entrusted with funding the pursuit of knowledge, David Truman stands as one of a handful of political scientists who have shaped the discipline as we know it today. As a member of the Social Science Research Council's Committee on Political Behavior, he played a major role in initiating the series of studies that now continue as the National Election Studies. Both the 1952 and 1956 studies came into being because of the efforts of Truman and his fellow committee members. Truman was also central to the funding of the collection of data from congressional candidates that made possible the Miller-Stokes study of congressional representation in 1958. Although many in the world of higher education have direct and large reason to value the roles he subsequently played as provost of Columbia University, as president of Mount Holyoke College, and as president of the Russell Sage Foundation, our dedication of this volume is to David Truman, political scientist.

The vision, and the resources, that made our study possible would have come to naught had it not been for the superb performance of the senior staff members associated with the studies. We are particularly indebted to Dr. Barbara Farah, who was a mainstay in the first data collection, was solely responsible for the superb execution of the 1980 study, and provided valuable continuity and experience needed for the solution of the many problems encountered in the sequel, a data collection launched in 1985.

Although we attempt to recognize Barbara's contribution through our acknowledgment on the title page, only those who have worked with her on a number of studies over the years or who are familiar with her current activities as the survey director of the New York Times Poll can appreciate the many levels on which her interventions have shaped the ultimate form of our studies. She has been senior academic colleague, chief administrator, and major facilitator in a manner unique to her talents and experience.

Barbara Farah was ably assisted in the conduct of the 1980 study by Debra Dodson, who is currently a Ph.D. candidate at the University of Michigan, and who, in turn, directed the administration of the 1985 replication of the surveys reported in this book.

Both in the conduct of the data collections and in the subsequent execution of data processing, a host of other colleagues were involved. We must single out for particular attention Laura Stoker, who, along with Debra Dobson, provided invaluable assistance in a variety of computational activities.

We were also blessed with the cheerful and efficient services of Kathleen Dorando at the University of Michigan and Dr.-to-be Ed Bez and Ph.D.-to-be David Malin of Arizona State University.

Among other individuals who should be singled out for particular mention for their central contribution to our efforts, first and foremost is Raburn Howland, Assistant Director for the Center for Political Studies, who has seen to it that the resources put to our disposal were efficiently used. More broadly, the Center for Political Studies has provided the administrative and technical home for our work, and, despite Raburn's best efforts, has occasionally been called upon to extend the financial support provided in such large part by the Russell Sage Foundation. Other CPS colleagues, including Phil Converse, Edie Goldenberg, and Mike Traugott, provided professional counsel in the early days of our work.

We also express our appreciation for the close, critical reading of penultimate versions of the manuscript by John Kessel, David Mayhew, Austin Ranney, and Byron Shafer. As the footnotes to this volume suggest, we relied heavily on John's book *Presidential Parties*, as well as on his personal comments, but all four colleagues passed the truest test of friendship with their severe criticism of our too many omissions and misstatements in earlier drafts of the manuscript. Following a careful response to their admonitions, our work was given over to Priscilla Lewis and her staff at the Russell Sage Foundation. We are in their debt for the careful attention to transforming word processed prose and figures into precise and more esthetically pleasing printed words and tabular materials.

Finally, a prominent note of appreciation is due Peter de Janosi and Marshall Robinson who, as senior officers of the Russell Sage Foundation, not only saw to the implementation of the grant which has produced this volume, but have subsequently made certain that our lines of inquiry will be extended into the Reagan era. Thanks to their good offices and the support of their Board of Trustees, the Russell Sage Foundation funded a sequel data collection in 1985. It will add another data set to the archives in the form of panel data for the 1972, 1976, and 1980 delegates, and a new data collection from the participants in the nominating conventions of 1984. Appropriately, this data collection was made possible with the commitment to place the data in the public domain without delay. Consequently the new data collection, as with those of 1972 and 1980, will be available through the Inter-University Consortium for Political and Social Research.

With so many stellar and significant institutions involved, the following volume should be without flaw. To the extent that sins of omission or commission intrude on this expectation, the authors accept full responsibility.

The book itself is the product of the collaborative efforts of the authors. Following extended discussions informed by preliminary analyses, an initial division of labor resulted in chapters 1–7 and chapter 11 being drafted by Warren Miller and chapters 8–10 being drafted by Kent Jennings. These initial efforts, however, were simply the beginning points for what eventually emerged as finished chapters. All of the chapters reflect multiple readings, revisions, and particular contributions by each of us.

WARREN E. MILLER
Tempe, Arizona

M. KENT JENNINGS
Santa Barbara, California

1986

PART I

The Structure and Mechanics of Elite Circulation and Candidate Preference

CHAPTER 1

Introduction: Background, Context, and Objectives

Thanks to the U.S. Constitution—which never once mentions political parties—the study of political parties in the United States is plagued by countless continuing problems of concept and definition. For our purposes, a political party exists if a group "however loosely organized [seeks] to elect government office-holders under a given label."[1] But this simple and straightforward definition, which by-passes problems of reconciling subjective identification with patterns of partisan behavior or with formal membership status, does not address the real origin of the difficulties that underlie the study of American parties. In the first place, the Constitution guarantees states' rights, and the federal system of government provides a multiplicity of state governments as well as a national arena for the development of political parties. And just as the structure of intergovernmental relations is confused, complicated, and often in flux, so the relationship of state and national parties is multifaceted and complex. The U.S. Constitution also provides for the classic American separation of powers, which adds to the complexity in-

[1] Leon D. Epstein, *Political Parties in Western Democracies* (New Brunswick, NJ: Transaction, 1979), p. 9.

troduced by federalism by separating presidential politics from congressional politics—at least where electoral politics is concerned. This adds another potential set of 535 elections to be shaped by yet another set of political parties. When one adds counties or parishes or townships or municipalities to the roster of sites where elections may be held and where, therefore, some body of citizens may attempt to secure the election of one or more persons identified with a "party" label, the final array of structurally unconnected, more or less organized political parties in the United States is awesome to contemplate, let alone study.

This book, therefore, contemplates the study of just one segment of the American party system, but it is a crucial segment because it is concerned with presidential selection. However, individual contenders for the presidency, whose paths to glory or defeat shape much of our story, are not treated by our analysis. We are concerned instead with convention delegates who, in large numbers, attend the nominating conventions, choose presidential candidates, and then, upon frequent occasion, lend their resources to general election campaigns.

It is important to note at the outset that our interest in convention delegates is almost exclusively an interest in their role as campaign activists—as one vitally important set of participants in the long, drawn-out quadrennial process of selecting a president. They become publicly visible as strategic participants when they first campaign for their own election, or selection, as delegates, often, but not always, in behalf of a specific candidate for nomination. They are most visible in the selection process as they then participate in the national convention to set party rules, shape party platforms, and nominate a candidate who thereby becomes the national party leader. Finally, after the convention, they devote their resources to the election of the party nominee or, in ensuing years, to the support of a candidate for another set of nomination and election contests.

There are many arenas in which national convention delegates could be studied. The present treatment is not a study of their selection as delegates; it is, moreover, not a study of their role as convention decision-makers. It is a study of their performances as campaign activists. In the best of all possible worlds this would be a book about *all* presidential campaign participants, not just that subset made up of convention delegates. In lieu of confirming evidence, we are content to presume that the delegates are similar to other elite participants in presidential politics. We think it reasonable to assume that their opinions and preferences are inordinately important in defining the political strength of individual candidates and in signifying the composition of the coalitions and factions which contest for party leadership. We also presume that they are like other activists who, although never delegates, have resources that are used on behalf of the major contenders in the presidential selection processes or that are withheld in influential demonstrations of their individual allegiances and preferences. The population of convention delegates is, therefore, of interest to us for what it can tell us about the universe of the political elites who participate in the activities that define presidential party leadership.

This book is about the changes in attitudes, opinions, preferences, and behaviors of the members of a political elite. However, it is not a specific study of the causes of stability or change in their attitudes or behaviors. It does present some strong inferences as to causal origins, particularly as to external causes which motivate, reinforce, or discourage their participation in the presidential selection processes, but we do not suggest any "causal models" to explain what we observe. In like manner, we are not primarily concerned with the future consequences of the changes we document, although at times we will speculate about the implications of various patterns of stability and change that can be discerned within the time period of our study. In short, the book presents a relatively extensive description of various changes that took place in the presidential elite in each of the parties at a critical juncture in American political history. The theoretical implications that follow from the observed changes are, we think, important both as a commentary on recent political history and as a possible foretaste of the future. The observed changes are important in their own right for what they tell us about the processes of change that accompany transitions in party leadership.

The cast of political actors on whom we focus our attention is important for many reasons. On the one hand, the actors reflect the waxing and waning of the fortunes of their champions, the would-be contenders for nomination. Thus, the delegates are indicators of the ebb and flow of power in the unending struggle for leadership and control of the national party, a struggle in which the winners become nominees for the presidency. At the same time that they mirror the struggle for leadership of party and of nation, the delegates are themselves part of the party's leadership, and they contribute to the process by their own decisions to fight the good fight in losing causes, to join ranks with the supporters of new champions, or to leave the fray—perhaps disappointed, sometimes triumphant but exhausted, or simply distracted by other challenges.

Beyond these reasons for studying convention delegates, we also assume that they, along with other participants whom we would like to study but who lie beyond the bounds of this investigation, are important because they provide a crucial link between presidential campaigns and the mass targets of those campaigns. This subelite is made up of those who are influential gatekeepers. The delegates are, almost without exception, rooted in the local and state politics of the nation, whether as publicly visible leaders such as governors, senators, and members of Congress, or as less visible representatives of groups and interests within the party rank and file. They are significant political figures whose opinions are attended to and who not only provide their own resources of time, money, and talent to the campaigns in which they participate, but who are crucial to the highly personal transactions that determine whether others in turn will make their resources available to one or another candidate.

It is doubtlessly true in the current times that the media-oriented general election campaigns of the presidential contenders are less dependent on the tens of thousands of presidential campaign activists than they were in times past; and yet it is reasonable to surmise that these activists are still important, if for no other reason than that their enthusiasms determine the flow of private contributions of money that provide necessary supplements to the public funding of the national campaign apparatus. It also seems likely, however, that the universe of presidential campaign activists that is the focus of our attention is made up of people whose declared preferences and whose expressions of loyalties and enthusiasms or the lack thereof are communicated to the strata of citizens whose decisions to vote in the primaries, caucuses, and general election in turn become crucial components in the national presidential selection processes. We presume, and we think with good reason, that it is the opinions and behaviors of such subelites that keep the multi-million-dollar efforts of a John Connally from being translated into delegate selection and support, that make possible the candidacy of a John Anderson or Gary Hart, or that keep the Hollingses and the Askews in the role of also-rans. At some stage in the selection process the popular divisions in mass support take over and determine the viability of candidacies. But it is also true that the effectiveness of this or that campaign organization, particularly in the primary selection season, must have rested on the ability of the candidate's representatives to elicit enthusiastic support from those who ultimately make up the local base of the candidate's strength.

Given our presumptions as to the political importance of the people we have chosen to study, we think it important that we know more about them, precisely because they are not, as a group, normally visible beyond their brief appearance on the stage of the nominating convention. Neither the political journalists nor the academic researchers have paid much attention to individuals who are not occupiers of formal positions of authority and influence or who do not possess national reputations of at least symbolic importance. And yet, beyond the small groups at the center of each faction or individual candidacy, American politics rests on the efforts of those who provide leadership for national politics by their hometown activities.

Where candidates are concerned, the transitions of leadership are determined by institutionally defined victories and defeats. Where the delegates are concerned, changes in party leadership are only partly dictated by the fate of national leaders or by the delegates' own electoral success or failure; they are more often a matter of voluntary decisions by the delegates to circulate into or out of the role of presidential campaign activist, to enter the lists on behalf of a champion, to do battle for one or another of various lines of contenders, or to retire from active combat.

Our analysis, perhaps more than most analyses of party leadership, emphasizes the informal, personal, voluntaristic nature of political activism. The subelite we are investigating is crucially defined by the members' formal selection (by election or appointment) as delegates to a national party presidential nominating convention. At the same time, our inquiry takes full advantage of the fact that entry into presidential politics as a campaign activist is usually a personal choice that precedes any formal designation, such as that of convention delegate. Former delegates' exits from the ranks of the presidential campaigners are equally voluntary removals dictated largely by individual decisions to withdraw. As formal participants in the nominating process they not only participate in the official selection of a presidential nominee, but they usually honor their involvement in party affairs at least by actively engaging in the campaign in the year of delegateship. Prior to becoming a delegate, however, they customarily have already manifested their interest in presidential politics by taking part in an earlier presidential campaign; and in most cases—with some interesting exceptions we shall discuss in detail—their active involvement carries over into election campaigns in the years after their formal role as a delegate has terminated. Our inquiry is unique inasmuch as it brings these individual, noninstitutional decisions and their consequences into view.

Our inquiry also draws attention to the continuity of presidential politics. Although the public presentation of presidential politics in the mass media is highly episodic and generally occurs only for a brief period every four years, the episodes are demonstrably connected through the continuity of the personnel involved. And behind the episodes that we will examine—the campaigns of 1972, 1976, and 1980—there is even greater continuity in the struggle for leadership within each party. The struggle may well be temporarily suspended within the party of an incumbent president, at least early in the term of the president. But the Reagan challenge to President Ford's nomination in 1976 and the challenge from President Carter's left within the Democratic party in 1980 illustrate the persistence and continuity of the contests for leadership. Neither the Republican nor the Democratic challenge waited for the respective nominating convention to take shape; both rested on weeks and months of planning and quiet or not-so-quiet campaigning well before the conventions.

The terms of the ongoing, intraparty contests for leadership vary with time, context, and party. Our inquiry is sharply bounded by both time and context, but it encompasses enough variability in the circumstances faced by the national Democratic and Republican parties to offer some promise of conclusions that will be generalizable and applicable to other times and circumstances. We observed the Republican presidential party at a time when a new ideological wing captured the fancy of the party as its leader captured the fancy of the national electorate. On the Democratic side, our inquiry occurred as that party attempted to reestablish itself through a redefinition of leadership while suffering four defeats between 1968 and 1984 in seeking national approval at the polls.

The aftermath of both the Republican successes and the Democratic failures highlights the centrality of electoral victory as *the* crucial term in the contest for party leadership. Ideology and preferences for specified public policies motivate many of the participants in presidential politics, while the well-being of the party and its ability to reward the faithful with position if not power energize other supporters. But all other rewards pale beside those that flow from a presidential victory. And the dark side is evident in the lack of credibility in party circles which is tendered the McGoverns and the Goldwaters on the morning after their defeat. Our inquiry embraces both victory and defeat for Republican leaders, with emphasis on the Reagan victory in 1980. With our beginning date set in 1972 and ending in 1980, we learn something of Carter's short-lived victory in 1976 but even more about the aftermath of defeat among Democrats.

More generally, the two parties present us with a variety of contrasts, some of which become apparent only as we study the circulation of our delegates into and out of the ranks of those whom we shall designate as part of the presidential campaign elite. Other contrasts are evident as we simply review the recent history of the competition for leadership in each party. It seems to us that the interparty differences associated with the circulation of these campaign activists are very much a function of those histories of the battles among party giants. We are, however, acutely aware that an otherwise extensive analysis is limited by its temporal constraints as well as its novelty of design; and the associations we observe and discuss may turn out to be more idiosyncratic than we now imagine. As a prelude to our analysis, we begin with a brief review of the political antecedents that provided the real-life context for our study. First, we present our version of a relevant overview of the recent history of contexts for leadership of the Republican party. Next, we offer a selective synopsis of the parallel developments within the Democratic party.

Republican Transition

Our analysis of the transition in Republican party leadership captures at best only one of two dramatic turning points in recent

Republican history. The years between the 1930s and World War II were dominated by a two-faction competition in the Republican party between the moderate-to-liberal eastern establishment typified by Governor Thomas E. Dewey of New York and the conservatives of the Midwest, often led by Senator Robert A. Taft of Ohio.[2]

Following Dewey's defeat by Truman in 1948, General Dwight D. "Ike" Eisenhower, the hero of World War II, won the Republican nomination over Taft in 1952 and, with the selection of Richard Nixon as his vice-presidential candidate, laid the groundwork for part of our chronicle of leadership in transition. By 1960 a tripartite division among Republican party leaders had emerged with Nelson Rockefeller on the left, Nixon in the middle, and the Old Guard, represented largely by the convention platform committee of that year, on the right. Nixon's defeat, and the apparent squandering of the Eisenhower legacy, set the stage for the first, if short-lived, postdepression intraparty success of the conservative wing of the party.

A combination of Goldwater's intense work on behalf of the party between 1960 and 1964 and the belated and futile efforts of Lodge, Rockefeller, Romney, and Scranton to engage in the battle for leadership gave Goldwater the nomination in the bitter convention in San Francisco's Cow Palace in 1964. This time the crushing defeat of the Republican right in the Johnson landslide restored legitimacy to the center—albeit a distinctively conservative center. A resurrected Nixon then defeated the remnant of party liberals led by Governor Nelson Rockefeller in Miami and returned to the White House in 1968.[3] Our study begins with Nixon in the Presidency at the time of the 1972 campaign, and we do not encompass the contests of 1964 and 1968 which marked the demise—at least for some time—of liberal power (if not dominance) in Republican presidential politics. We first depict the Republican campaign elite at the height of Nixon's presidency when he administered a smashing defeat to the Democrats fighting under the McGovern banner.

Once again, however, party tragedy struck. Watergate, an im-

[2] See Charles O. Jones, *The Republican Party in American Politics* (New York: Macmillan, 1965), chap. 3.
[3] The struggles within each party from the 1960s onward are nicely portrayed in John H. Kessel, *Presidential Campaigns*, 1st and 2nd eds. (Hammond, IL: Dorsey Press, 1980, 1984).

pending impeachment, the humiliation of an entire administration, and a tight nomination struggle between President Gerald Ford and challenger Ronald Reagan gave the party's conservative center a handicap too great to be sustained, even in a contest with Democratic newcomer Jimmy Carter in 1976. Once more, electoral defeat, again a defeat of the established center of the party as in 1960, opened the way for a second internal triumph of the Republican right. In 1980, however, their dominance was complete as Governor Reagan ignored the Anderson liberal insurgency, overcame the remnants of the moderate or centrist leadership within the party, and capped the intraparty success of the "New Right" with a sweeping national electoral victory in 1980.

In the years between the mid-1950s and the mid-1980s, Republican party leadership was transported from a more or less liberal, eastern establishment dominated by the Brownells and Deweys to a midwestern conservative enterprise run by the Tafts, Dirksens, Nixons, and Fords, and on to a sunbelt-based right-of-center coalition initiated by Goldwater and brought together and held together, if not dominated, by Ronald Reagan. Our study misses the first Republican transformation. The essentially personal decisions of liberal leaders in 1964 and 1968 that marked the end of their visible contest for party control are scarcely reflected in our analyses. John Anderson or George Bush may have represented the threads of intellectual continuity tying 1980 liberal Republicans to the past, but they were scarcely more than pale surrogates for a Nelson Rockefeller; and those among our delegate population who preferred an Anderson, Baker, or Bush candidacy in 1980 are scarcely to be taken as surrogates for the earlier supporters of the Republican left wing.

Our portion of the Republican story begins in 1972 with the conservative-centrist Nixon-Agnew administration. It follows the nomination of President Ford as a candidate for election, against the opposition of the resurgent right under Reagan. It concludes with the Reagan nomination of 1980 and therefore only foreshadows the even larger success of the so-called New Right in its dominance of the 1984 Republican Platform Committee and the national triumph of its champion in the election of 1984. Given the fact that our data do not include the liberals of decades past, the divisions that we do observe within the Republican campaign elite are notable as a mild constraint on what has become a virtually monolithic bastion of conservatism, overwhelming in its support for Reagan in the search for national electoral success.[4]

In our view, the transition of leadership in the Republican party has been fueled by an ideological drive that has become politically viable through the failures of Republican liberals and centrists—personified by Rockefeller in 1964 and Nixon in 1960 and 1974—and has succeeded because of the disarray in the ranks of the Democratic opposition. The pressures to move to the right were, we think, not a response to an external demand but a logical extension of a constant internal yearning for a truly conservative party program that had previously been beaten down because of its presumed lack of national appeal. The various accounts of the internal contests for dominance of the Republican party are replete with references to the bitterness with which the Tafts and the Goldwaters greeted the Eisenhower nomination in 1952, the Nixon-Rockefeller accord in 1960, or the Rockefeller candidacy in 1964.[5] The transition to the dominance of the New Right does not, by any account, seem to reflect an opportunistic "Downsian" strategy intended to strengthen the party's national base. It seems, rather, to be an expression of ideological conviction, though one which—happily for the party—has reaped electoral profits.

Democratic Transition

The history of Democratic party leadership over the same thirty-year period is strikingly different, in part because of the durability of the Roosevelt legacy and in part because the conservative wing of a party dominated by liberals has been limited in both its geographic and ideological appeal. In brief, it seems to us that the contests for leadership of the Democratic party have consisted largely of challenges from outside the party establishment—challenges more sporadic and situational than the ongoing tug-of-war within the Republican party. Of course this interparty contrast

---

[4] Changes in the Republican elite do, however, seem to reflect striking alterations in the coalition composing the electoral base of the party. See John Petrocik, *Party Coalitions* (Chicago: University of Chicago Press, 1981); and John Petrocik, "The 1984 Election Results," *Public Opinion* 8 (December-January 1985): 23–42.
[5] See Theodore H. White's volumes on the 1960, 1964, and 1968 elections, *The Making of the President* (New York: Atheneum, 1961, 1965, 1969).

should not be overdrawn. Thurmond and the Dixiecrats in 1948 and George Wallace and the American Independents twenty years later represented real continuity in expressing southern interests. Nevertheless, except for the Kennedy interlude, the established Democratic party leadership was not seriously challenged until it was confronted by the turmoil of the late 1960s and early 1970s.

Speculation about political hypotheticals is always hazardous and often bootless. Consequently, we will not attempt any commentary on what would have happened to Democratic leadership coalitions had John Kennedy not been assassinated nor on what would have happened had he not selected Lyndon Johnson as his vice president. The fact of the matter is that Lyndon Johnson was a direct heir of Roosevelt's New Deal, a part of the Roosevelt-Truman-Stevenson-Humphrey lineage, and his program for the Great Society was massively supported within the Democratic party and at the polls in 1964. Aside from the pesky George Wallace, there was virtually no viable intraparty challenge to his leadership until popular protest erupted in the late 1960s. And whatever ironies followed from the New Left rejection of an administration that had crafted the aggressively liberal programs of the Great Society, remade national policy on civil rights, and resigned from office in order to facilitate the search for peace in Vietnam, a second fact is that Hubert Humphrey's defeat in 1968 was properly interpreted by the Democratic establishment as marking a crisis in party leadership.

The party's response to the crisis was not business as usual in search of a new party leader from among the established ranks of the Edmund Muskies or Henry Jacksons. Instead, the party undertook a series of reforms intended to restore legitimacy to its leaders by changing the process of their selection. That process has become the subject of a voluminous literature, increasingly devoted to documenting unintended and generally deleterious consequences for the Democratic party qua party.[6] Whatever the merits or demerits

[6] See especially Nelson V. Polsby, *Consequences of Party Reform* (New York: Oxford University Press, 1983); James Caesar, *Reforming the Reforms* (Cambridge, MA: Ballinger, 1982); Byron E. Shafer, *Quiet Revolution* (New York: Russell Sage Foundation, 1984); David E. Price, *Bringing Back the Parties* (Washington, DC: Congressional Quarterly, 1984), esp. chap. 6; Austin Ranney, *Curing the Mischiefs of Faction* (Berkeley: University of California Press, 1975); Robert T. Nakamura and Denis G. Sullivan, "Party Democracy and Democratic Control," in W. D. Burnham and M. W. Weinberg, eds., *American Politics and Public Policy* (Cambridge, MA: M.I.T. Press, 1978); and William Crotty, *Party Reform* (New York: Longman, 1983).

for the longer term, the thrust of the reforms (some impelled as much by the embarrassments revealed within the Republican presidential elite in the course of the Watergate inquiry) was to open the presidential selection process to wider public view and participation. The reforms had an impact on both parties, but the larger consequences have been visited on the Democratic party.[7] They did not prevent an extension of the Roosevelt line of succession to include Walter Mondale in 1984, but they clearly were instrumental in the nomination of two outsiders, McGovern in 1972 and Carter in 1976, and the strong run of a third outsider, Gary Hart in 1984, and they ensured a Democratic seach for new leadership after 1984.

Without our putting too fine a point on it, the followers of George McGovern and Jimmy Carter were at least as different from each other as were the supporters of Nelson Rockefeller and Ronald Reagan, but the Democrats were alike in their support of two candidates, who both stressed their role as outsiders, as new faces in the ranks of Democratic leaders. Of the two, the McGovern candidacy was perhaps the more striking in its challenge to the Democratic establishment. Although joined on the left by John Lindsay and Shirley Chisholm, McGovern's major contest was with Humphrey—joined by Muskie and Jackson as party centrists, and George Wallace again on the right. We pick up the story at this point. Our story contains no information about the 1968 Humphrey supporters who were not delegates in 1972, and we know nothing of the Robert Kennedy–Eugene McCarthy cadres of 1968. As of the campaign of 1972, however, we begin to follow the two major strains of the Democratic campaign elite—the McGovernites (whom we call the liberals), and the centrists (whom we call the traditional leaders). We note only briefly the schism within the party in 1972, although we return to this central fact of political life often in subsequent chapters. Our analysis follows the principal candidate support groups through 1972, 1976, and 1980 as they fit into the major lines of competition for party leadership in each of those years.

In 1976, Chisholm, Lindsay, and McGovern all disappeared

---

[7] See Nelson W. Polsby, *Consequences of Party Reform* (New York: Oxford University Press, 1983), Chap. 2, pp. 53–88. For an excellent concise comparison of reforms in the two parties, see Robert J. Huckshorn and John F. Bibby, "National Party Rules and Delegate Selection in the Republican Party," *Political Science* 16 (Fall 1983): 656–66.

from the head of the liberal file, to be replaced by a veritable horde of new would-be leaders of the left—Bayh, Harris, Shriver, and Udall, to be joined by Brown and Church too late to do more than embarrass each other. The traditionalists became the center, and a weak center at that, while Jimmy Carter—a national centrist but right of center among Democrats—took up the role of the challenger from the outside. Even more than in 1972, the contest was removed from the established corridors of party power and was spread across the countryside as convention and caucus were replaced by the freewheeling competition of primary elections. The technocratic former governor of Georgia seized the opening created by the post-1968 reforms, shrewdly challenged the left that had foundered under McGovern's leadership, and crafted a sequence of primary election victories that carried him to the nomination and on into the White House. The center—the old left wing in the days of the struggle against the southern conservatives—ran a weak third in the personal preferences of the party influentials as its more conservative members moved with alacrity to the side of the winner, Carter.

In 1980 incumbent President Carter, who had eschewed a major role as party leader while trustee to the nation, was mildly threatened by the third Kennedy on the left.[8] The threat was not viable but it did further differentiate leadership groups within the party. It drove remnants of both the new left and the old center to the support of the president, while leaving the Kennedy forces a very distinguishable but outnumbered band guarding the left flank in the tradition of McGovern and Udall from earlier years. Our analysis will reflect both the imprint of the ideological confrontations of Miami in 1972 and the modifying accretions of experience that subsequent campaigns imparted to the new Democratic left. The patterns of changing leadership in the Democratic party thus are notably different from those of the Republican party, where the challenges and responses were *internal* to recognized party leadership in contrast to the incursions from the outside that shaped party leadership choices for the Democrats.

[8] Carter *was* involved in party affairs after his election in 1976, notably in his influence on the Winograd Commission. That involvement, however, was largely in the interest of ensuring his own renomination rather than in a concern for the health of the party. See Polsby, *Consequences of Party Reform* (New York: Oxford University Press, 1983), pp. 174, 177.

The Origins of the Study

A concern with the circulation of party elites was foreshadowed by the beginnings of our inquiry in 1972. The study had a number of objectives related to political party organization and the changes that seemed to be under way at the time (especially those involving reform and the role of women). Specific topics included gender roles; intrapsychic needs for achievement, power, or affiliation; the structure of personal values; institutional constrainsts associated with caucuses, conventions, and primary elections; representational roles and related organizational linkages; policy orientations and candidate preferences; and political career lines, including holding public and party offices. All of these themes were present, in one form or another, in the study of delegates to the two 1972 major party nominating conventions.[9]

In the aftermath of that study it was apparent that hunches and hypotheses motivating the 1972 inquiry could be fully explored only with a panel design for a study which would include repeated measurements separated in time. The present study, executed eight years later, redeems part of that early expectation through a second collection of data in 1981 from the 1972 study respondents. More significantly for present purposes the 1981 collection also added to the early plans by including the new delegates to the 1976 and 1980 conventions as well. A quasi-panel design for the study of individual change is present for the added cohorts in the form of their recall of selected experiences in 1972 and 1976.

In addition to the shift in analytic options that follows from the availability of information from six sets of delegates selected to participate in the nominating process of the two major parties in three different presidential elections, we have made critical, substantive use of our panel study of the 1972 delegates, often exploiting their unique experience for our more general pursuits. The 1972 data collection is of paramount importance in another way, however, because of the information it provides, directly and by strong inference, on the efficacy of our mode of collecting data in 1981. At the heart of the 1972 study design was a strict probability

---

[9]The 1972 study has been reported in Jeane Kirkpatrick's book, *The New Presidential Elite: Men and Women in National Politics* (New York: Russell Sage Foundation and Twentieth Century Fund, 1976).

sample drawn from all delegates to both party conventions. The overall response rate was 86 percent, an exceedingly good return. As a supplement to the personal interviews, mail questionnaires were also sent to all of the delegates, with an overall response rate of 55 percent, quite good for mail surveys. Because a few questions were asked in identical fashion in both surveys, it is possible to compare the two. As reported in Appendix A, the two samples are very much alike in each party despite the lower questionnaire response rate. Because the 1981 data collection relies completely on mail questionnaires, these results are quite encouraging.

1981 Data Collection

The 1981 data collection was not flawless by any means, but we are satisfied that it did not introduce troublesome, to say nothing of disabling, biases into our study. We think the data to be highly representative of the values, beliefs, and behaviors of the populations they purport to describe.

The mail questionnaires were distributed in early 1981. Altogether we received usable questionnaires from 5,453 delegates spread over the three cohorts and the two parties.[10] The details of the 1981 data collection are described in Appendix B. Response rates are notoriously low in mail surveys. Bearing that in mind, and reflecting on the rather close fit between data based on personal interviews and mail questionnaires obtained in the 1972 collection, the results from our 1981 efforts are most reassuring. For each cohort we have taken as the base for calculating the response rate the total number of delegates within each party for each year. Convention repeaters (13 percent of the total) are included in each cohort for which they are members. Since there has been a small

[10] During the course of the three years we spent on analyzing the data, a handful of cases (N = 41) were ultimately discarded due to incompleteness of information and duplication of records. At any given point in the analysis to be reported on here, then, the total raw number lying at the base of the analysis might vary between 5,412 and 5,453. Given the smallness of the numbers involved, their spread across the various cohorts, the inefficiencies of replicating all of the pertinent analysis with the "final" purged data set, and the trivial to nonexistent impact the exclusion of the bad cases would have on the results, we have decided not to perform a complete reanalysis.

amount of "natural" mortality even among the recent cohorts, the resulting response rates are on the conservative side.

The response rates and the actual numbers of cases are presented below:

	1980		1976		1972	
	%	N	%	N	%	N
Republicans	56	1,126	44	985	39	519
Democrats	49	1,643	36	1,082	28	878

As mail surveys go, these are quite respectable rates and compare favorably with other studies of delegates, some of which employ purposive or quota designs.[11] Not surprisingly, the more recent cohorts had higher response rates—a result due, in small part, to the greater incapacitation or death of earlier cohort members. Republican elites tend to have higher response rates than do Democratic elites. For example, the original 1972 study had a response rate of 63 percent among Republicans compared with 51 percent among Democrats. Similarly, as the figures above demonstrate, the 1981 figures favored the Republicans across the board. Why this pattern emerges is by no means apparent. In any event, the larger message lies in the fit shown with the interview data in the 1972 data study and in the comparisons between our results and those based on other studies (see Appendix B).

A second set of response figures of relevance for us is that representing the 1972 respondents who also took part in our 1981 data collection. These individuals compose the 1972–1981 panel data within each party. For the Republicans the retention rate was 54 percent (N = 458) and for the Democrats it was 48 percent (N = 7.75).[12] Considering the eight-year interval between the surveys as

---

[11] See John W. Soule and James W. Clarke, "Issue Conflict Concensus: A Comparative Study," *Journal of Politics* 33 (February 1971): 75–76, for a summary of earlier studies; Thomas H. Roback, "Motivation for Activism Among Republican National Convention Delegates: Continuity and Change in 1972–76," *Journal of Politics* 42 (February 1980): 183; and M. Kent Jennings and Barbara G. Farah, "Social Roles and Political Resources: An Over-Time Study of Men and Women in Party Elites," *American Journal of Political Science* 25 (August 1981): 462–82.

[12] In principle, the individuals who make up the 1972 delegate cohort in 1981 should be the same as those who make up the 1972–1981 panel. However, there are 61 fewer Republican panel members than 1972 cohort members and 103 fewer Demo-

well as the amount of "natural" attrition, the retention rates within each party are very respectable. Moreover, comparisons of those delegates who stayed in the study versus those who dropped out—based on the 1972 observations—reveal only occasional minor social-demographic and political differences (Appendix C). Thus, we feel quite confident that the 1972 cohort respondents, the most distant in convention time from the 1981 data collection, are a remarkably faithful reflection of the full set of original 1972 respondents.

The Outline of Our Inquiry

Our study of continuity and change in these national presidential party elites will begin with attention to the pervasive contribution of presidential candidacies. From our survey of possible causes for circulation of people into and out of the ranks of campaign activists, it is clear that the candidates play a central role as their failures and successes provide the stimuli that provoke both continuity and change in the cadres of campaign activists. The description of interparty differences in continuity and change among the campaign elites also provides an opportunity to begin the study of contrasts in the transition of leadership within the two major parties.

Much of our interest in mapping the circulation of presidential campaign elites is grounded in the fact that whatever the causes of replacement within elites, their circulation often produces changes in the motives, goals, ideals, ideas, and patterns of organizational behavior that characterize national presidential politics. Consequently, after establishing an analytic scheme for the book, and observing the different patterns of recruitment, continuity, and disengagement associated with the participation of different candidate support groups among the delegates, we will note in some detail the dimensions of political ideology, policy preference, and political values that are associated with different groups of candidate supporters.

The description of changes in the ideological centers of gravity

---

cratic panel members. The reason for the discrepancy is that some 1976 and 1980 delegates had been delegates to the 1972 convention but had not taken part in our survey. Thus, they cannot be included in the panel analysis, but for many purposes they will be considered as 1972 delegates, as observed in 1981.

and the political perspectives of the party elites will introduce an analysis of elite support for party, issue commitments, and individual candidacies as expressed in the delegates' actual participation in the campaigns of 1972 and 1980. This analysis of the centrality of issues, party, and candidates in presidential election campaigns will be directly relevant to the task of exploring some of the consequences of institutional change that have accompanied the transitions in leadership in both parties.

Our interest in changes taking place within each party has obvious roots, origins that sustain each of the early chapters as we seek out consequences of reform—particularly among Democrats—or the correlates of change in party leadership—particularly among Republicans. As our analyses have developed, we have also become keenly aware of our ability to speak to two other closely linked but larger themes. To some extent, each party, and even particular elements within each party, may go its own way in dealing with the process of leadership selection. Many of the patterns of attitude and behavior we report seem more related to the somewhat idiosyncratic fates of particular candidacies than to structural properties of a competitive two-party system of politics. At the same time, the changes in elite attitudes and behavior do have consequences for the party system. We therefore move from the early chapters emphasizing intraparty phenomena to an analysis that centers on interparty differences. If the role of the party is to articulate and aggregate value preferences in order to structure an alternative for the voters' choice, what have the changes of party leadership, and movement into and out of the campaign elite, contributed to the definition of Democratic-Republican party differences?

Finally, because parties, nominations, and elections are the only institutions developed to link a mass-based electorate to its leaders, we turn to analyses of elite-mass relationships. These analyses provide a unique insight into the linkages that connect the amorphous and ill-defined arena of national elite politics to the preferences and predispositions of ordinary citizens. Our interest in the interconnectedness of political life will culminate in an examination of linkages which connect presidential politics to the goals of rank-and-file voters. In what is by now a traditional mode of analysis, we will examine the consequences of elite circulation for the representation of local expressions of mass policy preferences and political values in the stratosphere of presidential campaign politics.

CHAPTER 2

The Circulation of Campaign Activists

Defining a Presidential Campaign Elite

The generic task of setting boundaries to define an elite is classically given over to determining whether one or more of three criteria is met: (1) For the arena in question, does the individual in question hold a relevant formal organizational position? (2) Does the person exercise power and influence by virtue of decision-making authority? (3) Is the person accorded power status by reputation?[1] In matters of electoral politics these criteria are not always helpful. This is so because politics, and presidential election politics in particular, is anything but rationally or formally organized. The national parties are clearly more than the aggregation of in-

[1] The various formulations of political elites are especially prominent in the community power literature. See Floyd Hunter, *Community Power Structure* (Chapel Hill: University of North Carolina Press, 1953); Robert A. Dahl, *Who Governs?* (New Haven: Yale University Press, 1961); Edward C. Banfield, *Political Influence* (New York: Free Press, 1961); and Nelson W. Polsby, *Community Power and Political Theory*, rev. ed. (New Haven: Yale University Press, 1981). Few efforts have been made to examine the empirical overlap generated by these three approaches. For partial attempts, see M. Kent Jennings, *Community Influentials* (New York: Free Press, 1964); and Linton C. Freeman, *Patterns of Local Community Leadership* (Indianapolis: Bobbs-Merrill, 1968).

21

dividuals with formal memberships on the national committees. Those who exert power and influence in national presidential politics include more than the persons named on campaign organization charts. And not everyone named on somebody's chart participates as a part of the cadre of the national political elite.

Nevertheless, we share with many other students of American politics the inclination to define national leadership elites by formal organizational roles. In our case, the crucial role consists of having been selected as a delegate to a national nominating convention. The formal position of delegate carries with it decision-making authority, although the independence or autonomy with which that formal authority is exercised is a matter of continuing controversy.[2]

At the same time, we do not assume that the sheer fact of formal attendance at a nominating convention, whether early or late, is sufficient for membership in a given presidential *campaign* elite. To be included in our operational definition of the campaign elite of a given year, one must have been an active participant in that presidential campaign. The precise nature of the measure of campaign activity will be described in detail at a later point. A detailed description is necessary because campaign activity is not simply a criterion for inclusion in the study; it lies at the heart of our design for analysis. With it as a part of our operational definition of the campaign elite we have included two of the three classic criteria used to define the influential or powerful—formal position via the status of convention delegate and the exercise of decision-making authority via actions taken at the convention—and have substituted relevant activity for reputational nomination as a third criterion.

Because of our initial and continuing interest in the formal institutional changes that have been reshaping the presidential selection process, this is a study of delegates and not a study of county campaign chairmen, political consultants, or some other distinguishable body of campaign activists. The need for a clear specification of a population to be studied called for some organizational context with which to define the boundaries of our study. The membership of the nominating conventions provided that definition by centering on the individuals who would, next to potential

---

[2] See Nelson W. Polsby, *Consequences of Party Reform* (New York: Oxford University Press, 1983), esp. chap. 5.

presidential candidates, be most directly affected by many of the changes in the presidential selection process. And insofar as those changes are important for redefining the nature and role of the national political parties, the nominating convention delegates are, apart from national party committee members, the most inclusive, authoritative representation of the national parties. They are, therefore, well suited to our needs for a manageable yet meaningful population through which to study changes taking place in the national presidential selection process. They are also central to changes taking place in the leadership of the parties.

As we have already emphasized, and as will become increasingly apparent as we move through the analysis, we are only marginally interested in the convention delegates in their roles as delegates. Rather, we employ them as at least one-time members of the presidential elite and as a set of activists who represent middling-to-high levels within party politics. At the same time, the status of convention goer and the significance of the convention should not be slighted. It has become fashionable in these days of essentially bound, instructed delegates to see the convention as a mere ratifying process, something more akin to the gatherings of the electoral college in its nondeliberative nature. However, that portrayal is a caricature.

In the first place, conventions do make important decisions other than the (automatic) selection of the presidential nominee, and many of these decisions are by no means foregone conclusions. Decisions involving credentials, resolutions, the platform, party rules, and the vice-presidential selection often take on major significance and are not completely predetermined. During the three conventions covered by our study there was one big battle on credentials (the Democrats in 1972), one on rules (the Republicans in 1976), and at least two on the platform (the Republicans in 1976 and the Democrats in 1980). This is to say nothing of the minor skirmishes and bargaining which occurred, nor of the intense pressure surrounding the vice-presidential selection in several of these conventions.

Beyond these decision-making functions, conventions serve important functions with respect to intraparty processes. Even in the case of early candidate dominance, the fact that a convention is being held conditions the flow of the campaigns and the internal relationships of the party. Reflecting on the 1976 Democratic convention, where Carter was a foregone winner and had tight control of the convention, Sullivan et al. nevertheless note the many functions served by a convention.[3] Divisible prizes such as platform planks, rules changes, and a preferred vice-presidential candidate are available and, when achieved, help legitimate and encourage support among the less enthusiastic supporters of the nominee. By the same token, a convention offers the possibility of reconciliation in hotly contested fights, such as that between Ford and Reagan in 1976. Although the losers apparently did not ultimately work as hard as did the winners of that particular struggle, they did receive some solace from the platform and the selection of Robert Dole as the vice-presidential nominee.[4]

More generally, the conventions provide a setting for the party as organization. Agendas can be set, group integration can be achieved, and the policy choices of the nominee can be constrained. The conventions remain the one place where the diverse groups within each party can be represented in large numbers and where implicit and explicit agreements can be struck. Indeed, because the presidential nomination itself is virtually assured, the delegates may place even more emphasis on matters over which they do have some control. This was clearly the case in the Kennedy-led challenge to Carter at the 1980 convention and to the concessions (though modest in nature) made by the Reagan forces to Republican moderates in 1980.

Especially with the omnipresent eye of television, the conventions have become a showcase for the parties and their nominees and programs. It has been argued, in fact, that conventions now come closer to opening the campaign season than to closing the nominating season.[5] Beyond the decisions taken and the faces presented to the country, conventions thus provide the vehicle for energizing the delegates directly and would-be supporters and followers indirectly via the mass media.

All of this is not to say that the conventions are the great deci-

[3] Denis G. Sullivan et al., "Candidates, Caucuses, and Issues: The Democratic Convention, 1976," in Louis Maisel and Joseph Cooper, eds., *The Impact of the Electoral Process* (Beverly Hills, CA: Sage, 1977).

[4] Denis G. Sullivan, "Party Unity: Appearance and Reality," *Political Science Quarterly* 92 (Winter 1977–78): 635–45.

[5] Nelson W. Polsby and Aaron Wildavsky, *Presidential Elections*, 6th ed. (New York: Scribner, 1984), pp. 145–46.

sion-making bodies that they once were, if by that we mean nominee selections and brokered conventions. But neither are they negligible. This returns us full circle to the question of why we are utilizing delegates as our subjects for studying transitions in leadership. Delegates remain important political actors in their role as delegates. More crucially for us, however, they serve as activist representatives of the various factions, coalitions, and interests within each party. They are by no means representative of only the top echelons of the party, but neither are they drawn exclusively from the bottom levels. As Kirkpatrick said of them in regard to 1972: "Collectively, the delegates constitute a slice of American political life broad enough to include representatives of all political levels. No political leader is too important to attend his party's national convention, but in 1972 many a precinct leader or insurgent was important enough."[6]

Specifying our national political elite in terms of the nominating convention delegate's role obviously excludes from our study many who might well be included were the task only a matter of a conceptual definition of elite participants in presidential politics. Certainly in every election year many men and women of power and influence are members of that year's elite and yet are excluded from the role of delegate for one reason or another. Although in some instances this may have been because they purposefully chose not to contend for a delegate seat, in many other cases their exclusion is the result of failure to win election, whether in caucus or primary, or to be chosen by candidates as at-large or bonus delegates. We recognize, consequently, that the numbers and identities of those who would have preferred to be designated as delegates in recent years (and thereby be included in our study) were doubtless influenced, particularly in the Democratic party, by the changing rules for delegate selection that have been so prominent a part of reform in the presidential selection process. The consequences of their exclusion cannot be assessed by our inquiry.

Because of an unavoidable hiatus following our 1972 study, the second data collection—and the primary data base for this volume—took place in 1981. In order to minimize the consequences of the absence of a post-1976 study, our second data collec-

---

[6] Jeane Kirkpatrick, *The New Presidential Elite* (New York: Russell Sage Foundation and Twentieth Century Fund, 1976), p. 22.

tion was timed to come after the 1980 campaigns and elections and it was designed to include the participation of all delegates to the 1972, 1976, and 1980 conventions in the three presidential campaigns during that period. By extending the inquiry to ask about campaign activities in the 1972 and 1976 elections as well as the 1980 election, we enlarged the time frame and political context to include all three election campaigns in our study. Although our analytic building blocks are the campaign elites in three different elections, we treat our full complement of delegates as members of the 1972–1980 national presidential campaign elite, circulating into and out of presidential politics as their political fortunes—and those of their champions, the candidates for nomination—rise and fall over an eight-year period, embracing three presidential campaigns.

Because it was not practicable to try to contact delegates from the 1968 or earlier conventions, we accepted the 1972 campaign as a necessary early time boundary for the study. By asking delegates from 1976 and 1980, as well as our 1972 study participants, about their participation in 1972 we could tap at least three cohorts of delegates in order to study the 1972 campaigners. We could not, however, fully reconstitute that portion of the 1972 activists made up of some-time convention delegates insofar as that group had actually included many whose status as delegates (1) had been defined in 1968, 1964, or even earlier or (2) would be defined only as they became delegates in 1984, 1988, or even later. In like manner, our reconstruction of the 1976 or 1980 set of elite would be limited in representing participants who would eventually be delegates to later conventions, even though less hampered than 1972 in the representation of previously recruited into presidential politics. In any event, without extending our temporal boundaries to include both earlier and later conventions, we could not actually include in our study the full roster of delegates involved in the 1972, 1976, or 1980 campaign elites. The population we have studied is, therefore, clearly only a subset of all those whom we might ideally include in a campaign elite populated by all some-time delegates who engaged in campaign activities in 1972, 1976, or 1980.

Inasmuch as the campaign elite in a given year includes all of those some-time delegates who report having been active in the campaign of that year (whether or not they were delegates in that year), it also follows that a substantial portion of our representation of the 1972 presidential campaign elite is made up of people who did not become delegates until four or eight years later. Similarly, our "sample" of the 1980 campaigners includes large numbers of active participants whose delegate status had occurred four or eight years earlier. More generally, one of our first observations is that even within the conceptual boundaries and the limits of feasibility that define our subset of the campaign activists, the delegates for a given year constitute only a minority of that year's campaign elite, and, of course, an even smaller fraction of the combined 1972–1980 elite.

Turnover Among Campaign Activists

Broadening our operational definition of the national presidential political elite to include those who have been delegates in any one of our three consecutive election years *and* who reported participating in the presidential campaign in any one of the same three years allows us to shape our analysis around the theme of the circulation of campaign elites. The time span of our study makes it possible to examine only a limited replacement of elites, but it includes a time period in which both political parties experienced dramatic changes in political leadership. As our study unfolds there will be many instances in which we would clearly prefer to be able to anchor our examination of changing leadership in an earlier era. What were the delegates who campaigned for Hubert Humphrey like in 1968, in possible contrast to the Humphrey supporters of 1972? Did the bitter confrontation at the San Francisco Cow Palace in 1964 shape the nature of the 1968 and 1972 Republican campaign elites, and did Nixon's popular incumbency establish a different elite group in 1972 Republican national politics?

Our beginning year of 1972 is not totally devoid of connection with the past. On the Democratic side, the delegates to the 1972 election, although dominated by "the new presidential elite" brought in with George McGovern's candidacy, included many carriers of the older party traditions as personified by Senators Hubert Humphrey, Edmund Muskie, and Henry Jackson, or even Governor George Wallace. McGovern's defeat, of course, facilitated continuation of the transition of Democratic leadership, and the successful candidacy of Jimmy Carter in 1976 was the occasion for extending the campaign activities of former supporters of the traditional party leadership as well as of McGovernites mobilized during the 1972 contest.

On the Republican side, 1972 provides continuity with the past, but, paradoxically, it is of relatively little analytic use for two reasons. First, the popularity of the Nixon candidacy in 1972 obscured any latent division in the party. Not until 1976 does a division in Republican ranks give us some purchase on understanding the transition that produced the Reagan candidacy of 1980. Second, the disintegration of Nixon's presidency produced a crisis in leadership that is not foreshadowed in the 1972 selection of delegates. Consequently, the disengagement of Nixon supporters in 1976 and 1980 is in some measure the consequence of a totally abnormal change in party leadership.

If 1972 was a less than ideal situation in which to undertake the study of the contribution of disengagement and demobilization to the circulation of national party elites, it was not a bad year in which to begin a study of the mobilization of activists. However abnormal the McGovern candidacy and the end of the Nixon presidency, both parties carried on in 1976 and 1980 with a transition into the 1980s. They nominated new candidates, including a Reagan who challenged the twenty-year-old legacy of leadership by Eisenhower, Nixon, and Ford, and a Carter who shared little with his predecessor, McGovern, other than his justified claim to being another outsider and a newcomer to Democratic presidential politics. Consequently, we will focus considerable attention on the recruitment and mobilization of new cadres of activists who replaced the disengaged and thereby continued the circulation of elites in this era.

Given the necessary constraints on our study design, we will look to 1976 and 1980 for answers as to what happened to the McGovern supporters after the debacle of 1972, and in the face of the Carter candidacy and incumbency four and eight years later. Our study of the Democratic transition to Jimmy Carter will be matched by our interest in the evolution of support for Ronald Reagan and the demise of moderate leadership in the Republican party in the face of a Reagan-led conservatism. At times we will examine changes in the preferences and commitments of individuals who participated in presidential campaign politics throughout the period of our study. However, our attention will often be given to the consequences of turnover in the membership of the presidential campaign elites. Who drops out of active participation and with what consequences for the values and political perspectives articulated by the next campaign's active participants? And how is the next election year shaped by the mobilization of those previously not active as participants in national presidential campaign politics? What happens to support for party, for issues, or for other political perspectives as a result of the circulation of elites that results when those who disengage are replaced by the newly mobilized?

Analysis Design

Although most delegates were delegates in only one of the three years embraced by our study, 13 percent served as delegates in multiple years. In order to avoid double counting and to preserve our theoretical focus, ordinarily we have assigned delegates to that year in which they were *first* selected as delegates. The 1972 cohorts, therefore, contain a visible set of individuals (22 percent among the Democrats and 33 percent among the Republicans) who also were delegates in 1976 or 1980. On the other hand, our 1980 cohorts consist only of people who had never been delegates before. This assignment rule was established with our interest in studying changing elites in mind, and it was made in order to clarify intercohort differences. For example, 1972 delegates who were also delegates in 1976 and 1980 are counted only in the 1972 cohort and do not influence our characterizations of the delegate cohorts first chosen in 1976 or 1980.[7] This decision will not intrude on our analysis of elite circulation because our fundamental analytic scheme emphasizes campaign participation rather than behavior in the delegate role as such.

The measure of campaign participation is based on each delegate's responses to the following questionnaire item: "We are interested in knowing the reasons for your political involvement over the past three *presidential* election periods. For each campaign in

---

[7] If our analytic interests were centered on the comparison of conventions, the focus on cohorts, of course, would not be appropriate.

which you were involved, please indicate how much of your activity was motivated by commitments to the party, to the candidate, or to an issue position or special group. If you were not at all involved in the campaign, please indicate [this in the first column]." The questionnaire format thus allowed delegates to describe their involvement in each of the congressional, senatorial, and presidential election campaigns from 1972 to 1980. Our definition of the presidential campaign elite is based on delegates' reports of their own participation—or noninvolvement—in the three *presidential* elections of 1972, 1976, and 1980.[8]

Table 2.1 specifies the participation patterns that can be generated from the delegates' reports of their presidential campaign activities. (We will examine the focus of that activity—party, issue, or candidate—in chapter 7.) Each pair of cohorts (Democrats and Republicans) has a unique pattern of campaign participation across the three years.

The delegates to the 1972 conventions will provide our most extended view of the consequences of demobilization or disengagement from active campaign participation. Table 2.1 documents one striking and not altogether unexpected difference between the Democratic and Republican delegates of that year. More than two fifths of the 1972 Democrats had dropped out of active campaign participation by 1980. A quarter had dropped out by 1976, and the remaining one fifth dropped out by 1980. A very small subset (7 percent) participated in the campaign of 1972, sat out 1976, but were reactivated in 1980. Only one in two were active all three years.

On the Republican side, the picture is quite different: Only one in six of the 1972 Republicans (compared with one in four Democrats) failed to participate in a subsequent campaign. Republicans dropped out between 1976 and 1980 at only half the rate of their Democratic counterparts. About the same proportion of Republicans and Democrats participated in 1972 and 1980 but were

[8] By restricting our definition to presidential campaigning, we purposely circumscribe the domain of the elite activity we wish to study. At the same time, we make it relatively easy for the delegates to enter the activist stratum, for they have only to cross what is probably a low threshold of campaign involvement. Consequently, differences between activists and nonactivists to be reported in all likelihood underestimate the range of contrasts because the campaign activists could have been divided according to degrees of involvement had the appropriate questions been asked.

Table 2.1

Patterns of Delegate Participation in Presidential Election Campaigns, by Party Cohorts

	Participation			Party Cohort Total	
	1972	1976	1980	Republican	Democrat
1972 Cohorts	Yes	Yes	Yes	69%	51%
	Yes	Yes	No	9	18
	Yes	No	Yes	6	7
	Yes	No	No	16	24
				100%	100%
Unweighted N				(519)	(879)
1976 Cohorts	Yes	Yes	Yes	75%	60%
	Yes	Yes	No	6	14
	No	Yes	Yes	12	15
	No	Yes	No	7	11
				100%	100%
Unweighted N				(848)	(937)
1980 Cohorts	Yes	Yes	Yes	65%	58%
	No	Yes	Yes	17	20
	Yes	No	Yes	4	4
	No	No	Yes	14	18
				100%	100%
Unweighted N				(852)	(1,387)

inactive during the 1976 campaign. Among the 1972 Republicans, however, almost seven out of every ten were active campaign participants in all three presidential election years, a rate 18 percentage points higher than that found among the Democrats.

Where the 1972 cadres provide the base for analyzing discontinuity or disengagement, the 1980 cohorts provide the major foundation for our analysis of recruitment or mobilization of campaign elites. Although roughly 60 percent of the 1980 delegates (58 percent of the Democrats and 65 percent of the Republicans) were active in all three years, approximately one in three did not participate in 1972 but were subsequently mobilized either by the 1976 or 1980 campaign. Party differences were least extreme between the 1980 Democratic and Republican cohorts, but the Republican edge in continuous campaign activity was maintained among the delegates of that year as well.[9]

Although we shall eventually return to the separate analysis of each of the cohorts, our major scheme for studying the circulation of campaign activists is provided by an aggregation of the patterns of participation across all three cohorts. We will concentrate our attention on the continuity and the changes that link or differentiate 1972 and 1980. The distribution of stability and change in the campaign elites over that eight-year span will involve all but one of the twelve subsets of delegates portrayed for each party in Table 2.1; those members of the 1976 cohorts who participated *only* in 1976, the year they were delegates, are not included.[10] Across the eight-year span the continuing core will come from those delegates in any of the three cohorts who reported active participation in both 1972 and 1980, including persons in the 1972 and 1980 cohorts who participated in both of those years but not in 1976. Disengagement will stem from the deactivation of two categories of the 1972 cohorts (YYN and YNN in 1972, 1976, and 1980, respectively, in Table 2.1) and one category of 1976 delegates (YYN). Mobilization, in turn, is captured in two of the categories of the 1980 cohorts (NNY and NYY) and one 1976 category (NYY).

In order to aggregate across cohorts and characterize the campaign participants in any given year, or in order to assess the circulation of activists through time, it is necessary to make one further operational assumption. We will treat the cohorts of delegates as being equal in size where their contribution to each year's campaign is concerned. There are variations from one election year to another and between the two parties in the numbers of delegates selected to attend the conventions; however, interparty differences pose no problem for us because most of our analyses treat the two parties separately, chapter 8 being the one exception, and even there the size of the party groups does not affect our analysis. There

[9] As our analysis focuses on either mobilization or disengagement, we will tend to emphasize either the 1980 or 1972 cohorts. The 1976 cohorts do give us some additional purchase on both analytic problems. Among the Democrats in particular, we have enough cases so that we could replicate the participation patterns of the 1972 delegates who participated in 1972 but dropped out in 1980, and we could replicate the mobilization pattern for the 1980 elites who were inactive in 1972 but mobilized for participation in 1980.

[10] If we were focusing on change between 1972 and 1976, the group excluded would be the last category of the 1980 cohorts, those who participated only in 1980—some 6 percent of our Democrats and 5 percent of our Republicans.

also may be variations from one election year to another *within* either party in the numbers of active campaigners whom our delegates are representing in this study, or in the proportion of all campaigners that comes from our population of delegates. However, we know of no way to establish the parameters for the latter figures.

Finally, the response rates from each cohort did vary somewhat, with more cooperation from the more recent delegates and less cooperation from the 1976 cohorts. There is no reason to allow that variation to affect our depiction of the contribution which a given cohort, or its active campaign component, makes to the totality of elite campaigners in a given year. This is particularly so in the absence of any apparent bias among our nonrespondents.[11] Lacking any clear rationale for assigning differential weights to given cohorts, we have adopted the practice of weighting all cohorts equally within each party.[12] Throughout our analysis we deliberately do not attempt to combine the two parties in order to constitute a single national presidential campaign elite. We have not attempted to address the question of whether there are more Republican campaigners than Democratic campaigners, and the equal weight of cohorts is maintained only within each party.

Therefore, it is possible to constitute the campaign elite for a given party in a given year by combining the appropriate patterns of participation from all three cohorts for the specified year. The 1972 campaigners thus consist of all the (active) 1972 delegates, plus the first two groups (Table 2.1) within the 1976 cohorts plus the first and third groups within the 1980 cohorts. The 1976 elites, in turn, consist of all 1976 delegates, those from the first two patterns within the 1972 delegates, and the first two patterns within the 1980 delegates. Finally, the 1980 campaign activists include all 1980 delegates and those in the first and third patterns from both the 1972 and 1976 cohorts.[13]

---

[11] See Appendix Table B.1.

[12] As we noted in the text, this decision has no impact when treating each cohort separately, for there the original Ns are retained. When the cohorts are "pooled," as in analyzing circulation patterns, the consequence of equal weighting is to make the analytic N *smaller* than the actual number of cases upon which the analysis is based. This is so because the 1972 cohorts, the smallest ones, were taken as the base for weighting of the other cohorts. In effect the 1972 cohorts are self-weighting and the remaining cohorts are given noninteger weights of less than 1 to make them approximately equal in size to the 1972 cohorts.

[13] Table 2.3 shows in tabular form the combinations that make up our major classifications of participation patterns.

The Continuity of Personnel in Presidential Campaigns

The distribution of each year's campaigners, by cohort, is presented in Table 2.2 in order to repeat a simple but important point: The campaigners for any given year are numerically dominated by activists who were *not* delegates to that year's conventions. This is true even without including the active campaigners who were delegates before 1972 or the campaigners who were to become delegates at some future time (1984 or beyond) and thus would be conceptually included within our representation of a presidential campaign elite. Although there are minor variations between the two parties, the delegates for a given year constitute only some two fifths of that year's campaigners, even when the boundary defining activists is truncated, as it must be in our inquiry, to include only those who were delegates during one of the three years under study. Conversely, activists whose delegate status was at least eight years removed from the elections of 1972 or 1980, made up at least one quarter of each year's roster of activists.

Past research on convention delegates, usually based on a single year's delegates, has tended to emphasize the uniqueness of each cohort. It now becomes clear, though, that there is much more continuity in the composition of the campaign elite than meets the

Table 2.2

Contribution of Cohorts to Presidential Campaign Elites

		Campaigners		
		1972	1976	1980
Republicans	1972 Cohort	41%	30%	29%
	1976 Cohort	33	38	33
	1980 Cohort	26	32	38
		100%	100%	100%
Unweighted N		(1,790)	(2,001)	(1,945)
Democrats	1972 Cohort	42%	28%	25%
	1976 Cohort	31	41	32
	1980 Cohort	27	31	43
		100%	100%	100%
Unweighted N		(2,409)	(2,609)	(2,680)

casual eye. It is doubtless true, as Johnson and Hahn report, that most *conventions* are made up of delegates participating in a nominating convention for the first time; but delegate members of the *campaign* elites of 1972, 1976, and 1980 were largely repeaters, not novices.[14] Even if each cohort is different because of the politics of "their year" as delegates, the distinctiveness of any given cohort of delegates is diluted by the larger numbers of the others who have participated in multiple campaigns. The year 1972 has been characterized as unique for the Democratic party because of the delegates who assembled in Miami to nominate McGovern. However, even with our limited ability to account for the 1972 campaign activists, the Miami delegates were outnumbered three to two by those active campaigners who were to become delegates four or eight years hence, and who, as we shall see, sometimes differed in substantial and politically important ways from the 1972 delegates.

Our basic analytic scheme involves assembling the full array of components who contributed to continuity and change in each party between 1972 and 1980. The scheme centers on what Lasswell and his associates term "personnel circulation" as it separates continuing participants from those who disengage and drop out or those who are mobilized and replace the disengaged.[15] The relatively limited numbers of those who circulate into and out of the campaign elite, detailed in Table 2.3, immediately provide another means of emphasizing the continuity of American national politics. This theme is particularly notable within the Republican party where almost three out of every four Republicans who participated during the change from the party of Nixon to the party of Reagan participated as active campaigners *both* in 1972 and 1980. Of all Republican delegates to the three conventions, only 10 percent contributed to change between 1972 and 1980 by dropping out of presidential campaign politics after the 1972 election; and the transition from Nixon to Ford to Reagan was accomplished even though fewer than 15 percent of the total set of delegates involved at one

[14] Loch K. Johnson and Harlan Hahn, "Delegate Turnover at National Party Conventions, 1944–68," in Donald R. Matthews, ed., *Perspectives on Presidential Selection* (Washington, DC: Brookings Institution, 1973).

[15] Daniel Lerner, Harold D. Lasswell, and C. Rothwell Easton, *The Comparative Study of Elites: An Introduction and Bibliography* (Stanford, CA: Stanford University Press, 1951).

Table 2.3

Contributions of Cohorts to the Circulation of Campaign Activists, 1972–1980

Cohort Year	Participation Pattern 1972	1976	1980	Continuously Active 1972–1980 Republican	Democrat	Disengaged after 1972 Republican	Democrat	Mobilized after 1972 Republican	Democrat	Other (1976 only) Republican	Democrat
1972	Y	Y	Y	23.1%	17.2%						
1972	Y	N	Y	2.1	2.2						
1976	Y	Y	Y	25.1	20.2						
1980	Y	Y	Y	21.9	19.2						
1980	Y	N	Y	1.2	1.5						
1972	Y	Y	N			3.0%	6.0%				
1972	Y	Y	N			5.3	7.9				
1976	Y	Y	N			2.0	4.5				
1976	N	Y	Y					4.0%	5.0%		
1980	N	Y	Y					5.7	6.8		
1980	N	N	Y					4.5	5.8		
1976	N	Y	N							2.1%	3.7%
Totals: Rep				73.4		10.3		14.2		2.1		100%
Dem					60.3		18.4		17.6		3.7	100%
Weighted N				(1,088)	(1,344)	(140)	(415)	(208)	(338)	(31)	(68)

Notes: Participation is defined as a single dichotomous variable: Yes or No. The measure does not reflect variations in intensity or level of campaign activity.

In equating the sizes of cohorts within party, our weighting procedure reduced each of the larger cohorts to the weighted equivalent of the smallest. Therefore, each Republican cohort was reduced to 519 cases, for a weighted total of 1,557 (against an unweighted total of 2,219); each Democratic cohort was reduced to 879 cases for a weighted total of 2,637 (against an unweighted total of 3,203). (Where numbers of cases in subsequent tables vary from these base line figures, it is the result of excluding cases with missing data.) Projections are carried to one decimal place to avoid rounding errors.

36

time or the other made their contributions through their mobilization *after* the 1972 election year.

Within the Democratic ranks the lower rate of persistent participation that was noted in our cohort-by-cohort inspection (Table 2.1) is reflected in the fact that only 60 percent of those who contributed to the transformation from the McGovern years to the Carter years participated in the election campaigns of both 1972 and 1980. It also comes as no surprise that a large proportion of the 1972 participants (42 percent of the 1972 delegate cohort, 18 percent of our total for the 1972-1976-1980 elite) had dropped out eight years later. They were, however, virtually replaced by equal proportions who were mobilized in time for the 1980 contest.[16]

Finally, across the entire set of delegates under study, 70 percent of the Republican campaign elite participated in all three presidential year campaigns and only 12 percent were active only in a single year, the year in which they were delegates. Among the Democrats, 57 percent were continuing participants in all three years while 17 percent were one-time participants, including almost 8 percent who participated only in the 1972 campaign.

It is useful at this point to attempt to forestall future confusion by delineating the different ways in which we shall approach the study of change over time in this volume. For example, our depiction of changes in campaign activity in Table 2.3 is based entirely on data collected in 1981 after the 1980 campaign. However, relying on the delegates' memories of 1972 and 1976, as well as 1980, we reconstruct patterns of individual behavior and treat the data as "pseudo-panel" data. At the same time, preserving the identity of each of the three cohorts within each party makes it possible to examine intercohort differences for evidence of cohort effects that persist in the 1981 indicators. Individual-level reconstructions with pseudo-panel data will be pursued in analyzing (1) campaign activity and (2) candidate preference. Recall data were collected in 1981 for both of these domains precisely to permit us to reconstruct the circumstances of 1972, 1976, and 1980 for each delegate and then estimate changes over time.

In all other content domains, including (3) ideological self-placement, (4) public policy or issue preferences, (5) values at-

---

[16]This conclusion obviously rests on the assumption that the cohort totals were of about the same size in all three years.

tached to political activity, (6) assessments of politically relevant groups, (7) evaluations of political leaders, and (8) personal, socio-economic attributes, the basic data were collected with reference to one point in time for all delegates, 1981, and have no other time referrent. Intercohort differences may be interpreted as residual differences from the initial effects, but, for the 1976 and 1980 cohorts, there is no possibility of any measure of change over time.

For the 1972 cohort, however, there are occasions when two time points are available for the measurement of identical or very similar indicators. In a limited number of instances, 1981 measures were collected from 1972 delegates who had also participated in the earlier 1972 study. These 1972 delegates are members of a true panel who responded first in late 1972 and second in early 1981. Thus, for the 1972 cohort, and for them alone, some of our assessments of individual level attributes are from direct observations at both points in time.

CHAPTER 3

Candidate Preferences

The presidential candidates play a major, if often indirect, role in determining the personnel of our campaign elite. In the first instance, they initiate their own candidacies and, by becoming visible alternatives for political leadership, they attract followers. Subsequently, as viable candidates they are responsible for primary election and caucus decisions that ultimately select delegates who thereby enter our population of campaign activists. The candidates, or their organizational representatives, may indeed intervene directly in the ultimate selection of personnel as they assemble slates that compete in primary elections or local nominating conventions or as they dictate the selection of "super delegates" on the Democratic side. Indeed, the enhanced role of candidates and their representatives in establishing the composition of convention delegations is one of the most serious developments cited by the critics of the new rules for presidential selection.

Our next depiction of the circulation of presidential campaign activists centers on patterns of participation associated with delegates' preferences for candidates in the 1972–1980 period.[1] For this

---

[1] While most studies of convention and presidential campaign activists solicit candidate preferences or pledges for a given year, virtually none attempts to develop a

aspect of our inquiry (as with the analyses of social and partisan composition), we ignore any formal prescriptions by which delegates may have been bound or committed to support a given candidate at a national nominating convention. Instead, we turn to the delegates' recall of their personal preferences. Following a series of questions about how the delegates were selected, we asked, "Whether committed or not, whom did you *most prefer* as your party's nominee for President in the last three presidential elections?" Our best evidence of the reliability of delegates' recall of past preferences is provided by our 1972 cohort members who had first revealed their 1972 candidate preferences to us in the 1972 data collection. The juxtaposition of their 1972 and 1981 reports, presented in Appendix A, gives evidence of both the reliability of the 1981 recalls in the aggregate *and* the relative absence of bias produced by the failure of many of our 1972 respondents to return their mail questionnaire to us in 1981.

Even more persuasive in terms of reliability is the match between the two years at the individual level. Four fifths of the Democratic delegates gave exactly the same response in 1981 as they had in 1972.[2] Mismatches occurred primarily between ideologically adjacent pairs, thereby affecting very little our ultimate construction of preference patterns.

Republican Patterns of Candidate Preference

Among Republicans, the patterns of preference for presidential candidates across the three years are relatively easy to reconstruct. This stems in part from the fact that there was a virtually unanimous preference for Richard Nixon in 1972. Meaningful differentiation occurs subsequent to 1972 and reflects the nearly even division of sentiment between President Ford and, then candidate, Ronald Reagan in 1976. This is followed by a division of preferences between the moderate candidates of 1980—including Bush,

---

history of candidate preferences. Given our longitudinal approach to activity and given the central role of candidates in focusing the campaigns, our decision to construct patterns of preferences is a logical necessity.

[2] If we consider the lack of opposition to Nixon in 1972, the Republican reports, while overwhelmingly identical at both points in time, are far less persuasive than those for the Democrats.

Baker, and Anderson—initially arrayed against Reagan's second candidacy. The task of defining unique and discrete patterns of preference is complicated, however, by the fact that not all delegates had a clear preference all three years. Even so, grouping the supporters of the three "moderate" candidates in 1980 permits an exhaustive disaggregation of Republican delegate preferences into nine groups. Three of the groups preferred someone other than Reagan in both 1976 and 1980. The largest group consists of those who preferred Ford in 1976 and someone other than Reagan in 1980. A tiny set of Republican delegates could not choose between Ford and Reagan in 1976, but opted for a moderate candidate in 1980. A third, somewhat larger, set preferred Ford to Reagan in 1976 but had no 1980 preference. A fourth group, consisting entirely of 1972 delegates, never appears in the Reagan column because these delegates preferred incumbent president Nixon in 1972 and had *no* subsequent preference in either of the next two years.

On the other side of the Republican party ledger, Reagan supporters of 1980 were made up of three groups distinguished by their 1976 preferences. The smallest of the three groups consisted of those who could not choose between Ford and Reagan in 1976. A much larger group moved from Ford in 1976 to Reagan in 1980. The largest category of Reagan supporters in 1980 consisted of those who had also supported his candidacy four years earlier.

Finally, despite the clear strength of Reagan sentiment in 1980 and the dominant shift from Ford to Reagan between 1976 and 1980, two visible fragments of the Republican elite moved away from Reagan following a 1976 preference for his candidacy. The larger of these two groups simply expressed no preference among the 1980 candidates; a slightly smaller contingent had preferred Reagan to Ford in 1976, but preferred a moderate Reagan opponent four years later. The distributions for the nine groups of Republican delegates are presented in Appendix Table D.1, with the three cohorts separated.

Republican Preferences and Circulation Patterns

The dynamics of changing support for presidential candidates in the Republican party between 1976 and 1980 are summarized in

Table 3.1

Circulation of Republican Campaign Activists, by Patterns of Candidate Preference, 1976–1980

	Patterns of Candidate Preference		
Circulation Patterns	Moderate Only	Former Reagan	Reagan Only
Continuously Active			
1972 Cohort	35%	20%	19%
1976 Cohort	22	47	27
1980 Cohort	12	11	34
Core Totals	69%	78%	80%
Disengaged after 1976	20	7	4
Mobilized after 1976	11	15	17
Totals	100%	100%	100%
Weighted N	(499)	(87)	(811)

Table 3.1. For this presentation, delegates are allocated to one of three groups: (1) the so-called moderates who never preferred Reagan; (2) the small middle group who had preferred Reagan in 1976, but moved away from that preference in 1980; and (3) those who became Reagan supporters in either 1976 or 1980.[3] Circulation of the activists is reflected in five categories of participants first introduced in Table 2.3. The first three categories consist of the core participants who were active in the presidential campaigns of both years, distinguished only by the year of their first delegateship. A fourth category of campaign activists consists of those who disengaged between 1976 and 1980. The fifth category presents the other side of the circulation coin and contains all of those who, although nonparticipants in 1976, were recruited to active presidential campaign participation by 1980.

Table 3.1 is organized to show the participation records of the groups defined by pattern of candidate preference. The contrast between the moderate delegates and the Reagan delegates is most striking where dropout rates are concerned. The persistence of participation among Reagan supporters is noteworthy: Only 4 percent of the total group disengaged following participation in 1976,

---

[3] In terms of Appendix Table D.1, these three categories represent a combination of, respectively, 1–3, 4 and 5, and 6–8.

whereas five times as many supporters of the moderate candidates had been activists in 1976 and had dropped out by the 1980 election campaign. Somewhat more in line with expectations, the group of moderate supporters mobilized in 1980 after having been inactive in 1976 is relatively small compared with the groups of Reagan supporters who were mobilized in the same interval. It is also significant that the deviant fragment which moved away from a Reagan preference in 1976 was not much inclined to withhold participation. Only 7 percent of the group (9 percent of those active in 1976) dropped out of the ranks of the activists following the 1976 campaign.

Large differences in candidate preference associated with the three different cohorts are also apparent in Table 3.1, but they can be highlighted by examining the distribution of preferences within the cohorts (looking at distributions within rows rather than within columns as presented in Table 3.1). Among the core participants from 1972, a clear majority (59 percent) preferred a moderate candidate to Reagan *even in 1980*. The Reagan ascendancy is marked by a favorable balance of sentiment within core participants in the 1976 cohort and by an overwhelming dominance of the preferences of the 1980 delegates. Those who contributed to the circulation of the elite, rather than to continuity, simply reflect the patterns observed in Table 3.1. The demobilized and disengaged were overwhelmingly moderate supporters (in a ratio of three to one in 1980), while Reagan counted almost two out of every three who were newly mobilized for participation in the 1980 campaign.

To some extent these data must also be interpreted as reflections of the political fortunes of the delegates. The disengaged were concentrated among the supporters of those who bid for and lost the nomination in 1980, and the mobilized were those whose preferred candidate was the 1980 victor.[4] If we keep in mind, how-

---

[4] This is a longer-term variant of the proposition that fervent backers of losing candidates "sit out" the ensuing general election and thus dampen their party nominee's prospects. Most of the evidence on this score is impressionistic and anecdotal, though surely it holds in varying degrees. We found little clear evidence for this poor loser syndrome in the election year accompanying convention attendance, but the evidence presented here and below suggests a longer-term effect if factional preferences are realized in subsequent years. Sullivan found some reported occurrences of this phenomenon among 1976 Reagan supporters: Denis G. Sullivan, "Party Unity: Appearance and Reality," *Political Science Quarterly* 92 (Winter 1977–78): 635–45.

ever, that *campaign participation* remained a voluntary act throughout, it is not true that supporters of moderate candidates were precluded from participation in the 1980 campaign any more than the supporters of Reagan had to wait until 1980 to be mobilized as campaign activists. Just as their mobilization was a voluntary act, so the disengagement of the supporters of the defeated was largely a reflection of their subsequent lack of motivation to participate.[5]

Although combining the various patterns of candidate preference in order to create the tripartite division of Republican delegates does serve the purpose of simplifying the data, and thereby highlighting the substantial differences associated with elite circulation that we have observed, the procedure also obscures some meaningful variations among the original discrete patterns of candidate preference. For example, among the delegates whose preferences were limited to the more moderate candidates in 1976 and 1980, the rate of disengagement was only 13 percent among the large group who supported moderate candidates in both years. However, there was a 25 percent drop among the 1976 supporters of President Ford who had no preference in 1980. And there was a 50 percent decline among the delegates who preferred Nixon in 1972 but had no subsequent preference. The interpretation seems quite straightforward: Campaign participation may be motivated by commitment to party or policy, but in the absence of a clear preference for a presidential candidate, participation drops off.

The Ascendancy of Reagan

These and similar details associating differences in disengagement or mobilization with differences in patterns of candidate preference are descriptively interesting and generally make intuitive sense. It is, however, easy to become lost in the minutiae of the data and thereby lose track of the larger contours. To return to the larger

---

But the most direct and convincing demonstration of this effect is provided in a panel study of *state* convention delegates. See Walter J. Stone, "Prenomination Candidate Choice and General Election Behavior: Iowa Presidential Activists in 1980," *American Journal of Political Science* 28 (May 1984): 361–78.

[5] In a separate analysis we have determined that although some part of demobilization is a consequence of aging and poor health, it is not an explanation for the differentiation in dropout rates among the candidate preference groups.

canvas we reorganize the data that were summarized in Table 3.1. We maintain the distinctions among core participants, those who drop out of campaign activity, and those who are mobilized. However, instead of the tripartite division of candidate preferences, we will create a fourth category of subdividing the 1980 Reagan supporters into those who had not supported him in 1976 (groups 6 and 7 in Appendix Table D.1) and those who preferred his candidacy in both 1976 and 1980 (group 8 in Appendix Table D.1). With this subdivision of the 1980 Reagan supporters, we can classify each delegate in terms of the presence or absence of a preference for Reagan, in both 1976 and 1980. This new classification will, in turn, help us understand the nature of Reagan's rise to preeminence within the party.

By a small margin the largest of the four analytic categories among all Republican delegates consists of those who preferred Reagan in both 1976 and 1980 (40 percent of the total). This group is almost matched in numbers by those who did not prefer Reagan in either year (37 percent). The shorthand tale of Reagan's ascendance to leadership is consequently presented in the differential size of the other two groups. Delegates whose *change of preference* represented a gain for Reagan outnumbered those who moved away from Reagan between 1976 and 1980 by a ratio of more than five to two.

In 1976, as Ford sought reelection, Ronald Reagan was the preferred candidate of 48 percent of our total set of delegates who were to be active in that campaign. Four years later, he was the preferred candidate of approximately 59 percent of the delegates who were active campaigners in the election of 1980. All told, Reagan gained over 10 percentage points in support from the campaign activists between 1976 and 1980.[6]

Table 3.2 presents the full array of information about changes in preference *and* participation between 1976 and 1980 for all of the Republican delegates who took part in either presidential campaign. With the full set of information before us, it is now possible to address a basic question pertinent to the change in the titular

[6] Anticipated shifts such as these undoubtedly affect the behavior of candidates in the prenomination phase. John H. Kessel contrasts Reagan's strategic considerations and decisions in 1976 and 1980 in terms of his (Kessel's) four phases: early days, initial contests, mist clearing, and the convention. See his *Presidential Parties* (Homewood, IL: Dorsey Press, 1984), chaps. 8 and 9.

Table 3.2

Composition of Preferences for Reagan, by Circulation Patterns, 1976–1980

Preference Patterns	Continuously Active 1976–1980	Disengaged after 1976	Mobilized after 1976	Total
Never Reagan	29	5	4	37
Dropped Reagan	5	1	*	6
Went to Reagan	14	*	2	16
Always Reagan	37	1	2	40
Totals for 1976–1980	85	7	8	100%

Note: Entries are the proportion of the total number involved in the 1976 or the 1980 campaign and for whom preference patterns are available. Weighted $N = 1,405$; * = less than 0.5%.

leadership of the Republican party: Was the nomination of Reagan the outcome of a successful insurgency in which supporters were mobilized to supplant and replace the old party loyalists, or did Reagan capture the minds and hearts of the opposition and come to power because old-timers changed their minds about him?

Both types of change, conversion and circulation, added to Reagan's support in 1980; but well over four fifths of the increase came from conversion within the ranks of the continuing participants. Within each of our three circulation components one can note the consequences of individual conversion. Among the continuously active participants, a subset amounting to 5 percent of the total moved *away* from Reagan between 1976 and 1980. This movement against the dominant flow was disproportionately located among 1976 delegates and scarcely to be found at all in the 1980 cohort. Those shifting their preferences away from Reagan were heavily outnumbered by the group who changed preferences in order to support him in 1980. This net gain for Reagan through conversion of the continuously active delegates was some 9 percent of the total 1976–1980 campaign elite.

Within the much smaller set of some-time activists who disengaged from presidential politics between 1976 and 1980, the balance of *individual* change was in the other direction, with those who were moving away from Reagan slightly outnumbering those who were coming to his support. However, the very fact that the disengaged had deserted the campaign ranks by 1980 probably meant that this isolated erosion of support was not visible to the activists in the campaign. In terms of sheer numbers it was not a significant brake on the increase in Reagan support between 1976 and 1980.

The flow of individual changes favoring the Reagan candidacy was, not surprisingly, strongly reflected among those mobilized between 1976 and 1980. Although the sheer numbers involved in changes of preference among the mobilized were minuscule compared with the number of core participants who changed their preferences, the ratio of Reagan gains to losses (six or seven to one) was substantially higher among the mobilized.

The contribution of circulation to the ultimate increase in Reagan's popularity is, of course, the result of the trade-off between those who were mobilized and those who dropped out. The relative contributions of this trade-off and the growth in Reagan support through conversions of core activists is highlighted in Tables 3.3 and 3.4. Among the group of 1976 activists who disengaged after 1976, Reagan had been preferred by no more than 30 percent of the delegates in 1976. On the other hand, among those who were mobilized following the 1976 election, he enjoyed a clear, if slim, plurality of support in 1980. Almost half of that support had developed as the result of individual changes in preference. The crucial bottom line, however, is that Reagan gained only some 3 percentage points ($+3$ in the bottom row of Table 3.4) within the total Republican presidential elite as a consequence of the replacement of the unenthusiastic disengaged by the more supportive newly mobilized. Circulation of personnel was not the key to Reagan's success in the contest for party leadership and the party's nomination.

Among core participants, the individual-level change in candidate preferences gave Reagan almost an 18-point jump between 1976 and 1980 (Table 3.4). This is a consequence of those who moved to his support outnumbering those who moved away by a total of 9 percentage points (14 to 5 in Table 3.2, column 1).[7]

---

[7] Since we are working with only two alternatives, a single point of gain for one alternative is also a point lost to the opposition and, therefore, a double gain when expressed in terms of change in percentage points.

Table 3.3

Sources of Support for Reagan, 1976 and 1980

	1976 Activists		1980 Activists	
Preference Patterns	Continuous Participants	Disengaged after 1976	Continuous Participants	Mobilized after 1976
Non-Reagan	43	5	34	4
Pro-Reagan	42	2	51	4
Net Support for Reagan	−1	−3	+17	0

Note: Entries are proportions based on the total 1976–1980 set of Republican activists. Weighted N = 1,405.

With the two components of change now identified, it is apparent that the increase in Reagan's strength came in only small part as a consequence of elite turnover; rather, it had its basic origin in the change of sentiments within the individual members of the campaign elite. With no individual-level change on the part of the core participants who campaigned in both 1976 and 1980, the circulation we have observed could have narrowed the gap but could not have transformed Reagan's status from that of minority challenger in 1976 to that of clear majority choice in 1980. If we consider the limited numbers involved in the circulation and the relatively modest differences in support for him among the mobilized and disengaged, it is clear that the major source of his new-found strength

Table 3.4

Sources of Change in Support for Reagan, 1976–1980

	Continuous Participants	Disengaged/ Mobilized	Net Support
Net Support			
1976	−1	−3	−4
1980	+17	0	+17
Change in Net Support for Reagan, 1976 to 1980	+18	+3	+21

Note: Entries are proportions based on the total 1976–1980 set of Republican activists and are derived from Table 3.3. Weighted N = 1,405.

was less a function of turnover and much more a consequence of his success in generating enthusiasm for his candidacy and converting the loyalties of continuously active participants.

Additional insight into the phenomenon of individual-level conversion of candidate assessments can be offered by returning to our preference patterns and again disaggregating the continuously active participants into three cohorts that contribute to that core. Within the 1972 cohort Reagan was a distinct minority preference in 1976, receiving the support of only 32 percent of the delegates in the cohort. He did, however, enjoy a modest increase in support over the next four years, gaining the support of some 15 percent of the cohort while losing the support of only 5 percent. But by 1980 he was still *preferred* by only 42 percent of the 1972 cohort. The pattern of change within the 1976 cohort was visibly different. In the first place Reagan enjoyed nearly a three-to-two margin of support among those first elected as delegates in 1976. However, most interestingly, losses and gains within the 1976 cohort were almost evenly balanced over the next four years. He did not enjoy *any* noticeable improvement in his relative position with the 1976 delegates by 1980 (58 percent in 1976 and 57 percent in 1980).[8]

The imprint of differences among the cohorts is finally and predictably most evident among the 1980 delegates. In 1976 their enthusiasm for Reagan almost exactly matched that of the 1976 cohort (he was preferred by some 54 percent of the 1980 cohort who, by our operational definition, were not delegates in 1976). Four years later, however, the growth of enthusiasm for his candidacy was reflected in a gain of 25 percent, offset only by a loss of 2 percent. This gave him a three-to-one margin of preferences (77 to 23) within the 1980 cohort. Substantially more volatility was reflected in changes of preferences in the 1980 cohort than in the other cohorts; and the almost unanimous movement to the Reagan camp produced a striking difference between the 1980 cohort and

[8] This level of support among members of the 1976 cohort does not match Reagan's actual support at the 1976 convention because those who repeated as delegates in both conventions have been assigned, analytically, to the 1972 cohort. The contrast between the support given by the 1976 cohort—58 percent in 1976—and the majority support that actually nominated President Ford reemphasizes the possible political conseqences that flow from continuity of participation—in this instance as delegates—which dilutes the impact of mobilization. First-time delegates to the 1976 election would have nominated Reagan in that convention; Ford's support from 1972 holdovers who nominated Nixon was sufficient to give him the victory in 1976.

those delegates whose status originated in the earlier years. And, of course, it was the 1980 cohort that gave Reagan the Republican nomination and the nation the image of a party in the midst of a radical change of leadership.[9]

It is a dramatic commentary on the processes of political change that at the very time the 1980 delegates nominated Reagan, and contributed to the general view that support for moderate candidates has virtually disappeared within the Republican party (dropping to 23 percent among 1980 delegates), the large cadre of still-active campaign participants from the 1972 cohort shared only a minor part of the enthusiasm for the new leader as their *preferred* candidate. Rather, they maintained a strong majority of preferential support for their leaders of the party's moderate wing. As a consequence of the political reality of Reagan's ultimate success in 1980, the extent of continued support among veteran campaigners for the moderate Ford legacy prior to the nomination did not receive anything like the public attention given to the demands of the newly mobilized. The postelection picture of a radical insurgency with a resounding mandate for change might have been modified with greater awareness that by no means all of the Republican campaign activist had shared in the swing to the new enthusiasm, and that the plurality of intraparty support for Reagan among these party activists was even less than the plurality of his interparty victory in November.

Nevertheless, Reagan's stock had gone up enormously in an absolute sense among the 1972 delegates, which gives added credence to our argument about the importance of conversion rather than replacement in the ascendancy of Reagan throughout the 1970s. In chapter 2 we noted that the 1972 delegates represent the one cohort for whom we have data collected prior to 1981. By introducing information as reported by the 1972 delegates in 1972, we can offer a complementary and persuasive argument that individual changes in personal affect provided a major thrust in the Republican elite's swing toward Reaganism.

---

[9] It is of interest to note that Reagan support in the 1980 cohort is the result of changing preferences within the cohort in part because it argues that our design, which omits nondelegates, did not, therefore, overemphasize Reagan stalwarts from 1976 who were finally elected in 1980 while missing converts who were not delegates because they moved to Reagan only in 1980.

We cannot utilize candidate preference reports, as was done in the preceding section, because Reagan was not a candidate in 1972. However, he was a prominent Republican personage, partly because of the late boomlet for his nomination in 1968 and partly because of his general prominence among Republican conservatives. As a consequence, Reagan's name was included in a list of names evaluated in the 1972 study through the use of the so-called feeling thermometer. Because Reagan was also included on the 1981 version of the questionnaire, where the same feeling thermometer was used, we have two soundings (based on identical measurement procedures) from the 1972 delegates who responded at both points in time. By coupling these evaluations with those made in 1981 by the 1980 delegates, we can obtain additional purchase on the contribution made by conversion versus turnover in Reagan's rise to the top. What should be emphasized, however, is that this new evidential base for our argument has its own limitations for our general analysis because it does involve moving from a relative preference among candidates to an absolute measure of affective reaction to a single candidate.

Our procedure uses three points of observation and follows the logic laid out in a study of French elites.[10] The net change in evaluations of Reagan between 1972 and 1981 will be represented by subtracting the 1972 delegates' *initial* ratings of Reagan from those provided eight years later by the 1980 delegates' ratings (as of 1981). This net change can come from two sources. To assess the place of conversion we can utilize the panel data collected from the 1972 delegates at both points in time. More precisely, individual-level change will be represented by subtracting the delegates' 1972 mean ratings of Reagan from their 1981 ratings—the larger the difference the greater the impact of conversion. On the other hand, to estimate the role of replacement, or turnover, we can then compare the 1972 delegates as of 1981 with the 1980 delegate cohort as of the same date. The 1980 delegates' scores minus the contemporaneous 1972 delegates' scores will be taken to represent the contribution of replacement. As the difference rises, the role of replacement looms larger.

[10] Roy Pierce and Thomas R. Rochon, "Attitudinal Change and Elite Circulation: French Socialist Candidates in 1967 and 1978," *American Journal of Political Science* 28 (May 1984): 379–98.

Presented below are the various means involved and the types of changes represented:

Mean Ratings of Reagan on 0–100° Scale

(1) 1980 Delegates in 1981	(2) 1972 Delegates in 1972	(3) 1972 Delegates in 1981	(4) Net Change $(1-2)$	(5) Replace- ment $(1-3)$	(6) Con- version $(3-2)$
90	68	85	22	5	17

Net change in Republican delegates' regard for Reagan over the decade was extraordinary, one of the largest changes recorded among a sizable number of groups and individuals judged at both time points. The blossoming of Reagan as a preferred candidate was echoed in these absolute evaluations of delegate affect.

Most crucial for present concerns is the apportioning of the change in these affective ratings. Quite clearly conversion among Republican delegates accounted for the lion's share of that gain—a shift of 17 points compared with one of only 5 points due to replacement. In terms of explained variance, conversion accounted for about three fourths of Reagan's gain in popularity and replacement for about one fourth. The ratio is very similar to the four-to-one ratio documented by the earlier analysis of sources of change in preferences; that is, in absolute as well as relative assessments, Reagan would have scored very large gains among Republican elites even in the absence of elite turnover. By 1981 the 1972 delegates were almost as enamored of Reagan as were the 1980 delegates themselves—at least in the wake of the 1980 electoral outcome.

All of this is not to say that Reagan's capturing of the nomination would have occurred in the absence of turnover, for it is clear that despite the sharp overall rise in Republican delegates' appreciation of Reagan, the moderate and disengaged contingents from the 1972 and 1976 cohorts would have preferred a moderate nominee in 1980. Rather, it is to note the collateral evidence that Reagan succeeded in winning the approval of many in the earlier cohort who had been lukewarm in their reactions to him in 1972. Processes of rationalization and dissonance reduction undoubtedly play a role in these absolute evaluations because there must be a strain between one's active involvement and attachment to a party on the one side and disapproval of the *successful* standard-bearer of the party on the other side. In large part these Republican elites apparently resolved any potential conflict by raising dramatically their evaluation of Reagan.

It is worth noting that conversion accounted for another dramatic movement among Republican delegates. Richard Nixon's fall from grace occurred after the original 1972 delegate study. At that time he stood high in the estimation of Republican delegates, having an average score of 92. By 1981 the 1980 delegates accorded him a mean score of only 52, for a precipitous 40-point drop. Virtually all of that decline could be attributed to conversion effects alone inasmuch as the mean score of the 1972 delegates as of 1981 was 51. Republican delegates joined their fellow citizens in devaluing their disgraced leader. Nixon's plunge and Reagan's ascendance portray in dramatic fashion the switch in the mantle of Republican leadership. A successful second Nixon administration would surely have helped keep the party control in the hands of traditional-to-moderate Republicans. Instead, the way was paved for Reagan's climb to the top and with it control of the party by conservative elements.

Defining Patterns of Democratic Candidate Preferences

Although it is reasonably easy to reconstruct the transition of Republican leadership by following a limited number of patterns of presidential candidate preference, the comparable task is much more difficult on the Democratic side. In 1972 there were six major candidates. In 1976, with a substantial change in the cast of characters, the field of major candidates was even larger. Only 1980 saw the Democratic choices simplified because of the incumbency of President Carter and a single serious challenge to his leadership led by Senator Edward Kennedy. When all of the discrete combinations of preference are mapped across the three years, the proliferation of patterns must be seen either as rich in texture or as overwhelming in detail. The map of patterns of change can, however, be made more manageable with some intuitively reasonable and inductively defensible groupings of the candidates from the first two years. We have three themes to guide our reconstruction of the patterns of change.

Reflecting in part the beginning date for our study, we will initially follow the fortunes of the liberal wing introduced in presidential politics in 1968 as Senator Eugene McCarthy and Robert Kennedy challenged the tradition represented by the candidacy of Hubert Humphrey. The liberals were established as a force in American politics with the successful challenge by Senator George McGovern four years later in 1972. They were strongly represented with a multiplicity of candidates in 1976, led by Congressman Morris Udall; and it was the liberals under the banner of Senator Edward Kennedy who mounted a futile challenge to the renomination of the incumbent President Jimmy Carter in 1980.

A second theme, the waning of the leadership tradition that began with Roosevelt (and was reconstituted in 1984 with Mondale) can also be documented, although less effectively because our study begins in 1972 rather than 1968 and ends in 1980 rather than 1984.[11] Consequently, we can only follow the temporary eclipse of the traditional wing of the party as it battles the liberal wing in 1972, is overwhelmed by the combination of Carter and the Liberals in 1976, and is left without its own candidate for nomination in 1980. As a third theme, we will follow the evolution of support for the Carter candidacy, at least in part as a second study of a successful insurgency.

In 1972 the liberal cause was championed by Senator McGovern. The traditional leadership that was successfully challenged in Miami was represented by Hubert Humphrey, supported by Henry Jackson, Wilbur Mills, and Edmund Muskie. Leadership for the extreme right was provided by Governor Wallace, although with less success than in his effort in 1968. Four years later, Chisholm, Kennedy and McGovern had disappeared from the ranks of the leading challengers on the left and were replaced by the sextet led by Congressman Morris Udall, flanked by Governor Brown, Senators Bayh, Church, and Harris and, maintaining the

[11] The tracing of the Mondale genealogy will await the completion of our analysis of data gathered in early 1985 from delegates to the 1984 (and 1972–1980) conventions. One clue, however, emerges from examining the evaluations of Mondale on the feeling thermometer. Compared with evaluations of Carter, McGovern, and Ted Kennedy, the ratings of Mondale were considerably less affected by the delegates' candidate preference genealogies; the eta statistic for Mondale was .23 compared with etas in the .50 range for the other three. Hence, Mondale did appear to be less tied to the coalitional structures of the 1970s and was, perhaps, a vestige of the New Deal coalition.

Kennedy banner, Sargent Shriver. The traditional moderate candidates, running a weak third in the preferences of our activists, were once again Humphrey and Jackson.[12] To the right of both of these groups of candidates, but well to the left of the foundering efforts of Wallace, was the insurgent and ultimate winner, Governor Jimmy Carter of Georgia. In 1980 the contest was reduced to a two-person competition between Kennedy on the left and Carter in the center.

Analyzing the rise and fall of candidate support produced by the circulation of the Democratic presidential campaign activists is once again further complicated by the fact that many delegates, for a variety of reasons, had no preference among contending candidates at one or another point in time. So, for example, a substantial number of those who supported the liberal wing in 1972 had no preference between the alternatives presented eight years later. Reversing the time frame, we see that a substantial set of those mobilized on Carter's behalf in 1980 were unable to reconstruct a preference among candidates in the earlier years. If one therefore adds "no preference" as an option in each of the three presidential election years, even the grouping of candidates suggested above means that there are four alternatives possible in 1972, five in 1976, and three in 1980.

Fortunately for descriptive and analytic purposes, many of the sixty possible combinations of preferences across the three years were empirically nonexistent or were represented by idiosyncratic patterns of preference expressed by such a small number of delegates as to make possible an early decision not to attempt further analysis. With the elimination of the idiosyncratic patterns (such as Chisholm-Wallace-Kennedy), and with some further collapsing and combining of other patterns of preference whose adherents were more like each other than different, it is possible to first reduce the full array to twelve categories depicted in Appendix Table D.2). We shall typically reduce this still large number even further, but for present purposes the twelve categories supply meaningful information.

Gross differences across the three cohorts provide a first description of the dynamics of changing candidate preferences and thereby give us a crude reconstruction of the recent history of com-

---

[12] Humphrey was not a formal candidate in 1976, which was doubtlessly responsible for his weak showing in activists' preferences.

petition for Democratic leadership. The cohort differences are, in general, not as sharp as those that characterized the Republican party. The alienation of members of the 1972 cohort, which occurred when supporters of Chisholm, Kennedy, or McGovern, as well as supporters of traditional party leadership, found themselves with no candidate preference by 1976 or 1980 (group 3 in Appendix Table D.2), was virtually absent from the ranks of the 1980 delegates. Conversely, the new support for the liberals and the mobilization of support for Carter were almost entirely a function of the mobilization of the 1976 and 1980 cohorts and, by definition, a function of political circumstances that could not be reflected among 1972 delegates.

There is, however, a rather remarkable uniformity among the cohorts in the representation of those who maintained a commitment to the liberal wing or who moved from liberal candidates or the support of traditional candidates to the support of Carter across the three cohorts. Changes of preferences among Democrats show nothing like the reduction of the moderates and the growth of support for Reagan that are captured in the cohort differences among Republican delegates. Despite the heterogeneity of claims to leadership of the Democratic party across these years, and despite the party's warm embrace of institutional reforms, the delegates who populated each of the three Democratic conventions did not differ—one year from another—as much as did the three comparable Republican cohorts.

The implications are not clear. It may be that the sequel to reform is fractionation of the politically active that will be hard to unite in any new coalition. It may be that we are only viewing another consequence of the failed efforts of the outsiders McGovern and Carter. And it may be that we are simply observing a political elite that will not respond easily to new definitions of leadership until the viability of new alternatives is more apparent.

Democratic Preferences and Circulation Patterns

We can facilitate a more explicit attention to mobilization, continuity, and disengagement among our categories of candidate preference by further combining some categories of candidate support without losing essential information. Several pairs of groups that do not differ substantially in their patterns of circulation can be combined. Consistent and predominantly liberal supporters can be joined, as can two groups of liberal supporters who moved to a preference for Carter. Two categories of delegates who moved to support the liberal wing of the party can be combined, as can both categories of traditional supporters who moved to Carter. Consequently, we can depict the impact of candidate preferences on elite participation while considering only the seven categories of candidate preference presented in Table 3.5.[13]

Activists in four of the eight patterns of candidate preference were very much alike in the extent to which they were core participants, active in all three presidential election campaigns. They differed in understandable ways in their patterns of circulation into and out of the ranks of the active campaigns. Within the four groups that contributed most heavily to sustained participation in presidential election campaigns, the two groups that had been liberal supporters in 1972 differed from the other two both in the extent to which they subsequently disengaged and dropped out of active campaigning and in the limited extent to which they contributed new personnel to the presidential elite of 1980. The two remaining groups were very much alike in all respects even though they represent strikingly different patterns of change in candidate preference. Both those who were newly arrived at a preference for Kennedy, the leader of the left in 1980 (the "Recent Liberals"), and those who moved from the support of traditional Democratic leadership to the support of Carter contributed heavily to the new participants who were recruited into elite politics and made minimal contributions to turnover in elite circulation by dropping out.

The other three patterns of candidate preference deviated in equally understandable ways. First, former supporters of liberal candidates who had no candidate preference in 1980 ("Alienated Liberals") provide the sharpest confirmation of the expectation that many of the McGovernites of 1972 ultimately dropped out of presidential politics. More than half of these "Alienated Liberals" carried their alienation to complete disengagement. Despite this fact, a strong minority of the 1972 cohort continued as core participants in the 1980 campaign. A similar phenomenon, although not as ex-

[13] In terms of the categories given in Appendix Table D.2, this means combining, respectively, categories 1 and 4, 2 and 5, 6 and 7, and 8 and 10. We also drop from separate consideration the 34 delegates in the "other combinations" category.

Table 3.5

Circulation of Democratic Campaign Activists, by Patterns of Candidate Preference, 1972–1980

Circulation Patterns	Liberal Only	Liberal to Carter	Alienated Liberal	Recent Liberal	Traditional to Carter	Carter Only	Alienated Traditional
Continuously Active							
1972 Cohort	23%	19%	31%	18%	18%	1%	25%
1976 Cohort	17	23	8	21	23	9	19
1980 Cohort	26	20	5	23	24	34	6
Core Total	66%	62%	44%	62%	65%	49%	50%
Disengaged after 1972	23	20	52	10	7	2	35
Mobilized after 1972	10	15	2	24	24	46	7
Other	1	3	2	4	4	3	8
Totals	100%	100%	100%	100%	100%	100%	100%
Weighted N	(542)	(302)	(193)	(366)	(630)	(154)	(190)

treme, occurred within the "alienated" (with no preferred candidate) among the traditional party supporters. A full third of them
had disengaged by 1980. Where high rates of disengagement account for the low level of continuity in those two groups, the third
group that made minimal contribution to continuity in the Democratic presidential elite was predictably made up of delegates
whose only expressed candidate preference was for Carter. Almost
half of that group represented a new contribution to the campaign
activists as they were mobilized some time after the 1972 elections.

The Decline of the Left

In order to summarize our analysis of the impact of circulation
on the representation of the support for liberal leadership, we have
rearranged the information from Table 3.5 to highlight the ebb and
flow of preferences for liberal candidates. This follows exactly the
format and strategy used earlier for our depiction of the evolution of
support for Reagan among Republicans. In the present instance,
represented by Table 3.6, we again work with four categories of
candidate preference anchored by the criterion of preference for
liberal leadership.[14]

The impact of the politics of the late 1960s and early 1970s is
dramatically presented by the preference patterns of delegates who
circulated into and out of the Democratic elite between 1972 and
1980. At one time or another almost 60 percent of all campaign
participants preferred a representative of the left, but by 1980 that
proportion had been reduced by more than a third (from 59 percent
to 38 percent).

If the continuously active participants in Table 3.6 are separated into the familiar three cohorts from 1972, 1976, and 1980, the
support for the liberals is, perhaps surprisingly, invariant across the
three cohorts. Despite the origins of the new thrust in 1972, core
support for and core opposition to liberal candidates varied scarcely
at all across the three cohorts. Perhaps even more surprisingly, the
pattern of individual-level changes in Table 3.6 does not reflect any
substantial net loss of support for liberals among continuously ac-

[14]The category labeled "Never Liberal" is formed by groups 8–12 in Appendix
Table D.2; "Dropped Liberals" by groups 2, 3, and 5; "Went to Liberal" by groups 6
and 7; and "Always Liberal" by groups 1 and 4.

Table 3.6

Composition of Democratic Preferences for Liberal Leadership, by Circulation Patterns, 1972–1980

Preference Patterns	Continuously Active 1972–1980	Disengaged after 1972	Mobilized after 1972	Total
Never Liberal	25	5	10	41
Dropped Liberal	12	7	2	21
Went to Liberal	10	2	4	15
Always Liberal	16	5	2	23
	63	19	18	100%

Note: Entries are the proportion of the total number involved in the 1972–1980 campaigns. Weighted N = 2,339.

tive delegates, and this pattern is again remarkably consistent across the three cohorts. Nevertheless, liberal leadership clearly lost strength between the years of the McGovern candidacy and Carter's bid for reelection.

The origin of the decline in liberal strength in the Democratic party stands in stark contrast to the nature of the decline in support for moderate leadership among Republicans. It is much less a consequence of individual-level change and much more a consequence of circulation. Those who disengaged from campaign activities following the 1972 election had given candidates of the left a margin of support in 1972 equal to about 6 percent of the total delegate population (Table 3.7). Among their replacements, who were mobilized following the 1972 election, support for liberal leadership was eclipsed and outweighed by a comparable margin (–7).

In both years liberal leaders were supported by only a minority of the core participants. Despite the near balance in individual-level changes among the core participants (the gain of 10 percent and the loss of 12 percent shown in the first column of Table 3.6), the slightly diminished enthusiasm for liberal leaders between 1972 and 1980 cost those leaders some 4 percentage points among the elite preferences (–8 to –12 in Table 3.8). At the same time, the exchange of the newly mobilized for the disengaged resulted in a decrement of almost 13 points. Thus, the net decline of support for the left, summarized in Table 3.8, is three to one (13 to 4), a

Table 3.7

Sources of Support for Liberal Democratic Leaders, 1972–1980

	1972 Activists		1980 Activists	
Preference Patterns	Continuous Participants	Disengaged after 1972	Continuous Participants	Mobilized after 1972
Nonliberal	35	6	37	13
Liberal	28	12	25	6
Net Support for Liberal	−8	+6	−12	−7

Note: Entries are proportions based on the total 1972–1980 set of Democratic activities. Weighted N = 2,339.

result of circulation rather than a matter of shifting of candidate preferences.

Although there was a provocative parallel in an apparent "drift to the right" in support for presidential candidates in both parties in 1980, it is now apparent that the processes of change were dramatically different on the two sides. Despite limited circulation among Republicans, dramatic changes in individual preferences for presidential leadership resulted in a major shift of leadership support. Among Democrats, the relative stability of preferences for both liberal leaders and traditional leaders among continuously active campaigners was offset by the relatively high rate of turnover

Table 3.8

**Sources of Change in Support for Liberal Democratic Leaders,
1972–1980**

	Continuous Participants	Disengaged/ Mobilized	Net Support
Net Support			
1972	−8	+6	−2
1980	−12	−7	−19
Change in Net Support, 1972 to 1980	−4	−13	−17

Note: Entries are proportions based on the total 1972–1980 set of Democratic activists and are derived from Table 3.7. Weighted N = 2,339.

among activists with very different preferences for national leadership. The disengagement of those supporting the left and the mobilization of support for Carter resulted in the loss of support for liberal candidates.

While turnover thus accounts for much of the shift in the changing preferences of the Democrats, disillusionment with their 1972 standard-bearer in an absolute sense suggests some additional contribution of conversion effects in moving the party to the right. The fate of George McGovern mirrors almost perfectly the history of Ronald Reagan during the 1970s and depicts the dwindling fortunes of the New Left since 1972. Again, evaluations on the 0–100° feeling thermometer provide compelling evidence. Whereas the 1972 delegates rated McGovern at 75° in 1972, the 1980 delegates scored him at 54° in 1981 for a net loss of 21 points. Meanwhile, the 1972 delegates had lowered their own evaluations of him to 56°.

Despite a great amount of turnover in the Democratic elites, the overwhelming source of McGovern's loss came as a result of individual-level change (18 points versus 3 points for replacement). Much of this decline can undoubtedly be traced to McGovern's devastating loss in 1972. It is nevertheless significant that the very convention that had nominated him so soundly deserted him—if not much of what he stood for—a few years later. Indeed, McGovern's rating in 1981 by the 1972 delegates was only marginally better than the 51° accorded the deposed Nixon by his 1972 delegates.[15]

The Tenuous Hold of Jimmy Carter

In a clear demonstration that there are many degrees of freedom for the analysis of change in leadership support, the growth of support for Carter in the 1980 campaign was more like the growth of support for Reagan. The process was one of change of individual preferences more than the turnover of activists produced by the circulation of campaign activists. There was, however, a profound difference in the magnitudes of change relative to the 1980 nominees of the two parties. In 1980 Reagan was the first prefer-

[15]Time heals many wounds. McGovern's stature appeared to improve during the 1984 nominating season, but it seems unlikely at this time that he will be resuscitated to the extent that a fellow landslide victim, Barry Goldwater, was by his Republican colleagues in 1984.

ence of almost 60 percent of the entire set of 1980 Republican campaigners after having been the favorite of about 48 percent of the 1976 elite. That 1980 plurality came in only very minor part from the replacement of those who disengaged from presidential politics after 1972 in favor of those who were mobilized by 1980. Because of the conversion of individual preferences, Reagan became the preferred candidate for those who were continuing members of the Republican elite involved in the eight-year span of presidential elections.

Carter, on the other hand, was only marginally the majority preference among the *1980* elite and, as Table 3.9 also reveals, among the entire set of delegates contributing to the Democratic circulation between 1972 and 1980, he was the preferred candidate of only about 45 percent of the total set of sometime activists (as against Reagan's support from 57 percent of the total Republican elite). If the consensus supporting Reagan at the time of the 1980 elections was qualified by a substantial minority who either preferred a different candidate or had no preference at all, Carter's campaign evoked minimal enthusiasm among many potential Democratic activists and he was, in a very real sense, a minority candidate within his party. Insofar as the enthusiasms for presidential candidates are nurtured and spread by the support of the national party activists, this insight into the sharp party differences of 1980 suggests a prime reason for the ultimate triumph of Reagan and for the decisive defeat of Carter at the polls.

Table 3.9

Evolution of 1980 Preferences for Carter

Preference Patterns	Continuously Active 1972–1980	Disengaged after 1972	Mobilized after 1972	Total
Never Preferred Carter	34	14	7	55
From Other Preferences to Carter	26	5	8	39
From No Preference to Carter	3	—	3	6
	63	19	18	100%

Notes: Entries are the proportion of the elite who participated in the 1972 or 1980 campaign. Weighted N = 2,339.

Scores of less than one half of 1% are not reported.

PART II

Changes Within the Parties

CHAPTER 4

Party Reform: Social Composition and Party Attachment

The circulation of campaign personnel in the period following 1972 is central to many of our analytic concerns. Among other interests, it provides a first insight into some of the extended consequences of the movement to reform the presidential selection process. "Reform," especially within the Democratic party, included broadening the representation and increasing the participation of social groups that had presumably been excluded by white male dominance of party organization decisions. The Miami convention of 1972, with its collection of counterculture people and their often flamboyant public appearances, provided a colorful image of the consequences of including groups previously only minimally represented in Democratic nominating activities. More formally, the rules adopted by the Democratic party following the violence-ridden convention in Chicago in 1968, and the ensuing defeat of the establishment candidate Hubert Humphrey, literally established quotas to ensure the numerical representation of women, the young, and racial minorities. Again, in Lasswellian terminology, the reform efforts to open participation in the nominating process were efforts to promote "social circulation" which would change the demographic composition of the elite.

By 1972 social circulation had, indeed, already increased the numbers of blacks, women, and the young among the Democratic convention delegates (and of women among the Republicans).[1] Subsequent disputes over the imposition of quotas resulted in a relaxation of some of the rules for delegate selection; but continued emphasis on the openness of participation and the encouragement of heretofore underrepresented groups were still very much the Democratic party norms in 1976 and 1980.[2] Our interest is in the question of whether the formal attempts to change group representation at the conventions were subsequently reflected in voluntary decisions to engage in, or disengage from, campaign activity. However successful the reforms in changing the social composition of conventions, to what extent did the same reforms establish new norms that guided individual decisions to move into or out of the 1972–1980 presidential campaign elite?

Although the Republicans were not torn asunder by fights about the methods of selecting delegates, they, too, initiated reforms of a more moderate and voluntary nature in order to encourage "positive action" in creating broad participation in the composition of delegations.[3] Even these moderate movements were tempered by conservative-led modifications, but the Republicans have not been impervious to the effects of reforms initiated by the Democrats. Moreover, certain reforms, such as direct primaries, have in some instances been forced upon the GOP by state law. Finally, it should be noted that the apportionment scheme for allocating delegates to the states has been working in an exorable way in recent times to enlarge the Republican conventions though, in general, at the expense of moderate factions within the party.[4]

---

[1] For a description of changes in the representation of minorities at the conventions between 1964 and 1972, see John S. Jackson III, "Some Correlates of Minority Representation in the National Conventions, 1964–1972," *American Politics Quarterly* 3 (April 1975: 171–88. Distributions for each party during the 1968–1980 period are presented in Warren J. Mitofsky and Martin Plissner, "The Making of the Delegates: 1968–1980," *Public Opinion* 3 (October-November 1980): 37–43.

[2] See David E. Price, *Bringing Back the Parties* (Washington, DC: Congressional Quarterly), esp. chap. 6. In 1980 the required representation of women among the delegates was actually more stringent than in 1972.

[3] See Robert J. Huckshorn and John F. Bibby, "National Party Rules and Delegate Selection in the Republican Party," *Political Science* 16 (Fall 1983): 656–66.

[4] Moderates and the Ripon Society in particular have challenged the apportionment formula on the grounds that it deviates from the norm of equitable delegate representation according to state population size and applies a bonus rule that has tended

Thus, the Republican party, too, merits attention with respect to the question of the fallout from reform.

Our line of inquiry is sharpened within each party by attending to the influence of the candidates on personnel circulation. We will examine the social circulation of campaign elites within two broad groupings in each party, groupings distinguished by tendencies to support one or another wing of each party. For the Democrats, the two clusters of delegates are made up of those who, in general, supported the waning liberal leadership represented by George McGovern, Morris Udall, and Edward Kennedy, and those whose allegiances lay with the traditional party leadership represented by Hubert Humphrey, Edmund Muskie, and Henry Jackson.[5] On the Republican side we separate the followers of centrist candidates such as Ford, Anderson, Baker, and Bush from those who supported the candidacy of Ronald Reagan, representing the new and dominant right wing of the party.[6]

The expectation (or hypothesis) which makes this separation of delegates into opposing camps appropriate is that the social circulation of supporters of Republican moderates and Democratic liberals should be more likely to reflect the goals of reform than would turnover among the followers of the more conservative of the parties' leaders, traditional Democrats and right-wing Republicans. The context provided by the politics of the 1970s would, by extension, lead us to expect sharpest evidence of social circulation among supporters of liberal Democrats and least evidence of the reform spirit among the more conservative followers in Republican ranks.

The most dramatic evidence that reforms in the social composition of convention delegates were followed by commensurate changes in the social composition of the campaign elites is pro-

---

to favor smaller, or less competitive, states. For impassioned statements on this issue, see Josiah Lee Auspity, "A Republican View of Party," *Public Interest* (1982); and Sidney Blumenthal, "The Right Rules," *New Republic* 191 (July 16 and 23, 1984): 18–20.

[5] In terms of Appendix Table D.2, the liberals are composed of categories 1–5 and the traditionalists of categories 7, 8, 10, and 11. Although we will analyze the mobilization of support for the Carter candidacy of 1976, our major focus of attention within the Democratic party will be on the changing roles of the liberal supporters of McGovern and the supporters of "traditional" party leadership.

[6] The moderates are made up of categories 1–4 in Appendix Table D.1, and the conservatives come from categories 5–8.

vided by the changing incidence of women within these various subsets of campaign activists. If we survey the evidence across both parties, it comes as no surprise to observe that the strongest representation of women is within the cadre of delegates who supported the Democratic left (see Figure 4.1). The gender difference between the two groupings within the Democratic party is evident in all three components of the campaign elite, the mobilized and the disengaged as well as the continuously active. However, of most interest for the analysis of social circulation, the intraparty difference is sharpest within the *mobilized* activists who entered the campaign elite after 1972.

The impact of the mobilization of a disproportionate number of women activists is further accentuated by the fact that, in comparison with the continuing participants, in each wing of the party there is a lower incidence of women among the disengaged. Thus, among liberals and traditionalists alike, Democratic women were less often numbered among the *disengaged* and more often numbered among the *mobilized.* The net result was a double gain for the representation of women *following* the 1972 campaign. This provides clear evidence that although the reform efforts were spearheaded by liberal delegates to the 1972 convention, those efforts were subsequently reflected in both segments of the Democratic party, with a notable increase in the proportion of women campaigners as a consequence of social circulation in the party's campaign elite.

Social circulation of men and women among Republicans differed dramatically from that among Democrats. Within the Republican campaign elite, women were *more* likely, not less likely, to drop out of the activist role between 1972 and 1980, and thereby diminished their relative numbers. The more striking difference between the two parties, however, lies in the fact that mobilization in both wings of the Republican party moved even more heavily to favor male representation as almost three out of every four of the newly mobilized were men.

A sharp contrast between the two parties' concern with reform may be deduced from the fact that as Democrats relaxed some of their formal rules for delegate selection, their efforts to engage more women were rewarded by the informal voluntary increase of campaign activity among women while the rate of female participation in Republican campaigning dropped despite the recruitment

Figure 4.1

Presence of Women Among Campaign Activists, 1972–1980

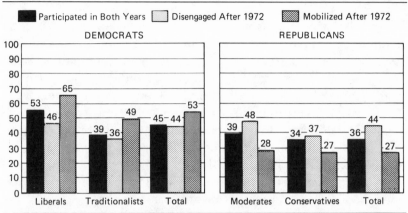

Note: Entries are the proportion of women within each category; for example, of all liberal Democrats who were campaign participants in 1972 and 1980, 53 percent were women. The weighted number of cases on which the percentages in this figure and in Figures 4.2–4.5 are based are as follows, reading from left to right in the figure: liberals—625, 283, 97; traditionalists—723, 142, 250; total—1,573, 481, 460; moderates—419, 75, 76; conservatives—674, 71, 134; Total—1,136, 160, 219. The number of cases varies slightly from figure to figure because of differing amounts of missing data.

of larger numbers of women as convention participants. It is a commentary on the impact of post-1968 reforms and of the women's movement, however, that even their reduced share for women was still well beyond the overall delegate share for women at the 1968 convention, namely, 16 percent.

Figure 4.1 also suggests a modest interparty parallel in the tendency of women to be engaged more often on behalf of moderate Republican candidates than on behalf of the new conservative alternative offered by Reagan. In anticipation of analyses of political perspectives that will be presented in later chapters, it is worth noting that the women who dropped out of the Republican elite were quite clearly less conservative in their views than were their male counterparts who disengaged following the 1972 election, and less conservative than women who remained active. (Given the conservative mode among all groups of Republican delegates, we think it appropriate to describe the female dropouts as less conservative rather than more liberal.) This was particularly

true among the Reagan supporters, and it provides an early intima-
tion of a subsequent conclusion that the circulation of Republican
campaign elites moved the Republican elites marginally to the
right.

The impact of this aspect of social circulation on the 1972–1980
Republican campaign elite as a whole was minimal, nevertheless,
simply because the numbers involved were so limited. Even
though women disengaged more often than did men, and moderate
women more often than conservative women, the entire component
of circulation involved in disengagement consisted of no more than
one in ten of the total Republican elite. Nevertheless, the evidence
that social circulation can have a marked influence on the character
of an elite is clear; and especially within the Democratic party the
evidence is more than suggestive that social circulation may, indeed, be a reflection of larger institutional changes.[7]

Turning to the second group targeted for increased representation in Democratic party reforms, we see that the data in Figure 4.2
show directly parallel findings concerning the presence of nonwhites in the Democratic campaign elites. The evidence is more
subdued but still fits the pattern observed for women. In the Democratic elite, nonwhites disengaged less often than whites, while at
the same time increasing their representation among the newly
mobilized. The absence of special efforts to promote minority representation within the Republican party is reflected in the data
which suggest no visible change one way or another affecting the
limited representation of nonwhites in the 1972–1980 campaign
elites, regardless of party faction.

The third reform theme, caricatured among Democrats with
the rallying cry of "don't trust anyone over 30," is reflected in

[7] Greater representation of women undoubtedly carries with it great symbolic value
and both reflects and facilitates the entry of women into the political elite. With
respect to convention decision-making and prominent political issues, however,
gender has proven to be of only modest value in an explanatory sense. This was one
of the signal findings of Jeane Kirkpatrick's analysis of the 1972 data, *The New
Presidential Elite: Men and Women in National Politics* (New York: Russell Sage
Foundation and Twentieth Century Fund, 1976), chap. 13. Similar results appeared
in a comparison of men and women delegates from each party in Michigan both
before (1964) and after (1976) the onset of the women's movement. The notable
exceptions in 1976 were issues directly involving gender roles and politics. See M.
Kent Jennings and Barbara G. Farah, "Social Roles and Political Resources: An
Overtime Study of Men and Women in Party Elites," *American Journal of Political
Science* 25 (August 1981): 462–82.

Figure 4.2

Presence of Nonwhites Among Campaign Activists, 1972–1980

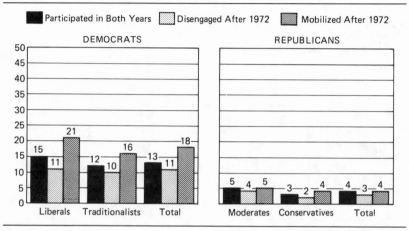

Note: Entries are the proportion of nonwhites within each category. See Figure 4.1 for base numbers of cases.

Figure 4.3, which displays the relative contributions of the younger cadres, those under 45 in 1980.[8] The social circulation of age groups is, however, more similar across the two parties than was the case where gender and race were concerned. Interestingly, the expected age differential between continuing core participants and those who dropped out after 1972 is virtually nonexistent in the ranks of Republican moderates and the Democratic liberals. Contrary to reasonable expectations, those dropouts were not visibly older than the core from which they disengaged. Continuing the interparty parallel, we see that an expected differential resulting from the disengaged being older than the continuing core was evident, however, in the more conservative wings of both parties. Moreover, in both wings of both parties the newly mobilized were almost inevitably visibly younger than the continuing core of campaign participants and, if we consider the age distribution of the conservative dropouts in both parties, the newly mobilized provide an extra impetus to social circulation in those wings of each party.

[8]The age of 45 was chosen as the dividing line for analysis to provide an uncomplicated reflection of differences, both intraparty and interparty, that roughly sorted out those over 30 in 1968 and yet avoided selecting a cut-off point that would be extreme for any of the four party factions in question.

Figure 4.3

Presence of the "Young" Among Campaign Activists, 1972–1980

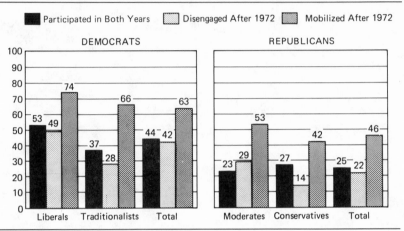

Note: Entries are the proportion under 45 years of age in 1980 in each category. See Figure 4.1 for base numbers of cases.

Among Democrats, reforms intended to change group representation among delegates attending nominating conventions had broader implications for the changing of party norms, and they spilled over to change the social composition of the campaign activists as well. Because of the relatively large proportions of Democratic delegates who participated in social circulation, by 1980 the Democratic campaign activists included substantially larger numbers of women, the young, and racial minorities than had the elite who participated in the McGovern campaign of 1972, to say nothing of the pre-reform campaign elites of the 1960s and earlier. The change was pervasive but was most dramatic within the cadres of the liberal supporters.

In many respects the Republican party participated in the reform movement right along with the Democrats,[9] but the circulation of Republican campaign personnel did not produce a social circulation to match that of the Democrats. Although the 1980 Republican cadres were younger than those of 1972, they were no less dominated by white participants and they were clearly more heavily populated by white males.

[9] See Robert J. Huckshorn, *Political Parties in America*, 2nd ed. (Monterey, CA: Brooks/Cole, 1984), pp. 111–13

The Eliteness of Campaign Activists

The efforts to open the presidential selection process to the participation of groups that presumably had been excluded in the past did very little to diminish the elite character of campaign personnel. The campaign activists in both wings of both parties continued to be composed of the economically well-to-do, well-educated, organization managers and members of the professions.[10] Although there was some marginal dilution of the homogeneity of the members of the Democratic left wing, the fact that they continued to be drawn from the social and economic elite is perhaps best represented in Figure 4.4, which shows the incidence of postgraduate education. In both parties the less conservative wings tended to contain the better educated, with the difference increasing among Republicans between 1972 and 1980, and diminishing among Democrats because of the disengagement of an exceptionally well-educated subset of the New Left.

More generally, the circulation of campaign personnel within the Democratic party produced a social circulation that did little to diminish the elite nature of activists while reflecting the new norms promoted by efforts to bring about reform within the party. On the Republican side, the circulation of personnel did not produce any substantial change in the background attributes of the campaign elite other than the paradoxical increase in the dominance of white males.

Campaign Activists as Political Elites

In both parties the campaign activists of our study were clearly members of the political as well as the social elite. Reports on their officeholding during the 1972–1980 period document this conclusion, but they also belie some of the more extreme characterizations of the presumed impact of the presidential selection process reforms on the political background and experience of convention delegates. Almost half of the delegates in both parties also held some public office during the same period. Moreover, four out of every five Republican delegates and three out of every four Demo-

[10] Jeane Kirkpatrick, *The New Presidential Elite: Men and Women in National Politics* (New York: Russell Sage Foundation and Twentieth Century Fund, 1976), Tables 3.1 and 3.2. Also see Appendix B for additional descriptive information about the 1972 and 1980 delegates as of 1981.

Figure 4.4

Incidence of Postgraduate Education Among Campaign Activists, 1972–1980

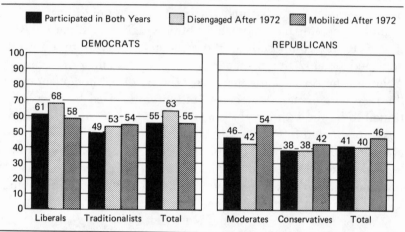

Note: Entries are the proportion who reported education beyond the undergraduate level. See Figure 4.1 for base numbers of cases.

cratic delegates held some party office during the period of our study.

Predictably, the core activists in both parties were, in general, more likely to be officeholders—particularly holders of party office—than were the sometime activists who participated in the circulation among the elites. Equally predictably, as Figure 4.5 reveals, the incidence of party officeholding varied with campaign activation more than did the incidence of holding public office. In both parties a further disaggregation of the data for an examination of circulation into and out of the ranks of party officeholders finds no more than one in five of those who became disengaged or mobilized as campaign activists nevertheless holding party office continuously between 1972 and 1980 (as against 40 to 55 percent of the core campaigners). Between 35 and 50 percent of those who disengaged from campaign activity after 1972 also dropped out of the ranks of party officeholders—and only 2 or 3 percent were drawn into party office; conversely, comparable proportions (35 to 45 percent) of those newly mobilized to presidential campaign activity were also newly inducted into party office after 1972 (with only 3–9 percent dropping party office as they were activated by a presidential campaign).

Figure 4.5

Officeholding Among Campaign Activists, 1972–1980

■ Participated in Both Years
☐ Disengaged After 1972
▨ Mobilized After 1972

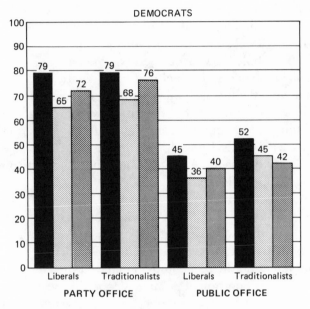

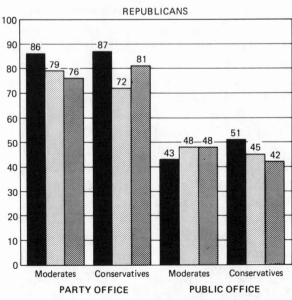

Note: Entries are the proportion who held some party or public office during the 1972–1980 period.

Among Republicans, this pattern of changes in party office-holding was simply not present where public office was concerned. Core campaign activists were no more likely to be continuous officeholders than were those involved in the circulation of campaign elites (some 15 to 20 percent in each group), and among the latter there was no coincidence of changes in public officeholding and campaign activity. Among Democrats the contrast between public and party officeholding was not quite as dramatic. Core campaign activists were visibly more inclined to be continuously in public office than were the disengaged or mobilized, and there was a modest but clear and consistent variation between changes in public officeholding and changes in campaign activity. Nevertheless, for Democrats as well as Republicans, it was true that presidential campaign activity was more closely tied to holding party office than to holding public office.

Much more surprising, not only were the various patterns of party and public officeholding very similar for Democrats and Republicans, but they were essentially the same for both major factions of both parties. It is true that the Democratic left boasted somewhat fewer public officeholders than did the Democratic center—just as the proportion of public officeholders was lower among Republican moderates than among the conservatives. And it was also true that among public officeholders the Democratic traditionalists had a larger representation of the elite state governors, U.S. Senators, and Congressmen than did the liberals. Nevertheless, the image of a Democratic party bereft of experienced leadership because of the triumph of left-oriented reform is not reflected in either the intraparty or interparty comparisons of the incidence of public officeholding among these campaign activists. And the denial is at least equally evident with respect to experience in party office. As with public office, the data in Figure 4.5 do not reveal the extent to which liberal and traditional party leaders differed in status—with the latter including more of the prestigious and most visible and recognizable state and national party leaders. Nevertheless, it seems clear that the widely cited contrast between "professionals" in the Democratic center and "amateurs" on the left was overdrawn.[11]

[11] Comparable data from the first phase of our study are presented in Kirkpatrick, *The New Presidential Elite: Men and Women in National Politics* (New York: Russell Sage Foundation and Twentieth Century Fund, 1976), Table 1.2. Those data suggest much sharper differences in 1972, particularly in interparty comparisons of Democrats and Republicans, than we observed for the full period of 1972 to 1980.

Subjective Commitment to Party

Critics of the efforts to reform the presidential selection process have argued that the base of participation may have been broadened but at the expense of diluting the participants' commitment to party. The full argument is complex and we shall return to it at many points in this book. We introduce it now in order to follow our analysis of changes in the social composition of the campaign elites with an immediate first-level search for correlative changes in levels of devotion to party.

Our measure of commitment to party is straightforward and borrows directly from a measure of party attachment used in the National Election Studies. Delegates were asked to locate themselves along a seven-point scale of attachment running from "not very strongly" (1) on one end to "very strongly" (7) on the other. While the bulk of the choices lay toward the "very strongly" end, there was sufficient variation to permit at least three categories of differentiation: strong supporters (7 on the scale), moderate supporters (5–6), and weak supporters (1–4). When these three categories are distributed across the two parties, the result is a six-point index running from strong Democratic supporters at one extreme to strong Republican supporters at the other. The results are as follows:

	Strong	Moderate	Weak	Weighted N
Republicans	55%	27	18	100% (1,537)
Democrats	41%	28	31	100% (2,594)

Considering that all of these respondents had crossed the threshold of partisan commitment to become convention delegates, and that most of them have impressive records of service to the party, the presence of substantial numbers of less than strongly committed partisans in each party is significant in itself.

Beyond that, the interparty contrasts command immediate attention. If we take the delegates as a whole, the GOP had more committed partisans. Establishing with certainty the origins of these party differences would require a more intensive line of research than we can undertake here. What we can do, however, is repeat the strategy adopted for the analysis of changes in the social composition of the party elites. For this first inquiry into the strength or level of party support, however, we will begin with the analytic components of our scheme for studying the circulation of the elites. Among the continuously active members of the 1972–1980 elites we will preserve the distinction among the three cohorts, those who were first-time delegates in 1972, 1976, and 1980, respectively. Following an inspection of the level of party support within each of the party's three cohorts, we will then turn to a further disaggregation of each party's sometime activists into the two factional groupings of followers used in the analysis of changing social composition.

Because there is a higher rate of turnover in the Democratic presidential campaign elite, the apparently stronger attachment to party among Republicans might be artifactual. Disengagement from presidential politics would seem to be prima facie evidence of lesser attachment, with the larger number of disengaged among the Democrats depressing the overall average for the party. By the same token, new recruits to the presidential elite (also more numerous among the Democrats) might be expected to have less commitment to their party than would the party veterans. This, again, might be particularly true of a Democratic elite which had undergone the changes in social composition we have just observed. Thus, if we disaggregate the two parties by participation profiles, we may discover that the overall difference between the parties stems from different levels of commitment among the new entrants. We may also find that the differences in party leadership patterns controlling the delegate selection process in specific years account for yet another portion of the overall party differences in level of attachment. In examining the impact of circulation patterns on partisan intensity little information will be lost by simply looking at the proportion of delegates who expressed very strong attachment. Those proportions are shown in Table 4.1.

These figures are extremely revealing on a number of counts. In the first place, they lay to rest the possibility that the greater overall attachment of Republicans to their party stems simply from divergent patterns of circulation. Republicans within each of the five activity patterns shown above feel closer to their party than do similarly defined Democrats.[12] The margin of interparty differences

[12] Evidence from other delegate surveys also suggests a basic difference between the parties in terms of party commitment, whatever the source of that difference might be. See Denis G. Sullivan, "Party Unity: Appearance and Reality," *Political Science Quarterly* 92 (Winter 1977–78): 635–45. It is also the case that at the mass public

Table 4.1

Strong Party Support and the Circulation of Campaign Elites

	Continuously Active			Disen-gaged	Mobil-ized
	1972	1976	1980	1972	1980
Republicans	55 (386)	59 (384)	64 (357)	37 (120)	46 (157)
Democrats	40 (498)	46 (525)	57 (529)	19 (354)	44 (326)

Note: Entries are the proportion in each category who described themselves as strong party supporters (numbers of cases are in parentheses).

varies considerably, however. It virtually disappears between the subsets of newly mobilized activists, among whom the contrasting changes in social composition might have produced the largest differences. At the same time, the higher rate of withdrawal among the Democrats clearly made a significant contribution to overall party differences. The disengaged Democrats constituted nearly twice as many of their party as did the disengaged Republicans of theirs (15.9 percent versus 8.5 percent), and the interparty difference was at its most acute precisely among the disengaged. Nevertheless, the higher rate of disengagement within the Democratic elites provides only one explanation for the overall difference between party.

Turning to the three cohorts of continuously active campaigners, we see the Republican edge over the Democrats reflected in each cohort. However, the interparty differences also diminish steadily across cohorts from 1972 to 1980; and in both parties the level of support is higher in each successive cohort from 1972 to 1980. Given that our measure of strength of party support was taken at only one point in time, early 1981, we have no direct evidence of change in levels of support and therefore cannot lay out and test the various possible ways in which this static picture may have been created. We can, however, take advantage of what we think we know already about the changing political composition of our campaign elites and we can search for a first-level explanation of our 1981 observations in the political composition of each of the three

---

level strong Republicans less frequently desert their presidential candidate than do strong Democrats, 1964 being the only exception between 1952 and 1980.

cohorts of each party. By decomposing each party cohort into the two major groupings representing the parties' major ideological factions we can, in fact, greatly increase our understanding of these patterns of party support.

First, and most simply, within the Republican party the similarities in the level of party support among the continuously active, in both major groupings of candidate supporters, are more impressive than are the differences. This is the first of numerous pieces of evidence that support our opening argument that Republican contests for party leadership were internal and did not pit "antiparty" forces against a "proparty" faction in the same manner as occurred in the Democratic party contests. Indeed, among the continuously active the single cohort that exhibits any intraparty difference between party factions is the 1976 cohort, in which the Reagan challengers appear to have been *more*—not less— supportive of party than were the party regulars who nominated President Ford. In 1972 and again in 1980, Republican moderates' enthusiasm for party was matched by the fervor of Reagan conservatives. The shift of the balance of numerical power to the latter group in 1980 did not, therefore, have any implications for increasing or decreasing the delegates' sense of subjective support for the Republican party.

In later chapters, with a variety of different indicators of the centrality of party in different contexts, this picture of Republican consensus over the importance of party will be modified but not contradicted. In the meantime, the disaggregation suggests that the overall cohort differences in strength of Republican party support may reflect enduring differences across the cohorts, but they are not the result of compositional changes resulting from the competition for party leadership and the nomination.

Among Democrats the story is more complex. There is strong evidence that party support is, in part, a reflection of the delegates' recent roles as supporters or challengers of established party leadership. There are sharp factional differences within the two cohorts that witnessed McGovern's nomination and Carter's renomination, differences that accord with the charge that those on the left who were dedicated to party reform were not themselves dedicated partisans. Their lack of partisan fervor is not only apparent in comparison to the level of support offered by the followers of traditional party leadership, but it is also responsible for another large portion of the Republican-Democratic differences that prompted this portion of our inquiry. In both the 1972 and 1980 cohorts, followers of traditional Democratic party leadership clearly matched the enthusiasm for party marked by Republican campaign activists. The large interparty difference within the 1972 cohort stemmed from the lack of party support offered by the dominant liberal Democratic faction of that year. The fact that interparty differences are smaller in the 1980 cohort was largely a consequence of the relatively smaller number of active liberals in the Democratic elite. Both the persistent interparty differences in level of subjective support for the party and the variation in those differences across cohorts are a function of the recent Democratic contests for party leadership. They contain only a mild suggestion of pervasive, qualitative party differences that would make Republican campaign activists generically more partisan than their Democratic counterparts; but they do reflect the compositional differences between the two parties during this era.

Having largely accounted for the party differences in strength of party support that were encountered as we began to investigate the consequences of the changing social composition of the Democratic party, we can now return to our point of departure. The disaggregation of our data to reveal intraparty, factional differences also modifies, at least slightly, an earlier conclusion. Although the total set of newly mobilized Democrats pretty well matched the strength of party support among newly mobilized Republicans, the entries in Table 4.2 suggest that the prime locus of changing social composition in the Democratic ranks was also marked by a slightly lower level of enthusiasm for party. Newly mobilized liberals included somewhat fewer strong party supporters than were to be found among newly mobilized traditionalists or newly mobilized Republicans. Nevertheless the magnitude of the difference is not great and it scarcely modifies the equally important reaffirmation of the conclusion that the circulation of campaign elites in the postreform era strengthened the sentiments of Democratic partisanship rather than extending the degeneration of party bonds.

The consequences of circulation for the level of subjective party support were, of course, most dramatic for Democrats. Even within the ranks of the liberals, new recruits were twice as likely as the disengaged to report themselves as strong party supporters. Nevertheless, with the data for both major factions of both parties

Table 4.2

**Strong Party Support and Circulation Patterns
Within Major Party Factions**

	Continuously Active			Disen-gaged	Mobil-ized
	1972	1976	1980	1972	1980
Republicans					
Moderates	58 (172)	51 (135)	65 (75)	33 (52)	45 (49)
Conservatives	61 (162)	64 (239)	64 (276)	48 (21)	47 (102)
Democrats					
Liberals	40 (168)	49 (171)	54 (176)	21 (121)	41 (84)
Traditionalists	57 (152)	47 (217)	68 (301)	20 (69)	50 (125)

Note: Entries are the proportion in each category who described themselves as strong party supporters (numbers of cases are in parentheses). This table is not simply a disaggregation of Tables 3.7, 3.8, and 4.1; the party factions as defined in this chapter omit some delegates, including those with missing data on candidate preferences.

before us it is apparent that the drama really lay in the absence of strong party attachment among the Democrats who had withdrawn from active campaign participation. Although disengaged Republicans were visibly less often stirred by partisanship than were the core activists, the absolute level of their enthusiasm for party clearly outstripped that among the disengaged Democrats. The latter, in turn, present the image of former partisans retreating after a demoralizing defeat. Against the double weight of preferring the losing faction in a defeated party, the show of party support by those newly recruited to the liberal Democratic faction—in part, at least, because they belonged to protected social categories—seems the more remarkable.

In later chapters we will return to the analysis of the level of party support provided by different candidate-preference groups. Our efforts thus far have been devoted to exploring the possible linkage between changes in social composition and changes in party commitment stemming from a common origin in the circulation of party elites. The first fruits of our analysis indicate that the reformation of the presidential selection process did indeed reflect rather pervasive norms that also influenced individual decisions to participate in—or withdraw from—the presidential campaign elite, at least within the Democratic party. However, the circulation of new personnel into the ranks of the campaign activists did not appear to dilute overall commitments to party but, to the contrary and particularly among Democrats, served to raise the level of partisan zeal.

CHAPTER 5

The Motivational Bases
of Political Involvement

Because changes in national party leadership ultimately re-
shape national politics as well as national governments, the professional student of American politics must be perennially concerned
with the institutional structures which channel the processes of
leadership selection. In the past decade the literature on American
politics has been preoccupied with the changes that have been
made in the rules governing participation in the presidential selection process. However much change may have been needed to
reestablish Democratic party legitimacy and power, much of the
interest in the changes stems from a fear that the process may have
been opened to a wider range of ideological confrontation or to
unorthodox candidacies at the expense of the parties themselves.[1]
Support for the parties as enduring institutions may have been replaced by support for particular causes or candidates. In our first

[1] There is considerable controversy about the relationship between rules changes
and the flavor of presidential politics since the mid-1960s. For a provocative argument that insurgency rather than alteration of rules accounts for the "different,"
more ideological presidential politics beginning with the 1964 Republican convention, see John R. Petrocik and Dwaine Marvick, "Exploring Party Elite Transformation: Institutional Changes and Insurgent Politics," *Western Political Quarterly* 36
(September 1983): 345–63.

response to this concern, the analysis of party support in chapter 4, we search for evidence that changing social composition of the campaign elite had been accompanied by a reduction in the absolute level of attitudinal support for party.

We will continue to examine the proposition, now from two additional perspectives. First, we will look at changes in elite attitudes relevant to a series of political orientations, including concerns with partisanship, with policies, and with more personal rewards. Second, in the next chapter we will describe behavioral patterns that reflect these different orientations and result in political activity that is variously directed at promoting the welfare of the party, the implementation of policy goals, or the election of particular candidates.

Our various indicators of the attitudinal underpinnings of elite political behavior reflect different themes. The first and most direct attack on the problem was presented in chapter 4. There we noted that while reforms had greatly altered the social composition of the Democratic party, they did not appear to have produced more than a minor reduction in the level of attitudinal support for party as expressed in the delegates' degree of subjective attachment to their party. The other two sets of indicators to which we now turn both have the advantage of providing a comparative basis for judging delegates' support of party *relative* to other competing commitments or objectives.

The second of our three sets of indicators of partisanship deals with the rewards sought through political activity of the individual members of our campaign elite. These rewards were described by Jeane Kirkpatrick in *The New Presidential Elite* as incentives to participation.[2] Both in the original data collection of 1972 and in our return visit in 1981, delegates were asked to assign importance to each of twelve statements that were presented as general "reasons for being involved in politics." The items were not at all focused on presidential politics; they were culled from the more general literature on political participation and were adapted for use with our elite population.[3] In addition to emphasizing political goals, and

[2] Jeane Kirkpatrick, *The New Presidential Elite: Men and Women in National Politics* (New York: Russell Sage Foundation and Twentieth Century Fund, 1976), chap. 4.
[3] Much of that literature, in turn, is indebted to the classic formulation of purposive, solidary, and material incentive systems as laid down in Peter B. Clarke and James Q. Wilson, "Incentive Systems: A Theory of Organizations," *Administrative Science Quarterly* 4 (September 1961): 129–66. Early examples of systematic research

the values attached to supporting party, issue, or candidate, the twelve statements included assessments of the importance of a variety of other values that might be enhanced by political activity. As we will note in more detail, the twelve items designed to diagnose reasons for elite participation in politics in fact reduced empirically to four dimensions for our political activists: (1) policy orientations, (2) partisan commitments, (3) social solidary rewards, and (4) personal career goals.

We will also turn to a third set of attitudinal assessments that is more sharply focused on political goals that might be sought through participation in presidential nominating conventions. These "instrumental" convention goals concentrate more directly than the twelve "reasons for political involvement" on two of the basic orientations underlying the contest for nomination in the 1972 convention of the Democratic party: maintenance of party and promotion of policy commitments. The particular measures that are used to capture these orientations were taken directly from the work of Richard C. Hofstetter, as inspired by the seminal volume by James Q. Wilson, *The Amateur Democrat*.[4]

This third set of measures was selected because of its apparent relevance to the changes that were sweeping the Democratic party in the late 1960s and early 1970s, changes that were prompted by dissatisfaction with past party performance in both domestic and foreign policy. The central thrust of Hofstetter's work was to distinguish between those activists who gave greatest weight to the central importance of party and those who would forego the rewards of partisanship in order to promote the primacy of issues in the selection of the party's nominee.[5]

---

on incentives for party recruitment and maintenance include Samuel J. Eldersveld, *Political Parties* (Chicago: Rand McNally, 1964); and M. Margaret Conway and Frank B. Feigert, "Motivation, Incentive Systems, and the Political Party Organization," *American Political Science Review* 62 (December 1968): 1159–73.

[4] *The Amateur Democrat: Club Politics in Three Cities* (Chicago: University of Chicago Press, 1966); Richard C. Hofstetter, "The Amateur Politician: A Problem in Construct Validation," *Midwest Journal of Political Science* 15 (February 1971): 31–56.

[5] In a related vein, see John W. Soule and James W. Clarke, "Amateurs and Professionals: A Study of Delegates to the 1968 Democratic Convention," *American Political Science Review* 64 (September 1970): 888–98; John W. Soule and Wilma E. McGrath, "A Comparative Study of Presidential Nominating Conventions: The Democrats of 1968 and 1972," *American Journal of Political Science* 19 (August 1975): 1501–17; and John S. Jackson III and Robert A. Hitlin, "A Comparison of

It should be noted that political scientists' preoccupation with the affairs of the Democratic party, particularly in the 1970s, has produced a possible bias in research and writings about party which may be reflected in both of our multi-item sets of attitudinal indicators. Until the early 1980s, the Republican party was virtually ignored in studies of the political parties, and the problems of the Democrats were often taken as a generalized definition of problems facing "the party system." It seems highly probable that a more balanced interest in the decades-old ideological struggle between Republican moderates and conservatives, and in the successful insurgencies of Goldwater and Reagan, might have generated insights relevant to Republican presidential politics that could now complement an inquiry that is heavily colored with ideas stemming from the competition for power in the Democratic party.

Given our analytic preoccupation with the circulation of political elites, the contest between established lineages associated with historical factionalism among Republicans might warrant the application of theoretical propositions such as might be derived from Pareto's insights into the perennial struggle between the lions and the foxes. But factionalism within the Republican party has not been very salient to the research community, and if the terms of their contests for power do differ from those underlying the current contest within the Democratic party, they have not been articulated and they are missing from our research.[6] On the other hand, Hofstetter, Wilson before him, and others who have written on changes in American parties have been preoccupied with distinguishing the issue-oriented insurgents who were intent on gaining control of Democratic party affairs from the political "pros" who were the traditional Democratic party leaders. Rather than depicting rivalries between elite factions, their concern has been explicitly

---

Party Elites: The Sanford Commission and the Delegates to the Democratic Mid-Term Conferences," *American Politics Quarterly* 4 (October 1976): 441–81. A more intuitive approach reaching similar conclusions is represented by Aaron Wildavsky, "The Goldwater Phenomenon: Purists, Politicians, and the Two-Party System," *Review of Politics* 27 (July 1965): 386–431.

[6] Thus, one of the few analysts who paid much attention to the Republicans during the 1970s used measures that echoed earlier ones based on studies of Democrats. These measures are not necessarily inappropriate for Republicans; rather, there may be other dimensions that have been omitted because of the scholarly concern with the Democratic party. See Thomas H. Roback, "Amateurs and Professionals: Delegates to the 1972 Republican Convention," *Journal of Politics* 37 (May 1975): 436–68.

defined by a contest between an established elite and popular insurgencies ostensibly driven by ideological conviction.

If we consider the political origins of the Democratic insurgents, their contest with established party leaders has not been
viewed as a struggle between the foxes and lions of established and
competing elite groups. As described by Wilson and eventually by
Kirkpatrick, the contest was between novices, newly come to nomination politics, and experienced veterans, who represented continuity with party traditions. Moreover, the so-called amateur-
professional antithesis, which has been used to characterize the
recent contest between ideological innovation and organizational
maintenance within the Democratic party, has been less frequently
examined for its particular relevance to the contests for leadership
of the Republican party.[7] Nevertheless, it reflects the principal set
of ideas that shaped our research as well as that of others.

Our intent here is not to add fuel to the smoldering dispute that
revolves in part around matters of terminology and in part around
matters of interpretation. Various dichotomies and ideal types have
been proposed and labeled: amateurs versus professionals, purists
versus politicians, ideologues versus pragmatists, idealists versus
realists, candidate versus party loyalists, and so forth. Although we
shall occasionally use a shorthand term for the sake of parsimony
(our favorite is "purists" versus "pragmatists"), our inclination is to
avoid labels for three reasons. First, there is great confusion over
their dimensionality, their referents, and the interchangeability of
the various pairings.[8] Second, the empirical literature is not always
convincing in showing the expected regularities and corollaries
accompanying classifications into one or another of these types.
Purists do not necessarily put ideology above everything else and
pragmatists do not necessarily eschew firm policy preferences. Per-

---

[7] But see Thomas H. Roback, "Motivation for Activism Among Republican National
Convention Delegates: Continuity and Change 1972–1976," *Journal of Politics* 42
(February 1980): 181–201; and, on a more limited scale, Denis G. Sullivan, "Party
Unity: Appearance and Reality," *Political Science Quarterly* 92 (Winter 1977–78):
635–43.

[8] The literature is a quagmire. For two reasonable efforts to bring some order into the
chaos, see David E. Price, *Bringing Back the Parties* (Washington, DC: Congressional Quarterly, 1984), pp. 25–32; and, at a conceptual level at any rate, E. Gene
DeFelice, "Separating Professionalism from Pragmatism: A Research Note on the
Study of Political Parties," *American Journal of Political Science* 25 (November
1981): 796–807.

haps the most convincing evidence on this score comes from a study of delegates to thirteen state conventions in 1980, in which it was demonstrated that the perceived electability of a candidate was of *greater* importance than was ideological proximity—this despite a preponderance of purists among delegates of both parties.[9] The third reason for avoiding mutually exclusive labels follows directly from this point. If multiple dimensions are involved and if their salience can vary according to situation,[10] it is at least equally plausible to stick with separate, generic dimensions. Thus, we will find it more useful and less confusing to employ such concepts as party orientation, issue emphasis, candidate focus, social incentives, and personal rewards.

Changes in Incentives for Political Involvement

We shall shortly take advantage of the fact that within each of the two sets of attitudinal measures there are clusters of interrelated items that permit us to summarize most of the information contained in the individual items with a limited number of indices. It is, however, instructive to begin with a brief survey, item by item, of party and cohort similarities and differences. The overwhelming central message of the data (presented in Appendix E) is that while there is variability in the importance assigned to each of the twelve motivations, there is a striking similarity in the patterns of response by both Democrats and Republicans, and across all

[9] A partial replication yielded similar results for the 1972 national Democrats. See Walter J. Stone and Alan I. Abramowitz, "Winning May Not Be Everything, But It's More Important Than We Thought: Presidential Party Activists in 1980," *American Political Science Review* 77 (December 1983): 945–56.

[10] An analysis of the 1972 Democratic delegates, for example, revealed that the strength and competitiveness of local party politics strongly conditioned the relationship between an amateur-professional index and various attitudinal and role orientation variables. This same analysis, using the 1972–1981 Democratic panel also uncovered a very modest relationship between a delegate's classification in 1972 on the index and the likelihood of dwindling political activity after 1972 (tau-b = .17). See Debra Dodson, "The Mediating Impact of Sub-National Party Organization Strength on Reform Era Politics," paper presented at the annual meeting of the Midwest Political Science Association, Chicago, 1983. Jeane Kirkpatrick notes the unlikely probability of the same sort of single dimension characterizing party elites of different levels and at different times: *The New Presidential Elite: Men and Women in National Politics* (New York: Russell Sage Foundation and Twentieth Century Fund, 1976), pp. 133–37 and pp. 154–55 (notes 20–23).

three cohorts within each party. Given some of the sharp differences to be noted later that separate Democrats from Republicans, and that differentiate the cohorts in terms of policy-related candidate preferences, the homogeneity of elite responses to these twelve reasons for political involvement is impressive.

The pattern of uniformity as of 1981 is all the more remarkable because there have been visible and apparently systematic changes within the parties on virtually every one of the twelve statements between 1972 and 1980. Our primary insight into the nature of changes in response to questions about personal motives for political involvement is provided by the subset of the 1972 cohorts who participated in this study in 1972 and again in 1981. As we suggested in chapter 2, although that subset is only about one third of the original total set of 1972 delegates, it appears to be essentially an unbiased subset. As further evidence of the unbiased nature of our 1981 representation of the 1972 cohorts, Appendix Table C.4 makes possible a comparison of their *1972* responses to our twelve statements with the responses of their 1972 colleagues who did not respond to our 1981 questionnaire. The comparison indicates virtually no difference between panel and nonpanel membership in 1972. Consequently, we assume that any 1972 to 1980 changes in the attitudes of the panel subset reflect changes for the entire cohort.

These changes, along with the 1972–1980 cohort changes, are reflected in Table 5.1. The patterns of change (columns 1, 2, 4, and 5) often differ by party. In general, Democrats *increased* their sense of the importance of partisan rewards *and* their appreciation of solidary values; Republicans reflected a *decrease* in the importance attached to party, along with a *decrease* in the relevance of politics for personal careers. Both partisan groups reduced their sense of the importance of issues, Democrats more than Republicans.

The *intra*cohort (that is, 1972–1981 delegate panel) changes between 1972 and 1981 seem more significant when one reviews the *inter*cohort comparisons of the 1972 and 1980 cohorts (columns 2 and 3, 5 and 6). As of 1981, Republicans and Democrats in the 1980 cohort did not differ markedly in their attention to party *or* to issues; but 1980 Democrats were somewhat *more* inclined than 1980 Republicans to value the solidary benefits and personal career rewards associated with political activity. The contrast with interparty differences in 1972 is dramatic. Eight years earlier the Demo-

Table 5.1

Incentives for Involvement in Politics, 1972 and 1981

	Democrats			Republicans		
	Panel in 1972	Panel in 1981	1980 Delegates in 1981	Panel in 1972	Panel in 1981	1980 Delegates in 1981
Policy-Oriented						
To Support Policies	90	81	82	79	71	82
Elect Particular Candidates	97	97	95	94	95	96
Partisanship						
Strongly Attached to Party	59	58	74	90	78	80
Politics a Way of Life	72	73	84	80	73	77
Civic Responsibility	74	68	78	91	78	80

93

Social						
Friends and Family						
Active	26	37	41	33	37	30
Enjoy Social						
Contacts	57	61	72	68	65	67
Fun and Excitement	55	55	67	64	60	63
Personal Career						
Make Contacts	9	10	18	10	7	8
Political Career	33	25	43	32	22	33
Close to Important						
People	39	35	47	47	38	41
Visibility and						
Recognition	28	27	38	36	26	29
Maximum unweighted N	(775)	(775)	(1,387)	(458)	(458)	(852)

Notes: Entries are the proportion who responded "extremely important" or "quite important."

Proportions who responded "extremely important to elect particular candidates" are 78, 61, and 60% for the Democrats and 65, 54, and 63% for the Republicans.

cratic delegates to the 1972 convention had assigned a higher value to concerns over policy questions and issues than did the Republican delegates who, in turn, accorded much greater importance to party than did the Democrats. And in 1972 the Republicans—not the Democrats—attached greater importance to the incidental rewards of sociability and the instrumental enhancement of one's personal career.

The transposition of party differences on the importance of personal and solidary values and the convergence of emphases on the importance of party and policy most probably reflect a combination of factors, including the socialization into elite politics of many Democrats who had only limited experience before 1972, and the response of both Democrats and Republicans to a very different political context in 1980. Most of the *intra*cohort changes between 1972 and 1980 resulted in bringing the attitudes of the 1972 cohorts more closely into line with the 1981 levels of importance attached to reasons for participation by both sets of 1976 and 1980 cohorts (see Appendix E). Two of the three notable exceptions to this were on the Republican side. The 1981 intercohort differences regarding both the importance of supporting a given candidate and the importance of influencing policy are the consequence of a decline from the importance which the 1972 cohort had attached to these themes eight years earlier (possibly a reaction of 1972 moderates to the ideological insurgency of Reagan in 1980). On the Democratic side, the limited emphasis given to the pursuit of political careers in 1981 is also the consequence of a 7-point decline from 1972 (perhaps reflecting some disillusionment among frustrated ideologues of 1972). With these exceptions, all of the 1972 to 1980 changes within the 1972 cohorts brought them more into line with the other cohorts within their respective parties *and,* at the same time, reduced the magnitude of interparty differences. The resultant uniformity of the interparty, intercohort assessments in 1981 coupled with the nature or direction of most change across the eight-year interval following 1972 suggest a pervasive sharing of political cultures on the part of these elites who, in turn, do so much to shape the course of national politics.

There are remaining interparty differences and patterns of intraparty differences that suggest other influences at work in shaping these attitudes (see Appendix E for data on party cohorts). This resulted in a tendency for the 1980 Democratic cohort to attach *greater* importance to such personal rewards as are associated with joining family and friends in political activity, having a political career, enjoying new business and professional contacts, and having increased visibility and recognition as a result of party work (differences of 5, 18, 12, and 11 points, respectively, between the 1972 and 1980 cohorts, and margins of 11, 10, 6, and 9 points between Democrats and Republicans in the 1980 cohorts). The trends across the cohorts seem a clear indication that the personal objectives motivating participation changed in the course of the eight years. Among both Democrats and Republicans, the 1980 cohorts also seem more committed to political careers (a 10-point difference for Republicans) and, reflecting a now familiar theme, 1980 Republicans became more interested in supporting a political candidate for election (up 9 points) and influencing policy (up 11 points) than were their 1972 counterparts. The latter intercohort differences add to the evidence that the 1980 contest mobilized conservative support for the Reagan candidacy and presented the delegates of that year with a different political context than that which prevailed in the renomination of Nixon in 1972. These intuitively understandable variations do not, however, add up to any major qualification of the larger sense that political elites from both parties who became delegates at different times and under quite different circumstances ultimately came to share expectations about the rewards attached to their individual participation in presidential politics.

We have, therefore, evidence that speaks directly and reassuringly to some of our earlier concerns. In particular, experience, socialization, or the sheer passage of time produced changes in the perspectives of the 1972 Democratic delegates. Preoccupation with issues was modified at the same time that greater importance was attached to party. These and other changes brought the Miami Democrats more in line with what appear to be national norms, shared across party and most probably very durable through time. The impact of reform on the Democratic party may have brought major changes in the candidate selection process, and may have influenced the social composition of the party elite, but the amateurs' enthusiasm for ideological purity at the expense of party was apparently short-lived.

Instrumental Goals for Nominating Conventions

Moving from the personal frame of reference to an examination of goals that might be expected to vary with the context of particular nominating conventions does not alter our impression of attitudinal patterns that reflect widely shared perspectives among the national political elites. In Table 5.2 we display for each cohort within each

Table 5.2

Instrumental Goals for Nominating Conventions, by Party and Cohort

	Democratic Cohorts			Republican Cohorts		
	1972	1976	1980	1972	1976	1980
Policy-Oriented						
Standing firm for position even if it means resigning from party	43	31	30	25	31	27
Playing down some issues if it will improve the chances of winning	58	66	62	70	73	71
Selecting a nominee who is strongly committed on the issues	95	94	95	93	95	96
Party-Oriented						
Counting service to the party heavily in nominating candidates	70	81	84	88	85	84
Working to minimize disagreement within the party	82	87	87	92	89	86
Minimizing the role of the party organization in nominating candidates for office	28	23	20	18	19	23
Encouraging widespread participation in making most party decisions	93	91	92	93	92	93

Notes: The seven responses were offered to the following question: In thinking about decisions that are made at the conventions, which positions do you favor and which do you oppose?

Entries are the proportion who responded "strongly favor" or "favor."

party the proportions who assigned substantial importance to each of the seven goals that might be sought in the course of choosing a party nominee for president. There are some intercohort differences, particularly among Democrats, that seem clear evidence of the uniqueness of the 1972 campaign experience. Even in 1981, veterans of the 1972 convention were more likely than their counterparts from later years to emphasize the importance of standing firm for their issue positions (over those of the party) and minimizing the role of the party organization in the nominating process, just as they were *less* likely to favor rewarding party services or favor minimizing issues in order to enhance the chance of electoral success.

An inspection of the same measures taken in 1972 extends these indications of the uniqueness of the 1972 experience, but it also again emphasizes the ameliorating effects of the passage of time. In 1972, only 47 percent of the 1972 Democrats thought party services should be rewarded in the process of nominating candidates; this proportion increased dramatically to 70 percent (first column of Table 5.2) by 1981. In like manner, by 1981 the 47 percent who in 1972 had favored minimizing the role of party organization in the nominating organization in the nominating process had *decreased* to only 28 percent of the cohort. Republican delegates showed much less evidence of change over time. There was significant movement on only two items: increased support for rewarding party service (up to 88 percent in 1981 from 78 percent in 1972) *and* for attributing high importance to nominating a candidate who is strongly committed on the issues (up to 93 percent in 1981 from 82 percent in 1972). As with most changes in attitudes toward personal incentives for participation, all of these changes, among both Democrats and Republicans, worked to bring the 1972 cohorts more closely into line with the sentiments of the 1976 and 1980 groups.[11]

Taken together, the nineteen individual attitudinal assessments generated in 1981 portray a great homogeneity of outlook

[11] Using the 1972–1981 Democratic panel data from this study, Dodson has calculated an overtime stability of .60 (tau-b) on a trichotomized index based on responses to the seven items contained in Table 5.2. So-called professionals were considerably more stable on the measure than were "amateurs" and "semi-amateurs." See Dodson, "The Mediating Impact of Sub-National Party Organization Strength on Reform Era Politics," paper presented at annual meeting of the Midwest Political Science Association, Chicago, 1983.

across what might have been very disparate components of the national presidential campaign elites. The striking similarities of attitudes, both between parties and across cohorts, seem significant for two rather different reasons. First, they suggest that both sets of partisan campaign elites have had very similar experiences in participating within the context of a truly national political culture. Despite many observations that emphasize differences between Democrats and Republicans in concerns undergirding party reform, the entire set of indicators we have reviewed, including some directly relevant to reform themes, belies the presence of sharp party differences. It is, of course, possible that the appearance of shared perspectives among Democrats and Republicans is the accidental consequence of sharply different experiences and contexts. We shall see suggestions of this possibility as we explore intraparty differences in incentives and goals among the major candidate preference groups in each party. Nevertheless, it strains the imagination to believe that near consensus on the relative importance of the various incentives and goals is strictly a matter of accident. This seems even more the case when we note that 15 out of 18 substantial changes in attitude on the part of the two 1972 cohorts were in the direction of movement toward national means, and only 3 (quite explicable) attitudinal shifts actually diminished the sense of interparty, intercohort uniformity.[12]

Beyond this strong suggestion of a pervasive national political culture with widely shared distributions of sentiments with regard to important norms and values, the configurations are of importance to the political analyst because they give a different context for evaluating the meanings that have been attached to at least some of our attitudinal measures. Virtually all of the items we have analyzed have been used in previous research to support the conclusion that the Democratic elite of 1972 was in significant ways a unique, even aberrant, intrusion on national Democratic party politics. In particular, as we noted earlier, the questionnaire items that we have described as reflecting attitudes toward instrumental goals of nominating conventions have been used to distinguish newly arrived liberal purists from the pragmatic old hands among the traditional Democrats. Although the distinction between the policy

---

[12]Moreover, within the presumably deviant 1972 Democratic cohort, 8 of the 9 changes were in the direction of greater conformity with national norms.

orientations of the newcomers and the party attachments of the old-
timers may be a matter of generic importance, the presumed
uniqueness of the "New Elite" in the Democratic party of 1972 is
tempered by the evidence of strong similarities between them and
their Republican counterparts eight years later.

An important part of the message rests on changes in attitudinal perspectives in both parties across the eight-year span. Even
before we consider the consequences of the circulation of delegates
into and out of the ranks of the politically active, the evidence of
changes in individual attitudes over time within the subset of panel
respondents provides a useful insight into, and caution against,
overinterpreting a single set of indicators for a single population at
a single point in time. The possibility that subsequent experience,
events, and changing circumstances will influence individual perspectives is now documented. The consequences of such change
modify expectations based on the earlier observations and qualify
interpretations which those observations produced. This is not
necessarily to contradict earlier descriptions of 1972 as producing a
new Democratic presidential elite so much as it is to suggest that
predictions of dire consequences for the Democratic party of the
future, based on those descriptions, may have been exaggerated.

The Dimensional Organization of Attitudes

Our sense of the homogeneity of attitudes representing personal incentives and political goals is sharply modified when we
return to the familiar theme emphasizing differences separating the
various candidate preference groups. Very much as with the policy
preferences that we examined in earlier chapters, there are pervasive differences in the attitudinal postures adopted by different
candidate support groups. In a manner, and to a degree, thoroughly
congruent with much of the post-reform analysis commentary,
there are clear differences among candidate preference groups both
on the importance of various personal incentives and in support of
instrumental convention goals. However, rather than review these
differences in detail at this point, we will hold such inquiry until
after we have moved to two important steps summarizing our data.
These summaries are necessary, or certainly useful, as simplifica-
tions to facilitate our subsequent analyses of the impact of circula-

tion on the representation of these attitudes in the campaign elites of 1972 and of 1980. Without summarization we would be faced with the task of relating nineteen different attitudinal measures to the circulation patterns of twenty different candidate preference groups.

To present the consequences of circulation, we have chosen to emphasize attitudes about convention goals rather than personal incentives for political participation. We have done so for a number of reasons. First, the choice accentuates evidence of change in the values emphasized by the campaign activists. The results of analyses centered on personal incentives are similar in all respects to those involving political goals, except that the findings are muted in the former case. This may be a consequence of differences in the measurement properties of the items used. It may also be a result familiar to the students of cognitive psychology who have documented the generalization that people are often not very insightful about the factors that govern their own behavior. They are, therefore, unlikely to be reliable sources of information about why they do or do not choose to engage in any given activity, including participating in politics.[13]

Second, the decision not to emphasize *reasons* for participation also conforms to our sense that we are better equipped to observe consequences flowing from the rise and fall of candidates for national leadership, and the results of the processes of delegate selection, than we are to provide explanations or causal models of change in elite behavior that rest on analytic insight into the motives and the causal factors that might underlie the patterns of behavioral change. Here, as in our analyses of policy preferences, we are content to limit our inquiry to the impact of circulation process on the representation of differing political values, goals, and perspectives.

Nevertheless, our primary reason for choosing to highlight data pertaining to political goals to be sought in the course of nominating presidential candidates rests on the fact that at the detailed level of the attitudinal measures used to reflect these goals, we provide greatest continuity with the literature focusing on the consequences of party reform. As we noted above, precisely the same

---

[13] R. Nisbett and T. Wilson, "Telling More Than We Can Know: Verbal Reports on Mental Processes," *Psychological Review* 84 (1977): 231–59.

items assessing the relative importance of party and policy have been used in others' characterization of differences between the supporters of liberal leadership and those favoring the traditional Democratic party leadership. We will observe, shortly, that those differences remained very real in 1980, and we have added confidence in this and related conclusions because they are based on totally comparable measurement devices that connect this analysis to a broader research literature.

Our measures of attitudes toward the instrumental goals of nominating conventions can be reduced to two indices reflecting two primary dimensions: party and policy.[14] However, factor analyses revealed that the clustering of items concerning possible political goals of the convention varied somewhat by party. Among Republicans, the highlighting of policy concerns in the convention is based on the three items emphasizing support for standing firm on one's own position, for selecting a nominee who is strongly committed on the issues, and for opposing the playing down of issues in order to improve chances of winning. Among Democrats, the first statement, offering a choice between policy and party, is not a part of the policy-oriented dimension and is replaced by the item emphasizing broader participation in party affairs. This interparty difference seems quite understandable *if* one assumes that Democrats viewed the first item as a test of party loyalty while emphasis on ensuring representation for women, the young, and ethnic minorities was seen as giving voice to their presumed particular policy issue concerns.

A second interparty difference in structuring comes in the party dimension. Among Democrats, the assessment of the importance of party rests on counting services to the party in nominating candidates, wanting to minimize disagreement within the party, opposing minimizing the role of party organization, and rejecting a firm stand for one's position even if it means resigning from the party. Among Republicans, however, no such clear structuring emerged. A detailed inspection of individual cohort patterns and experimentation with various combinations led us to use an index that included all but the last item (listed above) that went into the construction of the Democratic index of party importance.[15]

[14] See Appendix F for a discussion of the factor analysis and the loadings associated with various items.
[15] Indeed, as Appendix Table F.4 shows, the Republicans achieve a three-factor solution compared with the two-factor solution for the Democrats.

In addition to simplifying our analytic task by aggregating a subset of items to reflect a limited number of attitudinal dimensions, we shall also again aggregate our candidate preference groupings and examine only two clusters within each party. These aggregations were anticipated in our earlier analysis of candidate preferences. Here, as earlier, the decision to collapse the many discrete groups defined by patterns of candidate preferences across three elections was facilitated by the absence of systematic attitudinal variation among candidate preference groups *within* each of the ultimate clusters and the presence of clear differentiation *between* those clusters. On the Democratic side, we combine all of those patterns of candidate preference that *originated in or terminated in* support of liberal candidates. The other major group is then composed of all those whose patterns began with support of the traditional party leadership and thereafter avoided the liberal wing of the party. On the Republican side, the two groups are composed of those who were Reagan supporters in 1980 and those who were not. (These clusters were first presented in chapter 3, Tables 3.1 to 3.9.) We should emphasize that there was little variation, and no readily interpretable patterning of what variation there was, in the attitudinal preferences of discrete candidate preference groups within each of these clusters of preference groups. Consequently, the task of presenting the data in the next step of our analysis is greatly simplified with little or no loss of information pertinent to the generalizations important to our analysis.

Circulation and Political Goals

The net impact of the circulation of the presidential campaign elite on their representation of the various attitudinal assessments of incentives and goals is conditioned by three factors. First, it is limited because of the minor intercohort differences that we have just examined. Second, it is limited because the sheer number of continuing core participants dominates the elite of any given year, and only major differences between the disengaged and the mobilized will have any impact on the net result of elite circulation. Finally, as we shall observe shortly, although the representation of the major dimensions of both incentives and goals differed quite markedly among the candidate preference groups, they, in turn, differed sharply in their contribution to the circulation patterns.

The reader must also keep in mind the fact that we do not have individual-level measures of change for the 1976 and 1980 cohorts. Consequently, the changes we are about to discuss are only those that can be attributed to compositional change resulting from circulation—the effects of disengagement and mobilization.

✠ The Importance of Partisanship

Our assessment of change in the importance assigned to the role of party in nominating convention deliberations first reveals some familiar party differences. In both 1972 and 1981, members of the Republican campaign elite were more often inclined than their Democratic counterparts to assign a high degree of importance to the political party. That difference, in turn, was primarily a function of the limited role assigned to party by liberal Democrats. Just as we noted in chapter 3, factionalism among Republicans was not centered on the primacy of party. Whether measured in 1972 or in 1981, there was virtually no difference between moderates and conservatives in their judgment as to the importance of partisan concerns in the choice of a party nominee. And the level of importance assigned by the Republicans was of the same order as that assigned by the traditionalist camp of the Democrats. The Democratic left, however, was distinctive in its lack of concern for partisan considerations in the nominating process. The image of the McGovernites in 1972 as insurgents fighting party regularity remained a proper characterization of the liberal supporters of 1981.

The interparty differences of 1972 were, however, reduced between 1972 and 1980 as the consequences of convergence to which both parties contributed. Between 1972 and 1980, Democrats became somewhat more inclined to see the party as important and 1980 Republicans were slightly less inclined than their counterparts from 1972 to attach high importance to the role of party in the nominating process. In both instances, however, the magnitude of change was small.

The minimal evidence of change reflects, in the first place, the dominance of the core participants in both parties, but particularly in the Republican party. As we saw in chapter 2, roughly three fourths of the Republican elites in both 1972 and 1980 were made up of persons who participated in all three presidential cam-

paigns—1972, 1976, and 1980. The proportion of continuing participants among the Democrats was somewhat lower but ran slightly
above 60 percent in both years. Given the preponderance of core
participants, the consequences of mobilization and disengagement
could not be expected to be large unless the two groups exchang-
ing positions as party activists were very different from one another.

In Table 5.3 we can observe that in 1980 there were still
marked differences among Democrats between the liberal and the
traditional supporters where the centrality of party is concerned.
Party was clearly more important to the traditional wing than to the
supporters of liberal candidates. However, the separate analyses of
the two primary clusters of candidate preference groups in each
party reveal that the exchange of the newly mobilized for the disengaged had different consequences for the different clusters of candidate supporters. Because of the turnover in personnel, support for
party increased slightly (8 points) between 1972 and 1980 among
liberal supporters. The impact of that increase was muted for the
Democratic party as a whole because there was no comparable
change, indeed a small decrease, among supporters of the traditional leadership. And, of course, the contribution of the liberal
supporters to the Democratic total was proportionately less in 1980
than it had been in 1972 (columns 4 and 5 in Table 5.3). Among
Republicans, the 8-point decline in emphasis on party among the
moderates was, in turn, muted by the fact that the conservatives
showed less of a decline. And like traditionalists among Democrats, the relative number of conservatives increased in 1980,
further limiting the overall impact of the change among moderates.

All of this may explain why there was no more evidence of net
change in either party, but it also reveals that the convergence that
did occur was a function of change in the two minority wings of
both parties. The sharp contrast between the antiparty liberal Democrats and the proparty Republican moderates who disengaged (the
82-point difference between -53 and $+29$) was replaced by an
insignificant 2-point difference among those mobilized within the
same party wings (-22 to -20). At the same time, circulation
within the Democratic traditionalists and Republican conservatives
did nothing at all to reduce interparty differences (-5 to $+9$ in
1972 and -3 to -18 in 1980).

Table 5.3

Impact of Circulation on Importance of Party in Convention Decisions

Candidate Preference	Continuously Active 1972–1980	Disengaged after 1972	Mobilized after 1972	Faction Score 1972	Faction Score 1980	Change 1972–1980
Democrats						
Liberal	−26	−53	−20	−34	−26	+8
Traditional	+19	−5	−3	+16	+14	−2
Difference	+45	+48	+17	+50	+40	
Republicans						
Moderate	+12	+29	−22	+15	+7	−8
Conservative	+5	+9	−18	+6	+2	−4
Difference	−7	−20	+4	−9	−5	

Notes: Faction score entries are based on the appropriate combination of circulation components; that is, 1972 entries are based on the continuously active and the disengaged combined; 1980 entries are based on the continuously active and the mobilized combined.

Each entry is a Percentage Difference Index formed by subtracting the proportion who attributed little importance to party from the proportion who assigned great importance. Plus signs indicate greater importance.

The Salience of Issues in the Nominating Process

Where modest Democratic-Republican differences in the centrality of partisanship were largely the product of the limited concern on the part of left-wing Democrats, the marginal nature of interparty differences in the salience of concern for policy was the product of sharp but offsetting factional disagreements within both parties. In line with conventional expectations, liberals were more inclined than traditionalists to emphasize the importance of issue positions in the choice of a Democratic standard-bearer. At the same time, the magnitude of Republican conservative-moderate differences on the importance of issues were almost a perfect match for those separating the Democratic factions.

However, circulation had even less impact on the salience of issues as a criterion for nomination (see Table 5.4). Just as the circulation within the Democratic left did not result in a significant ideological shift, so the exchange of newly mobilized liberals for disengaged simply sustained the liberals' emphasis on the centrality of issues. As a consequence, because there was actually relatively higher level of concern with issues among the newly mobilized followers of traditional leadership by 1980 (compared with continuously active traditionalists), the net result was a modest increase in Democratic emphasis on issues in the renomination of Carter. The diminution of issue polarization among Democratic candidate groups between 1972 and 1980 was, then, clearly not the occasion for reducing the importance attributed to issue preferences in the nominating process.

Within the Republican party, the situation was very similar, with the exchange of personnel making no difference at all among moderates—who were the least inclined of all groups to emphasize issues in their deliberations about convention decisions. On the other hand, the mobilization of support for Reagan's election in 1980 was accompanied by a detectable increase in interest in issues. The mobilized conservatives actually matched the emphasis on issues within the Democratic left. As in other instances, however, the small numbers involved in the circulation of the Republican elites, and particularly the conservative elites, severely limited the overall impact of their greater interest in questions of public policy.

In addition to documenting the reasons for minimal net impact

Table 5.4

Impact of Circulation on Importance of Issues in Convention Decisions

Candidate Preference	Continuously Active 1972–1980	Disengaged after 1972	Mobilized after 1972	Faction Score 1972	1980	Change 1972–1980
Democrats						
Liberal	+10	+10	+7	+10	+9	−1
Traditional	−26	−42	−18	−28	−24	+4
Difference	−36	−52	−25	−38	−33	
Republicans						
Moderate	+44	−24	−23	−41	−40	+1
Conservative	−5	−9	+7	−6	−3	+3
Difference	−39	−15	−30	−35	−37	

Notes: Faction score entries are based on the appropriate combination of circulation components; that is, 1972 entries are based on the continuously active and the disengaged combined; 1980 entries are based on the continuously active and the mobilized combined.

Each entry is a Percentage Difference Index formed by subtracting the proportion who attributed little importance to issues from the proportion who assigned great importance. Plus signs indicate greater importance.

108

of elite circulation on the political goals of campaign activists, Tables 5.3 and 5.4 also document the pattern of sharp intraparty differences that distinguished the two subsets of candidate support groups within each party. Among the Democrats it is clear that, in line with conventional wisdom, party was much more important to the followers of traditional party leadership, whereas issues were of comparably greater importance to the followers of the New Left. Although these differences were marginally diminished between 1972 and 1980, they remained a striking contrast even in 1980. Within Republican ranks, in a manner parallel to the Democrats, the supporters of moderate candidates attached slightly greater importance to party than did the Reagan followers and were strikingly less interested in issues than were the Reaganites. However, the candidate-related differences about party were modest in the Republican party (and almost vanished in 1981) while the disagreement on the importance of issues remained virtually as sharp as it was within the Democratic party. Moreover, the intraparty disagreement among Republicans was not simply the result of the mobilization of Reagan supporters in 1980 but was apparently well established among the activists of 1972 as well.

The intraparty differences portrayed in Tables 5.3 and 5.4 bring us back to the larger canvas portraying the basic differences in the circumstances of Democratic and Republican changes in party leadership. Among Republicans the change was impelled from within the party establishment. The contending forces did not differ appreciably in their devotion to party, although the difference in the "Party Importance" score between the two groups who disengaged fits the theme of a successful Reagan insurgency that was accompanied by—if it did not produce—withdrawal of former participants who were very much committed to party. The dominant feature of the Republican landscape is, however, provided by the continuously active participants. Among them the candidate-related differences in the perceived importance of party were minor, as they were among those mobilized to participate in the Reagan nomination of 1980. The dispute between moderates and conservatives was not over the centrality of party.

Among Democrats, however, the contest between the traditional party leaders and the insurgent left included sharp differences in their appraisals of the importance of party in the nominating process. The net result of the circulation of left-wing supporters into and out of the ranks of the campaign activists softened the intraparty differences, but only moderately. Even as the liberals' challenge faded with the renomination of Carter in 1980, their lack of devotion to party remained notable and in clear contrast to the importance assigned by the inheritors of the legacy of party centrism. Because the turmoil in the Democratic party was so much a function of external criticism, and the reflection of a search for new legitimacy for party leadership, the competing factions arguing for and against change differed on the centrality of both issues and party, just as they differed in the substance of their policy preferences.

Intraparty differences in the centrality of policy questions complement the differences in assessments of the relevance of party to the choice of a presidential candidate. They fit our earlier sense of the contest for Democratic party leadership as a struggle in which the party establishment argued the primacy of party loyalty while denying the need to recognize new ideological orientations. The historically defined wings of the Republican party did not argue over whether party qua party was important, but they certainly disagreed on the question of the prominence that should be accorded to candidates' policy preferences when choosing a nominee. Their disagreement, with the previously dominant moderates denying a central role to issues, was every bit as spirited as the parallel disagreement among Democrats.

Personal Incentives

Before moving on to an examination of the behavioral emphasis on parties, issues, and candidates in presidential campaigns, two additional sets of attitudinal measures provide useful information for the characterization of our candidate preference clusters in the two parties. These measures are derived from the personal incentive items providing reasons for engaging in political activity, items that had no counterpart under the heading of instrumental goals for the nominating conventions. The statements reflecting the rewards for sociability and the enhancement of personal careers (see Table 5.1) provide further modest distinctions between the two clusters of candidate support groups within the continuing core of each party that make intuitive sense. Just as the Republican moderates and the

Democratic traditionalists joined together in a greater regard for the political party, so they were distinguished from the Democratic liberals and the Reagan conservatives in their greater appreciation of the rewards that follow from joining family and friends in the exictement of conventions and campaigns where they make rewarding social contacts. These traditional solidary benefits from political participation were less appreciated by the more issue- or candidate-oriented elements in both parties. In like manner, the programmatic emphasis on the part of the Democratic liberals and the Reagan conservatives was accompanied by core participants' somewhat lower interest in the personal rewards that stem from the business contacts, the personal visibility, and the association with the movers and shakers that might result from one's political activity.

In general, the circulation of personnel resulted in truncating these candidate-related differences. In the first place, among all Democrats the disengaged placed less value on both personal and solidary rewards than did core participants or the newly mobilized (who did not differ from each other on either dimension). But the minimization of these apolitical values was more extreme among the liberal dropouts than among the disengaged traditionalists. The net result was an absolute loss of personnel who were not inclined to value personal and social rewards as incentives for political involvement, and who were replaced by those who did. Thus, the cohort differences discussed earlier, in which 1980 Democrats emphasized personal and social instrumental rewards accompanying political activity more than the 1972 cohort did, were very relevant for sharpening the differences between the 1972 and 1980 campaign elites. The less political among the 1972 cohort dropped out of the campaign elite by 1980 and were replaced by members of the 1980 cohort who differed with them on the importance of the same apolitical, personal, and social rewards.

Just as disengagement made more difference to the ranks of the Democratic left so it made more of an impact on Republican moderates than on conservatives, where those who dropped out were not different from the continuing core with respect to the importance of personal rewards. But if the newly mobilized Democrats did not differ at all between candidate preference groups, and thereby tended to blur candidate-related differences among the 1980 campaigners, mobilization into the 1980 Republican campaign elite perpetuated intraparty differences. Although both conservatives and moderates among the newly mobilized were less taken with personal and social goals than were the continuing core partici- pants with whom they joined, they differed from each other as much as did the two core groups.

All told, the social circulation in both sets of elites maintained *intra*party candidate-related differences while producing the change in *inter*party differences discussed earlier. Disengagement within the Democratic ranks and mobilization into the Republican ranks were central to maintaining the intraparty differences, but both sources of change were necessary to produce the transposition of the parties as the Democrats of 1980 replaced the Republicans of 1972 as the elite group more inclined to emphasize the personal and social rewards from political involvement.

CHAPTER 6

The Place of Parties, Issues, and Candidates in Presidential Campaigning

In the previous chapter our analysis of the impact of intraparty struggles for leadership on the relative importance attached to goals and values associated with presidential politics was limited to evidence provided by attitudinal measures without a specific time referent. The analysis extended earlier research which had emphasized different perspectives associated with different patterns of candidate preference. It also demonstrated that turnover in the population of campaign activists was associated with changes of emphasis on goals and rewards between 1972 and 1981. The attitudinal analysis has been limited, however, in a number of particulars, all of which are likely to conceal the magnitude of differences that separated the perspectives of the activists of 1972 from those of 1980.

In the first place, most of the attitudinal measurements were taken in 1981 and therefore are removed in time from the campaign activity of those who disengaged immediately after the 1972 election or who were active well before the 1980 election. A second and even larger problem stems from the fact that we have thus far had no assessment of attitudinal change at the individual level extending across *all* of the cohorts to match our occasional analyses of the 1972 panel. This is particularly important because it has fore-stalled any investigation of changes within the continuing core of participants that might have flowed from their experiences in 1972 and the elections that followed. Our limited review of the changes in incentives to participate among the 1972 cohorts sharpened our awareness of this problem.

Finally, and perhaps most significantly, the perspectives that have been examined are, at best, *indirect* indicators of the relative prominence assigned to overtly political goals in the actual cam-paign activities of each year. The assessments of personal incen-tives were deliberately couched in terms of personal rewards at-tached to political participation *in general* and are not, therefore, direct indicators of the importance attached to various foci of en-gagement in *presidential* politics. Moreover, the instrumental goals for nominating conventions were presented to the delegates in the explicit context of *intra*party decision-making in a nominating con-vention, well separated from concerns with the general election campaign. Consequently, neither set of attitudes can be taken as providing direct measures of the importance attached to promoting party, issues, or the candidate when presidential politics moves out of party circles and convention politics into the public limelight of mass electoral politics.

All of these limitations can be minimized or overcome by re-turning to the reports on campaign behavior that were used in de-veloping the basic scheme depicting the circulation of our cam-paign elites. That scheme was introduced in chapter 2 by outlining each respondent's report as to whether he or she had participated in each of the three presidential election campaigns.[1] The questions that elicited this information, for each of the three years, were fol-lowed by an opportunity for the respondents to specify "how much [their] activity was motivated by commitments to the party, to the candidate, or to an issue position." The alternatives were: "A lot, some, or none." The format for eliciting this information was thus structured but permissive. A person who had been involved in a

[1] Kessel has reported limited reliability on activists' own descriptions of the level of their activities. Although we are mindful of this problem, our focus is not on fine discrimination among degrees or levels of activity, but on the reported motives for those who report *some* rather than *none* when we queried as to whether they were active in a given campaign. Personal communication from John H. Kessel, June 1985.

given campaign could indicate any of three degrees of motivation for each of three activities; working for the party, working in support of an issue, or working for the candidate. It was quite possible to indicate a highest level of commitment to any one or two or all three objectives. In fact, a good many delegates specified two foci for their participation in any given year, and, upon rather rare occasions, delegates gave equal prominence to all three.

From this detailed information, reflecting three possible levels of involvement in each of three domains in each of the three presidential campaigns, we have extracted and summarized data depicting the primary focus of campaign activities in 1972 and 1980. The emphasis for campaign activity varies among candidate-preference groups and between cohorts just as did political attitudes and policy preferences. However, inasmuch as the information on attitudes and preferences all pertained to a single year (1981, the year of data collection), the data on campaign behavior have a crucial added dimension. The reports on campaign activity refer to each of the years being analyzed, 1972 and 1980 for most of our present purposes. Consequently, the summaries depicting the foci for campaign activity make it possible to follow (recalled) individual-level change across the eight-year time span. Moreover, not only can persistence and change be mapped for the delegates who were active campaigners in both 1972 and 1980, but it is possible to describe the behavior of the disengaged in 1972, their last year of campaign activity, and the campaign foci of the newly mobilized can be captured as of the 1980 campaign. The ability to combine recall information from both year's thus adds to both the richness and the complexity of the next stage in our analysis of elite circulation.[2]

The analysis of each party will start by summarizing continuity and change in campaign focus for the continuously active participants. The summary of the campaign activities of the core participants in 1972 and 1980 will be followed with an exploration of the impact of replacement on net changes in campaign emphases for

---

[2] Curiously enough, few if any of the many studies dealing with activists' political styles have focused on motivations at the campaign stage. This would seem to be a glaring omission, given the stakes involved in a presidential election. For a provocative before and after study of *state* convention delegates, see Walter J. Stone, "Prenomination Candidate Choice and General Election Behavior: Iowa Presidential Activists in 1980," *American Journal of Political Science* 28 (May 1984): 361–78.

the two major clusters of candidate preference. Finally, the process of analytic aggregation will turn to overall summaries for the entire 1972–1980 campaign elite of the party.

Republican Campaign Behavior

As of 1972 there were no large differences in the focus of campaign activities among Republican candidate-preference groups. However, there was a regular pattern of variations across the three different cohorts. In 1972 the 1972 delegates placed relatively greater emphasis on party in their campaign activities, and the 1980 cohort of delegates-to-be provided the least emphasis. By 1980, however, these cohort differences had disappeared; the 1972 and 1976 cohorts reduced their emphasis on party and simply matched the relatively constant degree of emphasis given to party by the 1980 cohort. As a consequence, campaign emphasis on party declined between 1972 and 1980 among Republicans.

Across all cohorts and within all candidate-preference groups, the 1980 campaign was characterized by a slight increase over 1972 in the reported frequency with which active campaigners focused on issues. In line with what we have seen in earlier analyses, this was particularly noticeable among the Reagan supporters in 1980, and most particularly among those supporters from the 1980 cohort. However, the increased attention to issues was of modest magnitude, and it paled in comparison with the very large increase in emphasis on campaigning for the candidate in 1980 and the corresponding decrease in emphasis on party. Quite reasonably, the latter increase was most visible among the consistent Reagan supporters who worked on his behalf in the 1980 election.

Without differentiating among the cohorts, and returning to the two principal clusters of candidate supporters, the first part of Table 6.1 summarizes the changes for the continuously active campaign participants. It makes evident the extent to which changes in campaign focus were very similar for moderates and conservatives alike. It also becomes apparent that the changes that did occur in the patterning of campaign activities muted the 1972 moderate-conservative differences on the centrality of parties, differences which were minimal to begin with. On the other hand, the inter-year changes slightly accentuated candidate group differences in

Table 6.1

Campaign Focus of Republican Campaign Activists, 1972–1980

	Focus of Continuously Active				Focus of Disengaged(1972)/ Mobilized(1980)			
	Party	Issues	Candidate	N (weighted)	Party	Issues	Candidate	N (weighted)
Moderate								
1972	85	9	49	(455)	90	11	47	(109)
1980	71	12	62	(455)	48	13	71	(75)
Change	−14	+3	+13		−42	+3	+24	
Conservative								
1972	78	14	56	(633)	81	13	39	(31)
1980	69	21	74	(633)	39	22	87	(133)
Change	−9	+7	+18		−42	+9	+48	

Note: Entries are the proportion of each group, defined by candidate preference *and* role as a circulation element, who reported a particular campaign focus; for example, 85% of the moderates who were continuously active in both 1972 and 1980 indicated that they were motivated to campaign for a presidential candidate in 1972 because of their commitment to the party; 71 percent of the same group reported a comparable focus on party in 1980. In 1972, 90% of the moderates who would subsequently disengage emphasized party; in 1980, only 48% of the newly mobilized moderates emphasized party. Row totals are greater than 100% because many delegates ranked two, or all three, foci as equally important.

attention give both to issues and candidates, with the greater emphases in the conservative 1980 campaign sharpening the intraparty differences.

The 1972 activities of those who were to disengage following that election were patterned very much like those of the continuing core, with the perhaps significant exception of the conservative delegates' limited attention to the candidate (39 percent of the disengaged (from the second part of Table 6.1) as against 56 percent of the continuously active focused on the candidate). It may well be that their relative lack of emphasis on the Nixon candidacy was a prelude to disengagement from a political context in which another dominating personal candidacy, that of Ronald Reagan, was to become the center of attention eight years later.

Within both candidate-preference groups, the campaign foci for the newly mobilized in 1980 provided a sharp contrast, both with the disengaged and with the continuously active core which they joined for the 1980 campaign. In *both* wings of the party the newly activated were remarkably limited in their 1980 attention to party. They were commensurately uniquely preoccupied with Reagan's candidacy. Only in their attention to issues did they fit the campaign emphases of their respective sets of core activists.

Although the differences distinguishing the circulating elements from each other were quite similar among both moderates and conservatives, the impact of replacement was strikingly different in the two wings of the party because of the contrast in the size of the circulating elements. A small fragment (5 percent) of the 1972 conservatives dropped out prior to 1980, compared with almost 20 percent of the 1972 moderates. Conversely, the newly mobilized contributed more heavily to the conservative wing than to the moderate wing in 1980. As a result of the turnover, there was a modest decrease in the number of moderate campaign activists after 1972 while there was a substantial net increase in the number of conservatives active in the 1980 campaign.

The overall change in Republican campaign emphasis between 1972 and 1980 was a product of three factors: (1) shifting emphases among the continuously active, (2) sharp differences in the foci of the circulating elements, and (3) substantial differences in the *numbers* contributing to circulation within the moderate and conservative branches of the party.

If we take only the first of these factors into account, the net result of the 1972–1980 changes was virtually identical for both moderates and conservatives among the continuously active participants. In the first and fourth rows of the three right-hand columns of Table 6.2, both sets of campaigners show the by-now familiar pattern of a substantial de-emphasis on party, a modest increase in attention to issues, and a large increase in concern with the candidate that roughly matches the diminution of interest in party.

The net contributions of the circulating elements were, however, sharply different in the two wings of the party. Among the moderates the replacement of the disengaged with the newly mobilized sharply accentuated the decrease in attention to party. At the same time the replacement made no impact on moderate attention to issues or to the candidate; within the circulation elements exactly the same number reported those emphases in 1980 as they had eight years earlier in the Nixon-McGovern contest.

On the other hand, the mobilization of Reagan supporters for the 1980 campaign made a quite different contribution to the overall activities of conservative campaigners. Their increased numbers resulted in more emphasis in all three domains, but most sharply in attention to the candidate. The relative impact of the sheer number of the mobilized conservatives is perhaps most apparent in their contribution to the overall conservative emphasis on party. Even though they were much less inclined to campaign on behalf of party than the disengaged had been (39 percent against 81 percent in Table 6.1), their larger numbers meant that within the conservative ranks of 1980 they actually contributed to an increase in the proportion of conservatives campaigning on behalf of party, an increase that offset some of the diminished enthusiasm of the continuously active campaigners.

The net result of the sometimes countervailing changes in the two branches of the Republican elite was, nevertheless, a clear shift of Republican emphasis between 1972 and 1980. In 1980 Republicans were visibly less interested in supporting party, marginally more interested in campaigning for issues, and strikingly more attentive to their party's candidate. Both the continuously active campaigners and the circulating elements followed the same pattern, although the latter predictably contributed somewhat less to the overall result than did the continuously active campaigners. However, given the limited size of the circulating elements (10 percent disengaged and 15 percent mobilized), and the extent to which

Table 6.2

Change in Focus of Republican Campaign Activity, 1972–1980

	1972 Focus of Campaign Activity			1980 Focus of Campaign Activity			Change 1972–1980		
	Party	Issues	Candidate	Party	Issues	Candidate	Party	Issues	Candidate
Moderates									
Continuously Active	69	7	39	58	9	50	−11	+2	+11
Circulating Elements	17	2	9	6	2	9	−11	0	0
Total	86	9	48	64	11	59	−22	+2	+11
Conservatives									
Continuously Active	78	14	56	66	20	71	−12	+6	+15
Circulating Elements	4	1	2	8	4	17	+4	+3	+15
Total	82	15	58	74	24	88	−8	+9	+30
Combined Totals									
Continuously Active	72	10	47	63	15	61	−9	+5	+14
Circulating Elements	10	1	5	7	3	13	−3	+2	+8
Total	82	11	52	70	18	74	−12	+7	+22

Notes: Entries are the proportion of the total candidate-preference group who reported a specific campaign focus; 1980 entries are calculated on the 1972 base to reflect both changes in focus and changes in numbers due to replacement. "Circulating Elements" are those who disengaged after 1972 and those who were mobilized in 1980.

their behavior was different from those of the continuing core in both wings of the party, it is remarkable that their contributions added up to reinforcing the party-wide shift of elite concerns away from party and to the support of a conservative candidate.

It is tempting to argue that a key reason for the decline in party focus and the incline in candidate focus rests in the dramatically different nomination processes of the two years. With an essentially unopposed incumbent president running against a divided party, and with ideological fervor being at low tide within its own ranks, it is not surprising that the GOP campaign activists of 1972 would be so party-focused. The fairly sharp preconvention struggle of 1980, by contrast, generated strong candidate followers and more issue differentiation. The motivations for activity in the general election should reflect more of a candidate focus, as they do. That explanation, however, should apply more to adherents of the conservative wing because their candidate won and because he (Reagan) commands such devotion. To some degree that is true, but we have just seen that moderates *also* shifted their focus, though not quite as much. Now, some of these moderates may have been motivated by commitment to the moderate vice-presidential nominee, George Bush. More probably, they were caught up in the particular aura accompanying the Reagan campaign and in the more general phenomenon of a swing toward emphasizing candidates in the electoral process.[3]

Democratic Campaign Behavior

The description of Democratic campaign activities is once again more complex than that of Republican activities. This is true because we not only begin with more and larger differences among 1972 campaign behaviors associated with different candidate-preference groups, but within groups of candidate supporters there were also patterns differentiating among the three cohorts. Moreover, the potential for variations in patterns of change within the Democratic party was heightened by the substantially larger num-

---

[3] For an interesting discussion of how the particulars of a given year shaped the composition and perspectives of the convention leaders in the prereform era, see Dwaine Marvick and Samuel J. Eldersveld, "National Convention Leadership: 1952 and 1956," *Western Political Quarterly* 14 (March 1961): 176–94.

bers involved in circulation. While the contribution of circulating elements to change in the Republican party rested on some 25 percent of the 1972–1980 total, a full 40 percent of the Democratic elite was involved in the exchange of the mobilized for the disen-

A first inspection of the 1972 campaign emphases discloses striking differences in campaign behavior associated with candidate-preference groups (Table 6.3). The differences in emphasis among Democrats were greatest between the consistent supporters of the liberal leadership and the traditionalists who were to go to Carter. Everything that has been said about intraparty disagreements among Democrats in 1972 held for differences in the focus of their campaign activities that year. Traditionalists who were to prefer Carter eight years later were in 1972 much more likely than the consistent liberals to emphasize party in their campaign activities, 70 percent to 42 percent. The liberals, in turn, were more than twice as likely to concentrate on issues (49 percent to 23 percent). And their greater emphasis on issues was reflected in the absolute margin by which they outstripped traditionalists' attention to the candidate (80 to 54).

This general pattern of differences in emphases was further accentuated by intragroup *cohort* differences on the themes receiving the greatest attention. Thus, among the traditionalists the 1972 cohort was the most preoccupied with party, while among the liberals the 1972 cohort was strikingly most heavily committed to the promotion of issues and the McGovern candidacy. Intraparty differentiation in the focus of 1972 campaign activity was greatest in the ranks of those who attended the Miami convention and engaged in confrontational politics in person.

Eight years later, the cohort differences had totally disappeared. The passage of time and the change in political context resulted in a sharp diminution of attention to party within the 1972 and 1976 cohorts among traditionalists; in directly parallel fashion, the same two cohorts within the New Left reflected striking reductions in their concern with issues and the candidate. Within the 1980 cohort, changes in campaign focus between 1972 and 1980 were more modest. Nevertheless, the relatively greater increase in concern with party within the 1980 liberal delegates and the relatively greater increase in emphasis on the candidate within the 1980 traditionalists further softened the cohort differences so apparent in the 1972 campaign.

Table 6.3

Campaign Focus of Democratic Campaign Activists, 1972–1980

	Focus of Continuously Active				Focus of Disengaged(1972)/ Mobilized(1980)			
	Party	Issues	Candidate	N (weighted)	Party	Issues	Candidate	N (weighted)
Liberals								
1972	42	49	80	(622)	29	59	81	(232)
1980	53	38	72	(622)	44	37	74	(96)
Change	+11	−11	−8		+15	−22	−7	
Traditionalists								
1972	70	23	54	(722)	62	23	59	(133)
1980	67	24	67	(722)	53	25	76	(242)
Change	−3	+1	+13		−9	+2	+17	

Note: Entries are the proportion of each group, defined by candidate preference *and* role as a circulation element, who reported a particular campaign focus; for example, 70% of the continuously active traditionalists emphasized party in 1972 and 67% of the same group did so in 1980; 62% of the traditionalists who were going to disengage focused on party in 1972; 53% of the traditionalists mobilized after 1972 also focused on party.

For somewhat different reasons the passage of time and change of circumstances were also responsible for a muting of candidate-preference differences. Their polarization on the emphasis on candidates had been very sharp in 1972, but four years later it was virtually nonexistent. This happened, in part, because of the change just noted among the 1972 and 1976 liberal cohorts. An even larger contribution came from a general increase in attention to the candidate on the part of traditionalists, from 54 percent to 67 percent in 1980. The changes across cohorts were all in the direction of minimizing the distinctiveness of candidate-preference groups, and they were joined by the increase in attention to party on the part of liberals in all three cohorts and a minimal increase in attention to issues within the set of traditionalists to reduce intraparty differences in campaign focus by 1980.

At the same time, the process of homogenization did not erase fundamental differences in perspectives within the Democratic party. In 1980 the consistent supporters of liberal candidates remained conspicuous in their lower concern for party, just as traditionalists continued to labor on behalf of party (53 percent against 67 percent). If the 1972 cohort of liberals had reduced their passion for issues, liberals in the other two cohorts had not changed; and among traditionalists issues continued almost unchanged as a very weak third in their ordering of campaign priorities. Excitement over candidates was clearly the most volatile of the three dimensions of campaign activity. This is of fundamental importance to any analysis of contemporary presidential politics because, as we have seen, candidate preferences are reflections of the fundamental values and goals that create unity and lead to strife in party ranks.

Summarizing the detailed information by grouping candidate-preference patterns into the two familiar clusters, and ignoring cohort differences, reveals familiar patterns of change within the continuously active Democrats that at times are contrary to those noted for Republicans. For example, in contrast to changes in both wings of the Republican party, there was a general *increase* in emphasis on party by the liberal wing of the Democrats in 1980, which went hand in hand with their *decreased* attention to issues and the candidate. The traditionalist pattern differed from the liberal pattern in all three domains. As with the Republicans, there was, if anything, a *decrease* in their attention to party, a sharp *increase* in their attention to candidate, and no appreciable change with regard to issues.

Moving to an inspection of the two elements involved in Democratic circulation, we note in Table 6.3 patterns of change between 1972 and 1980 much like those among the continuously active within each branch of the party. However, the impact of elite circulation within each of the Democratic party wings was appreciably greater than had been true for Republicans. This was so because of the marked imbalance of the numbers involved. Within the combined ranks of the 1972 liberal campaigners, over 30 percent disengaged following that election, a number more than twice as large as those subsequently mobilized on behalf of the liberal candidates. Traditionalists lost proportionately only half as many from their 1972 ranks (16 percent), and their loss was more than compensated for by the mobilization of almost twice that number for the 1980 campaign. As a result, the left was reduced in size by 20 percent by 1980 while the traditionalists grew by 13 percent.

The combined impact of changing focus within the continuously active campaigners and the turnover resulting from the mobilized replacing the disengaged produced substantially different results within each wing of the party. As Table 6.4 indicates, there was a small upturn in emphasis on party by 1980 in both clusters of the candidate-preference groups; but within the liberal wing the increase came entirely from the continuously active— presumably socialized to a recognition of the importance of party in presidential politics. This was countered by a loss of concern for party in the exchange of circulating elements. Among traditionalists, on the other hand, *mobilization* produced all of the increased emphasis on party, an increase which was largely offset by the diminished enthusiasm for party among core participants.

Among the liberals the pattern of reduced emphasis on issues and candidate was accentuated by the changes coming as a result of circulation. Among the traditionalists there was again no significant increase in their attention to issues, but the very substantial increase in concern with the candidate in 1980 came in almost equal parts from the continuously active core and the exchange of the newly mobilized for the disengaged.

Somewhat ironically, the net result of greater intraparty differentiation and greater magnitude of change in the Democratic party was to leave the overall pattern of Democratic campaign emphasis in 1980 virtually unchanged from that of 1972, except for a modest *de*crease in the attention given to issues in the later year. Focus on party and candidate was unchanged because the shifts within the

Table 6.4

Change in Focus of Democratic Campaign Activity, 1972–1980

	1972 Focus of Campaign Activity			1980 Focus of Campaign Activity			Change 1972–1980		
	Party	Issues	Candidate	Party	Issues	Candidate	Party	Issues	Candidate
Liberals									
Continuously Active	29	33	55	36	26	50	+7	−7	−5
Circulating Elements	9	18	25	5	4	8	−4	−14	−17
Total	38	51	80	41	30	58	+3	−21	−22
Traditionalists									
Continuously Active	59	19	45	56	20	56	−3	+1	+11
Circulating Elements	10	4	9	15	7	22	+5	+3	+13
Total	69	23	54	71	27	78	+2	+4	+24
Combined Totals									
Continuously Active	44	26	50	46	24	53	+2	−2	+3
Circulating Elements	10	11	17	9	6	15	−1	−5	−2
Total	54	37	67	55	30	68	+1	−7	+1

Notes: Entries are the proportion of the total candidate-preference group who reported a specific campaign focus; 1980 entries are calculated on the 1972 base to reflect both changes in focus and changes in numbers due to replacement.
"Circulating Elements" are those who disengaged after 1972 and those who were mobilized in 1980.

two wings of the party effectively canceled each other out. Thus, despite having moved from 1972, with its sharp differences both among candidate groups and across cohorts, to a much more homogeneous party in 1980, with no cohort differences and attenuated candidate-preference differences, overall the relative balance of attention given to the three campaign domains was scarcely altered for Democratic activists over the eight years.

At the same time, it should be noted that the process of circulation virtually eliminated two of the major differences of perspective among Democrats. It is true that the liberals remained less focused on party in their 1980 campaign activities than were the traditionalists. On the other hand, the largest change among Democrats reflected the defusing of candidate-related polarization on the importance of issues and here the change was concentrated in the turnover elements. By 1980 the convergence of the traditionalists and the liberals, largely a function of disengagement within the left, produced virtual agreement on the importance of issues, and at a level only marginally greater than that expressed by conservative Republicans.

Intraparty differences among Democrats with regard to the centrality of the candidate remained at virtually the same level in 1980 as eight years earlier, but thanks largely to the circulation of the elites which resulted in the demise of liberal leadership, the locus of emphasis was reversed. Traditionalists in 1980 matched left-wing support of the candidate in 1972, while liberal interest in the candidate in 1980 dropped effectively to the same level expressed by traditionalists eight years earlier.

Candidate-preference differentiation had increased in the Republican party while it decreased in the Democratic party. Most notably, the Republican conservatives and moderates differed sharply on emphasis on issues in the 1980 campaign, not the Democratic left and traditionalists. But the same forces that produced Republican polarization also moved the entire Republican elite away from a preoccupation with party to a modest concern with issues and a strong interest in the candidate. Within the Democratic party, the pressures to change created rather massive shifts within each wing of the party, but they left campaign emphases in 1980 close to exactly what they had been at the height of the liberal surge in 1972.

Leadership transition in the Republican party was accomplished with great homogeneity of change in campaign focus across both wings of the party and among circulating as well as continuing participants. The uniformity in the changes was dramatically portrayed in Table 6.1; not so for the Democrats, as depicted in counterpart Table 6.3. The patterns of change are strikingly different in each of the party's factions, and those differences were accentuated by the circulation of participants between 1972 and 1980.

CHAPTER 7

Partisan Cultures:
Policy Preferences, Group Evaluations,
and Ideological Attributes

The struggle for the presidency is preeminently a struggle between and among individual candidates and their supporters. But
the rise and fall of candidate fortunes is also the rise and fall of
commitments to different policy choices. All of the post-World War
II contests for Republican party leadership and nomination were
contests between or among clearly delineated ideological factions
of the party. On the Democratic side, the picture is slightly more
ambiguous only because some of the personal contests, as between
Stevenson and Kefauver in 1956 or Kennedy and Humphrey in
1960, were contests for leadership of the liberal wing of the party.
Nevertheless, during the period embraced by this book most of the
contests for nomination were unmistakably contests rooted in different philosphies of government.

Although it is often the fashion of cynical commentators to
decry the significance of the choices ultimately presented to the
voters, the active participants in presidential politics not only di-
vide on their personal preferences and commitments to the contenders for leadership, but they are also sharply divided on the issues
of the day and on the values that will be enhanced by the pursuit of
different policy alternatives. And just as analyses of the circulation

of party elites reveal significant differences in the processes by which intraparty insurgencies may lay claim to party nominations, the same analyses depict significant changes in the policy-related values of these elites.

Although the term "political culture" has come under attack for its ambiguity, we will find it useful in this chapter for comparing factions within party and, in subsequent chapters, for comparing the two partisan elites with each other and with their respective mass publics. A political culture may be defined as a collection of values, beliefs, goals, and behaviors that, when combined, serve to distinguish one set of political actors (whether that be a nation or a political party) from another set.[1] No extensive documentation is required, for example, to argue that the priorities and behavior of party elites are demonstrably different from those of the average citizen. Politics in itself is highly valued by elites, and they devote a substantially larger portion of their time to politics than do ordinary citizens.

Our interest in political culture is more restricted than this, however. We are especially interested in what might be called issue opinion or policy preference cultures. While consensus politics in the form of agreement on basic norms and rules of the game provides a reasonably stable framework for the long-term conduct of politics, allocative politics deals with the stuff of everyday politics—issue preferences, group benefits, leadership evaluations, and the like. A prescribed role for political parties and party factions is to articulate and aggregate these differences about allocative politics. In the process of doing so they may develop what we shall call opinion cultures, sets of (interrelated) beliefs that appear to set off one party or one party faction from the other.

To establish the presence of such cultures we will examine opinions about sociopolitical groups, about political leaders, and about specific issues at both the elite and mass levels. We begin with a look at elites within each party as exemplified by our convention delegates. The following chapter will examine comparisons between the two parties. Chapters 9 and 10 will deal with mass-elite comparisons. In these comparisons we will use various

---

[1] Perhaps the best-known, and still relevant, use of the term in empirical work is found in Gabriel Almond and Sidney Verba, *The Civic Culture* (Princeton, NJ: Princeton University Press, 1963).

indices or scales to reflect the content of contemporary party and within-party cultures in the United States.

Indicators of Political Values

There are, of course, a multiplicity of values engaged by national presidential politics, with multiple dimensions and multiple indicators. We shall examine a variety of these indicators, but we will begin with a set of measures in which there are apparent underlying dimensions that accord with the contemporary political meanings attached to the labels of conservative and liberal.[2] Our set of summary indicators includes five scales or indices which have been created from a score of individual items evaluated by our delegates in the 1981 data collection.

As described more fully in Appendix F, factor analytic techniques were used to identify clusters of specific item responses that clustered together to form distinct attitudinal factors or dimensions. After identifying these several dimensions, simple additive indices were constructed based on summing the scores attached to the component items associated with particular dimensions.

Five summary indices will be introduced in this chapter. One is an issue index based on responses to five questions about current public policy issues: fighting inflation versus reducing unemployment, busing to achieve racial integration, protecting the environment or relaxing antipollution regulations, supporting the Equal Rights Amendment, and taking a strong stance against Russia. The factor analysis upon which this index is based isolated two additional items, a defense spending question and an abortion issue, as not belonging in the same cluster as the other five issues. Given the

[2] Defining the meanings of liberalism and conservatism is no easy task. Although the literature is vast, we have found a pithy statement by Carl Cohen to be a serviceable rendering of the dimensions involved. He puts forward five such dimensions of the left-right (liberal-conservative) continuum: (1) reform-conservatism; (2) democracy-authoritarianism; (3) collectivism-individualism; (4) socialism-capitalism, and (5) equalitarianism-system of merit. See Cohen's "Who's to the Left? What's to the Right?" University of Michigan, *Rackham Reports* (Spring 1983), p. 9. All but category number 2 would seem to characterize the contemporary left-right division across the parties and, in lesser degree, within the two parties. Our various measures capture at least portions of these four dimensions, although we share with other researchers the necessity of tapping these dimensions with imperfect measurement techniques.

wide diversity of issues contained in the index, it seems reasonable to call it a "Left-Right Issue Index." To facilitate comparisons with several other measures based on "feeling thermometer" ratings, we have converted the index scores to means having a range of 0 to 100—the higher the score the more conservative the attitude.

Three additional separate summary scores were derived from the evaluation of a number of sociopolitical groups which the delegates located on a "feeling thermometer" that ranges from 0° (very cold and negative feelings) to 100° (very warm and positive feelings). Each summary consists of the summed scores for the constituent groups divided by the number of groups in the index. All scores range from 0 (very liberal or nonconservative) to 100 (very conservative or nonliberal). Where necessary the particular group score was reflected so that it would run in a liberal to conservative direction. One group evaluation index measures responses to five "Traditional Left-Right Groups" and consists of ratings applied to conservatives, union leaders, business interests, Democrats, and Republicans. A second index, labeled "New Left Groups," summarizes the ratings applied to the women's liberation movement, gay rights, Blacks, antinuclear groups, environmental protection groups, and liberals. Another index, known as "Moral Groups," combines the evaluations given to the moral majority and pro-life groups. The only seemingly anomaly in the contents of these three indices results from the inclusion of conservatives and liberals in different measures.

The fifth measure to be used draws on the individual's self-location on a seven-point scale, anchored by "extremely liberal" on one end and "extremely conservative" on the other. These scores have also been converted to a 0–100 scale in order to make them comparable with the other indices.[3]

Within both parties, the representation of values underlying each of the five measures was influenced by the compositional changes in the party elites which resulted from their circulation into and out of the role of campaign activist between 1972 and 1980. There were also differences in scores which presumably reflect secular effects associated with the different cohorts' first years as

[3] On this and the other measures used to indicate opinion cultures, the amount of missing data was trivial. In most instances those respondents with missing data on one item making up the index were given a score standardized by the items to which they did respond.

delegates. Yet a third contribution to the ultimate configuration present in 1981 doubtless came from changes in individual delegate preferences and evaluations. In the latter portion of this chapter we will examine evidence of individual-level change which occurred between 1972 and 1981, but in the introductory analysis we will concentrate on compositional change by disaggregating the components of the 1972–80 campaign elites as of 1981.

As a first step we focus on the separate contribution of the three cohorts of the continuously active participants. The data are presented in a manner that will also permit, in passing, a first glimpse at interparty differences on the values represented by campaign activists' scores on our indices. A more systematic analysis of differences separating the Democratic and Republican party elites will be reserved for chapter 8.

The Republican Drift to the Right: Cohort Differences

The ultimate success of the conservative wing of the Republican party in nominating Ronald Reagan in 1980 is underscored by a persistent pattern of differences in ideological preferences across the three cohorts of continuously active delegates (Table 7.1). Those who were chosen as delegates in the year of Reagan's nomination were visibly more conservative than those first chosen in 1972 and 1976. Compared with interparty differences, the differences among Republican cohorts were not large; but the progression from 1972 delegates to those chosen in 1976, when Reagan first challenged Ford, and on to 1980 is evident on all five indicators, and the differences between 1972 and 1980 seem unmistakable and significant. The most striking differences across the cohorts all pertain to the new issues of the 1980s: the Equal Rights Amendment, women's liberation movement, the moral majority, and pro-life groups. Keeping in mind that the intercohort comparison is among sometime delegates who were active in all three presidential campaigns—1972, 1976, and 1980—and remembering that our measurements of these attitudes were taken in 1981 following the 1980 election, we are struck by the extent to which the three cohorts reflected differences in the ideological conflicts associated with the three campaign years.

Table 7.1

**Political Attitudes of Delegates Continuously Active
in Presidential Campaigns, 1972–1980**

	Democrats			Republicans		
Indices	1972	1976	1980	1972	1976	1980
Issue Positions						
Mean	30.2	36.5	34.2	71.1	73.7	75.2
Standard Deviation	20.8	19.2	19.0	16.4	17.5	16.6
New Left Groups						
Mean	34.7	36.7	34.0	72.5	73.4	74.0
Standard Deviation	22.2	21.0	20.4	14.1	13.9	13.5
Traditional Groups						
Mean	28.2	27.4	25.9	74.4	76.6	77.3
Standard Deviation	13.6	13.4	12.5	11.7	11.3	11.0
Moral Groups						
Mean	16.0	16.0	16.1	41.5	47.7	52.6
Standard Deviation	20.9	21.2	19.8	25.5	29.4	28.6
Liberal-Conservative Self-Placement						
Mean	31.9	36.5	34.1	68.9	72.4	74.4
Standard Deviation	23.0	21.7	20.8	16.4	17.3	16.5

Note: Entries are based on scores ranging from 0 (most liberal) to 100 (most conservative) and are derived from the 1981 survey.

Evaluations of the two symbolic groups most associated with the themes of moral assessment—pro-life groups and the moral majority—present the sharpest intercohort difference, a difference substantially larger than any other within either party. Moreover, the suggestion of an evolving intraparty conflict among Republicans is apparent in the assessments of intragroup *variation* provided by the standard deviations attached to the cohort means and shown in Table 7.1. On four of the five indicators of political values, all Democratic cohorts reflect greater dispersions of evaluations than do Republican cohorts. This greater dispersion of sentiment is in keeping with the popular impression that the Democratic party is more divided internally than is the Republican party. But among the Democratic cohorts there is no greater evidence of lack of consensus in attitudes toward the moral groups than on any other indicator of preference or assessment. Internal disagreement among

Republicans, however, is evident in this domain, both in the comparison with Democrats and in the contrast with the relative homogeneity of Republican positions on the other four indicators. Although gross statistics are seldom sensitive indicators of process, in this instance it seems worth noting that the move to the right implicit in the 1980 delegates' relatively positive appraisal of the moral groups was not the consequence of great homogeneity of sentiment within their ranks but at the expense of even greater intraparty disagreement.

The Absence of Change Among Democrats

If the evidence on the Republican side conforms to more general impressions of an ideological shift to the right between 1972 and 1980, the Democratic data belie an equally widespread notion that the 1972 convention in Miami had temporarily produced a cadre of party leaders substantially more liberal than those who were subsequently chosen in 1980 to nominate the centrist Jimmy Carter for a second term. Whatever their proximity to the Democratic rank and file in 1972, a question we shall confront directly in a later chapter, the delegates who nominated McGovern *and* who remained active in the 1980 campaign were, at least in 1981, not substantially to the left of their 1980 counterparts. Although marginally more liberal on the index of policy preferences and in ideological self-placement, the continuously active members of the 1972 cohort were also somewhat more supportive of traditional groups, and they were not different from the other cohorts on the remaining two indicators of ideological preferences.

Nevertheless, a trace indication of the change in the temper of the times in the Democratic party between 1972 and 1976 is evident in the preferences of the 1976 delegate cohort. On three of the five indicators—the issue scale, the index of attitudes toward New Left groups, and liberal-conservative self-placement—the delegates who first nominated Carter in 1976 were at least marginally more inclined to support conservative values than were either the 1972 or 1980 delegates.

In general, the continuing participants in the Democratic elite do not reflect any dominant move or drift, left or right, to match the 1972–1980 differences among Republican cohorts. We shall observe shortly that this is by no means the consequence of lack of disagreement on values among the various candidate preference groups supporting the succession of presidential aspirants within the Democratic party. To the contrary, we shall document policy and preference differences among Carter supporters, traditionalists, and the left that are every bit as dramatic as the striking differences that we shall observe between the moderate and conservative camps in the Republican party. The candidate-related differences within the Democratic ranks were, however, submerged in the two-time selection of a centrist nominee, while the Republican shift from Nixon in 1972 to Reagan in 1980 marked a significant movement from the leadership of the Deweys, Rockefellers, Nixons, and Fords to the party of Goldwater and Reagan.

Circulation and Changes in Values: The Republican Case

We noted in the previous chapter that the patterns of change that marked the demise of liberal leadership in the Democratic party and the successful insurgency of the conservative wing among Republicans were sharply different. In like but not quite parallel fashion, the circulation of the campaign activists had significantly different consequences for the representation of values and preferences within each of the two parties. For reasons of parsimony we again combine all of the continuously active participants, regardless of cohort, and compare them with the disengaged and the mobilized.

Among the Republicans, the policy preferences and group evaluations of the two analytic elements involved in elite circulation are predictably different (Table 7.2). Across all six indicators, the disengaged delegates, active in 1972 but nonparticipants in the 1980 campaign, were clearly more liberal than the continuously active delegates. Without exception, the dropouts reflected policy or value preferences that could have been inferred from the analyses of the last chapter, which reported that supporters of moderate candidates dropped out of active participation at rates four or five times greater than the dropout rate among Reagan supporters.

Without exception, those Republicans who disengaged were visibly less conservative than the core participants, and, corre-

Table 7.2

Political Attitudes of Campaign Activists, by Circulation Patterns, 1972–1980

Indices	Democrats			Republicans		
	Continuous Participants	Disen-gaged	Mobi-lized	Continuous Participants	Disen-gaged	Mobi-lized
Issue Positions						
Mean	34.9	36.7	40.2	73.3	65.1	74.3
Standard Deviation	19.7	20.6	19.6	16.9	18.3	16.2
New Left Groups						
Mean	35.1	36.3	40.1	73.3	67.2	72.2
Standard Deviation	21.2	21.7	21.0	13.8	14.5	15.0
Traditional Groups						
Mean	27.1	32.9	31.3	76.1	70.1	75.2
Standard Deviation	13.2	13.8	14.0	11.4	11.1	11.6
Moral Groups						
Mean	16.1	15.5	21.0	47.2	34.3	48.3
Standard Deviation	20.6	22.4	23.0	28.2	25.5	29.9
Liberal-Conservative Self-Placement						
Mean	32.3	33.7	39.6	73.0	64.8	74.1
Standard Deviation	21.3	22.5	21.5	16.2	18.1	18.1

Note: Entries are based on scores ranging from 0 (most liberal) to 100 (most conservative) and are derived from the 1981 survey.

spondingly, they were often most strikingly different from the 1980 cohort as described in Table 7.1. To the extent that the mood of the 1980 delegates dominated the atmosphere of Republican presidential politics in that year, it seems reasonable to conclude that disengagement (or the continued inactivity of those who had already dropped out by 1976) was at least in part a consequence of substantial disagreements with those who had moved into a dominant position within the party.

Differences of ideological position were pronounced on every policy question from detente through equal rights. The contrast was particularly dramatic with respect to such symbolic groups as the moral majority and pro-life groups. Both of these groups were supported by a clear plurality of the core participants among the 1980 Republican delegates, but were opposed by pluralities of comparable size among those from the other cohorts who chose not to participate in the 1980 campaign. The data provide dramatic evidence of the extent to which delegates with liberal sentiments left the Republican campaign trail prior to 1980. Their disappearance from the roster of activists clearly meant that the symbols of the right would receive more support in the Republican party elite as modal candidate preferences also moved to the right.

Furthermore, as one might infer from our inspection of the cohorts of continuously active participants, the mobilized (inactive in 1972 but engaged in the campaign of 1980) accentuated the party's conservative move as they replaced the relatively liberal disengaged. The newly mobilized were not only more conservative than the dropouts, but on three of our five indices they were marginally further to the right than the core of continuously active delegates. Interestingly, their unmistakable conservative preferences were, nevertheless, not quite a match for the positions of the 1980 delegates who had been active as early as the 1972 contest. The newcomers to presidential campaign politics were not necessarily in the vanguard of the conservatism that swept the 1980 convention, but they did sustain the thrust of the older hands who were new to presidential politics only in their role as first-time delegates in 1980.

Contrary to what might be expected, the newly mobilized were *not* as favorably inclined to the moral majority and pro-life groups as were the other 1980 delegates, and they were even less homogeneous in their evaluation of these groups. The new recruits to 1980 were not right-wing zealots, popular accounts notwithstanding. In their limited numbers, the newly mobilized could not add appreciably to the level of intraparty disagreement. And, indeed, the fact that they were not a totally unified group intent on pushing yet further to the conservative extreme may be as propitious for the party's future unity as the overall level of dispersion of sentiments in this domain is threatening.

By implication, the ubiquitous presence of numerous small contrasts between the 1980 core and those newly mobilized for 1980 reacquaints us with one of the limitations in our basic research design. If, as we have just suggested, the core participants in the 1980 cohort were homogeneous in the political attitudes *because* they were so predominantly Reagan supporters, it then follows that many others who might have been in the 1980 cohort but were not included in our study because they backed losing candidates (or were otherwise not chosen as delegates in 1980) may have been from the more liberal ranks of the supporters of moderate Republican leadership. Our design does not permit us to follow such possible activists, chart their subsequent participation or disengagement in 1980, and map their candidate preferences and political values. It may be that they are, in fact, already represented in our study by the other non-Reaganites in the 1972 and 1976 cohorts. If the formal fact of being a delegate has no intrinsic and unique consequences for activists, this could well be the case. On the other hand, to the extent that delegates are—or become—in some sense special people because of their experiences in a nominating convention, we are now alerted to the fact that the non-Reaganites in our 1972 and 1976 cohorts of sometime delegates are likely *not* to be fully representative of other activists who fall outside our particular definition of presidential campaign elite.

Circulation and Changes in Values: The Democratic Case

Circulation patterns among Democratic and Republican activists are in sharp contrast, at least with respect to expectations based on our inspections of cohort differences and our earlier depiction of the dynamics of changes in candidate support. In the first place, as Table 7.2 illustrates, delegates who dropped out of active campaigning after the 1972 election were not generally more liberal than those who remained active in the 1980 campaign. Only in their rejection of the moral majority and pro-life groups were the disengaged Democrats more proliberal, or anticonservative, than the core of active Democratic partipants. Their policy preferences, their self-designation as liberals or conservatives, and even their appraisal of groups identified with the New Left were all at least marginally more conservative than those of their former colleagues from 1972 who continued active participation in the 1980 campaign. Despite the fact that the relative decline in liberal candidate support among active Democrats was disproportionately a function of the *disengagement* of supporters of liberal candidates, as documented in a previous chapter, the consequence of their departure was not a general decline in support for liberal policies and social groups identified with the left within the Democratic campaign elite. To the contrary, the overall consequence of their departure from campaign activities left the continuing participants from 1972 and 1976 a slightly more liberal set of party leaders than they would have been had the disengaged left not retired from the fray!

The explication of this somewhat unexpected corollary to disengagement among Democratic delegates leads us to an intriguing exercise in the reconstruction of recent political history and the ideological structuring of elite subgroup relationships. The exercise begins with an explicit test of the presumption that it was the most liberal of the candidate support groups that suffered the highest dropout rates. Rather than return to any of the combinations of candidate support groups used in the various analytic summaries of past chapters, we shall examine the full set of twelve patterns of candidate preference, 1972–1976–1980, and documented in Appendix Table D.2. Using the issue index as the most unambiguous measure of contemporaneous ideological positioning, we can order our twelve patterns of candidate preference in a remarkably coherent and revealing fashion. The intuitive sensibility of the ordering is not complete, nor for our purposes need it be. However, in Table 7.3 the groups are politically anchored on the left by the McGovern-Udall-Kennedy supporters. With apologies to those in that group who actually supported Chisholm or Kennedy in 1972, or any of the Brown-Church-Harris-Shriver quadrumvirate in 1976, the pattern of unbroken preference for a candidate of the left is clearly associated with the most liberal of positions on all of our

Table 7.3

1981 Issue Preferences in Relation to Patterns of Candidate Preferences Among the Democratic Campaign Activists, 1972–1980

Candidate Preference Patterns	Continuous Participants		Disengaged		
	Score	N	Score	N	Difference
Consistent Liberal	21.7	(206)	21.6	(70)	−0.1
Liberal to Carter in 1980	26.5	(69)	27.0	(29)	+0.5
Alienated Liberal	26.4	(79)	33.3	(91)	+6.9
Wavering Liberal	29.1	(149)	29.0	(52)	−0.1
Liberal to Carter in 1976	31.7	(119)	32.3	(30)	+0.6
Others to Liberal	32.5	(42)	—	(0)	—
Traditional to Liberal	35.9	(187)	42.2	(33)	+6.3
Traditional to Carter in 1980	39.5	(182)	54.6	(22)	+15.1
Carter Only	39.9	(75)	—	(2)	—
Traditional to Carter in 1976	44.7	(216)	49.1	(18)	+4.4
Alienated Traditionalist	46.5	(95)	54.5	(65)	+8.0
Conservative	74.1	(18)	—	(7)	—
Total	34.9	(1,436)	36.7	(420)	+1.8

Notes: Entries are mean scores on the issue scale and range from 0 (most liberal) to 100 (most conservative). Candidate-preference patterns are documented in Appendix Table D.2.

No scores are reported with fewer than 18 cases (numbers of cases are in parentheses).

various indicators. The other extreme is equally—or better— defined by the handful of Wallace supporters who participated in our study.[4]

The *least* liberal of the left-wing candidate support groups are the two which most recently came to the liberal camp. The less liberal within this pair, in turn, consists of former supporters of traditional party leaders who preferred Senator Kennedy's candidacy in 1980 ("Traditional to Liberal" in Table 7.3). These delegates are, without much question, more liberal in their self-identifi-

[4] The relationship between candidate preference and ideology has, of course, been well documented for particular conventions. Perhaps the most graphic portrayals appear in Jeane Kirkpatrick's description of the 1972 Democratic delegate support groups. See *The New Presidential Elite: Men and Women in National Politics* (New York: Russell Sage Foundation and the Twentieth Century Fund, 1976).

cation than any other group *formerly* associated with the traditional Democratic leadership. But they are almost equally distinctively more *conservative* when compared with the other left-wing categories on our measure of policy preferences. Interestingly enough, this indication of relative conservatism within the liberal wing of the party is matched by their scores on left-right self-placement but is denied on all three evaluations of politically relevant groups. On all of those measures, the traditionalists who preferred Kennedy in 1980 challenge the pure liberal candidate groups for honors as the most liberal. Quite apparently their fellowship, if not the Kennedy leadership, was based as much on very positive responses to symbolic, group-oriented politics as their policy preferences.

A first real surprise, at least to the innocent observer, is provided by the relatively conservative position of those delegates who entered presidential politics on Carter's behalf in 1976 or 1980, having had no expressed preference among the contenders in 1972 ("Carter Only" in Table 7.3). Despite the arguments of commentators and analysts that Carter was a nonideological, pragmatic centrist, those mobilized to his support in 1976 or 1980 were markedly more conservative than the least liberal of the liberal support groups. On some specific indicators, such as their position on the self-defined continuum of liberal-conservative sentiment, they did look like followers of traditional party leaders; on other individual items, as in their attitudes toward abortion, Blacks, or the moral majority, they anchored the conservative position for mainstream Democrats. In general, the views of those delegates whose only preference was Carter suggest that it was a conservative Carter and a liberal left wing that provided the polar referents for the Democratic campaign elite in 1980.

The ordering within two other *pairs* of groups (among the twelve patterns of candidate preference) is consistent with this view of a distinctly conservative cast to the Carter candidacies. Among both the supporters of liberal leadership and the followers of traditional leadership, those who broke ranks first with a 1976 preference for Carter ("Liberal to Carter in 1976" and "Traditional to Carter in 1976") were visibly more conservative than the liberals and traditionalists who held fast through 1976 and came to a preference for Carter only as the party's incumbent candidate for reelection in 1980. Although in the previous chapter we suggested that candidacies are the engines of presidential politics, it now seems that we have clear evidence that value preferences may be both the prime mover, as in the case of the ideological homogeneity of the McGovern-Udall-Kennedy preference, and restraining forces, as in their brake on *both* liberal and traditional enthusiasm for Carter in 1976.

Two other patterns among the twelve share an unpredicted but explicable commonality that is central to our explanation of why disengaged Democrats were not a distinctively liberal group. Both the "alienated liberals" and "alienated traditionalists" (in Table 7.3) were visibly more conservative than their parent groups (represented by consistent liberals and all of the traditional groups). This is to say, quite simply, that those on the left who found neither Carter nor Kennedy to their liking in 1980 were quite apparently somewhat more conservative than their counterparts who did prefer Kennedy. In like manner, it was not that traditionalists who had no preferred candidate in 1980 did not have a sufficiently liberal alternative. Instead, if they understood Carter's positions to be reflected in those of his newly mobilized supporters, they apparently could not abide his lack of clear-cut commitment to conservative Democratic politics. The ideological location of the "alienated traditionalists" was clearly to the right of every other candidate group except the Wallace supporters. Other fragmentary pieces of side evidence suggest that the "alienated traditionalists" may have included some of the old-line centrists who, disillusioned with the insurgencies of McGovern and Carter and frustrated by traditionalists' loss of power, withdrew from party politics or even defected to the opposition. In any event, the "alienated traditionalists" were a thoroughly conservative group, by Democratic party norms, and their unhappy deviancy was marked by an exceptional rate of disengagement from presidential politics in 1980, a rate of 35 percent, second only to that of the 52 percent among "alienated liberals."

In line with the general thesis that alienation from party leadership was at least in part a function of their relatively conservative preferences, Table 7.3 records that those among the alienated (that is, those who had no 1980 candidate preference) who then dropped out of active campaign participation by 1980 were even more markedly conservative than their alienated counterparts who remained as active campaigners. Among the five liberal groups, the alienated disengaged were unique in being more conservative (by 7 percentage points) than those who remained active. As Table 7.3 indicates,

among the other four "early liberal" patterns, the scores of the
disengaged were not significantly different from those of the continuing participants. Whatever their rates of disengagement, and for
whatever reasons, the disengaged within other liberal candidate
preference patterns were essentially random subsets of their
groups when it came to the ideological cast of their political
values. Only "alienated liberals" among the disengaged were visibly
more conservative than their liberal colleagues who remained
active.

A quite different situation obtains among the various followers
of traditional leadership. Although the numbers involved in three
of the patterns are quite small, all four sets of the no-longer-active
traditional delegates were distinctly more conservative than those
who remained active as continuous participants (Table 7.3). It is not
immediately obvious why this should be, but in any event, because
of the sheer aggregated size of the two groups of the alienated who
disengaged after 1972, it is the *alienated* delegates who are largely
responsible for the slightly conservative cast of all the disengaged
among the Democrats.

The constant need to test logical inferences is exemplified by
our discovery that a disengagement dominated by McGovern supporters did not necessarily mean that the disengaged were more
"liberal" than those continuing in their roles as campaign activists.
And just as our initial analyses had not prepared us for the discovery that those who dropped out of the Democratic campaign after
1972 were not the most liberal of the 1972 activists, so the ideological positioning of those newly mobilized for the 1980 Democratic
campaign was not forecast as the result of our cohort-by-cohort analysis of the continuous participants. If the disengaged matched the
more conservative tenor of the 1976 cohort (see Table 7.1), the
newly mobilized delegates of 1980 were of an unmistakably more
conservative bent (Table 7.2). On all but one of the scales and
indices reported in Table 7.2 the Democratic delegates who had
not campaigned in 1972 but were active participants in 1980 were
dramatically to the right of the core of continuously active participants. It would appear that the 1976 campaign set the ideological
tone for mobilization of Democrats, in both 1976 and 1980. Given
the substantial numbers involved, the result could have been a
major move to the right within the Democratic party *if* the
mobilized had replaced a heavily liberal set of dropouts. As it was,

the disengagement on the left was not disproportionately left leaning in ideological terms and the mobilization of conservatives moved the entire set of Democratic activists only marginally to the right.

The Drift to the Right: Replacement and Conversion

On the Republican side, movement to the right between 1972 and 1980 occurred both because of the impact of the Reagan nomination on the 1972 and 1976 delegates and because the defeat of the moderates was accompanied by the disengagement of many of the more liberal Republican delegates. As Table 7.4 indicates, withdrawal from active campaigning accelerated the swing to the right promoted by the Reagan advocates at the Republican convention of 1980. The uniform pattern in Table 7.4 is clear and the net result was a politically as well as statistically significant removal of less conservative delegates from the campaign elite.

The Democratic move to the right was neither impelled by the previously active delegates of 1980 nor reinforced by the disengagement of 1972 activists. As far as compositional change was concerned, the increase in conservatism among Democrats was entirely the result of the recruitment and mobilization of *new delegates in 1976 and 1980*. Whether a lagged response to the recognition that Carter was really a conservative Democrat, or in anticipatory reaction to the rightward drift of the Republicans, Democratic delegates of 1976 or 1980 who had not been active campaigners in 1972 entered the lists in 1980 as the party's new center of conservatism.

Our analysis of the Republican party in particular has demonstrated a decided net drift to the right over time. Two sets of findings point in that direction. First, each succeeding cohort was more conservative than the preceding one. Second, the disengaged activists were much less conservative than the new cohorts, or the newly mobilized. Both of these findings suggest that it was change in elite personnel that fueled the GOP's rightward slide. Though less marked and of a more complicated nature, the Democrats also drifted to the right during the 1970s. There is presumptive evidence that this was largely a matter of elite replacement as rep-

Table 7.4

1981 Issue Preferences in Relation to Patterns of Candidate Preference Among the Republican Campaign Activists, 1972–1980

Candidate Preference Patterns	Continuous Participants		Disengaged		Difference
	Score	N	Score	N	
Consistent Moderate	61.9	(282)	60.5	(49)	−1.4
No Preference to Moderate	69.5	(20)	—	(0)	—
Alienated Ford	64.8	(51)	62.9	(20)	−1.9
Nixon Only	72.8	(38)	66.7	(38)	−6.1
Ford to Reagan	70.4	(147)	64.1	(14)	−6.3
Reagan to Moderate	73.1	(26)	—	(2)	—
No Preference to Reagan	76.1	(40)	—	(0)	—
Reagan Only	81.6	(446)	71.7	(16)	−9.9
Alienated Reagan	82.2	(30)	—	(4)	—
Total	73.3	(1,088)	65.1	(142)	−8.2

Notes: Entries are mean scores on the issue scale and range from 0 (most liberal) to 100 (most conservative).

No scores are reported with fewer than 14 cases (weighted numbers of cases are in parentheses; unweighted cases total 21 and 24 instead of 14 and 16 for smallest cells with reported scores).

resented by the greater conservatism of the newly mobilized, compared with the disengaged, coupled with the absence of much intercohort difference among the continuously active.

Important as elite turnover might be in aggregate attitudinal shifts of the elites, another source of change is to be found in changes in individual attitudes among the delegates. We saw in chapter 3 that individual-level change, or conversion, accounted in large part for Reagan's sharp rise in popularity during the 1970s. While the apparent shifts on issue stances and group evaluations were not nearly as pronounced as shifts in candidate evaluations, they are of sufficient magnitude on the Republican side and of sufficient complexity on the Democratic side to call for a more systematic look at the question of replacement versus conversion effects. To do this we will employ the technique introduced in chapter 3, one which takes advantage of the 1972 delegate study.

As there were scarcely any issue questions from the 1972 study that were repeated in 1981, our foray here is confined to eight group evaluations that were elicited at both times. Some of these groups appeared in the traditional left-right index, and some in the New Left group index (as used above). For present purposes we have constructed a new additive index based on the assessments of the six groups (omitting Democrats and Republicans) and running from 0 to 100: the higher the score, the more conservative is the attitude being expressed.

Table 7.5 presents the findings for Republicans and Democrats separately, with the final three columns supplying the three types of change scores of interest to us and the first three columns providing the bases for these change scores. Signs have been attached to entries in columns 4–6 in order to show the directional nature of the shifts (where + reflects a proconservative shift and − a liberal shift). The groups are listed for each party according to the amount of net change in the *conservative* direction (column 4) that occurred over the course of the two points of observation.

Not surprisingly, the Republicans registered more net change than did the Democrats, as shown by the summary index scores. Given the fact that the possible range is from 0 to 100, a net change of 9 points is substantial. As presaged by many of our previous findings, this shift was in the conservative direction. Moreover, the conservative tilt appeared with respect to each of the six groups evaluated, conservative groups gaining in affection and liberal groups losing. Especially pronounced were the alterations associated with ratings of liberals and conservatives on the one hand and union leaders and business interests on the other. Changing evaluations of these highly symbolic lodestars of the traditional liberal-conservative dimension in American politics provided sharp evidence about the shifting ideological cast of the Republican elite.

Net change on the Democratic side proved both more limited and, as we shall see, a bit more complex in its nature. And with these measures, as well as some of those examined earlier in the chapter, it was on balance slightly *liberal,* as denoted by the negative sign attached to the summary index change score. Perhaps the most significant development lay in a net gain of 7 points for the evaluation of the Democratic party itself (not shown). Indeed, in absolute terms the 1980 Democratic delegates felt as good about their own party as did the Republicans about theirs, an improve-

Table 7.5

Sources of Change in the Evaluations of Sociopolitical Groups

	1980 Delegates in 1981	1972 Delegates in 1972	1972 Delegates in 1981	Net Change (1 − 2)	Replacement (1 − 3)	Conversion (3 − 2)
Republicans						
Liberals	16	29	20	+13	+4	+9
Union Leaders	24	35	26	+11	+2	+9
Business Interests	72	62	70	+10	+2	+8
Conservatives	77	67	69	+10	+8	+2
Women's Liberation Movement	22	29	28	+7	+6	+1
Blacks	55	57	52	+2	−3	+5
Summary Index	71	63	68	+9	+3	+6
Democrats						
Business Interests	45	37	44	+8	+1	+7
Liberals	69	73	70	+4	+1	+3
Blacks	76	75	74	0	−2	+2
Conservatives	26	28	26	−2	0	−2
Women's Liberation Movement	66	58	66	−8	0	−8
Union Leaders	66	55	59	−11	−7	−4
Summary Index	32	34	33	−2	−2	−1

Notes: Plus signs indicate a proconservative shift and minus signs indicate a liberal shift.
Discrepancies in subtraction are due to rounding.

ment over the 1972 situation. However, whereas the Republicans moved unidirectionally over time with regard to all groups, the same was not true of the Democrats. They became more positive in their appraisals of a traditional constituent group—union leaders— and a new group—the women's liberation movement. But they also increased their estimation of business interests and their regard for liberals declined. Thus, the Democratic center of gravity shifted scarcely at all in terms of the overall index, partly because of countervailing movements within the party.

Turning to the sources of the net change, we see that both replacement and conversion effects were at work within the GOP. Somewhat surprisingly, however, the impact of conversion was even more substantial than that of replacement. Thus, of the 9-point net shift among Republicans on the summary index, the contribution of individual change doubled that of replacement. As the decade wore on, the 1972 delegates, presumably as a result of period effects rather than life-stage processes, became more conservative. Consequently, the political attitudes of Republican presidential elites would have shifted by 1980–1981 (assuming continued activity) even without a turnover in personnel, though turnover does make a difference.

This should not be taken to minimize the role of the newly mobilized Republicans nor the impact of the disengaged in changing Republican elites over the decade. A separate analysis of the 1972 disengaged shows, as expected, that they did not match the rightward tilt of their continuously active colleagues from the 1972 delegation (1981 scores of 65 for the disengaged and 69 for the continuously active). Still, the winds of change, the *Zeitgeist* of the era, worked to push the 1972 GOP contingents in a conservative direction. How much of this was due to serious self-examination and how much to the explosion of conservative proselytizing and electoral success cannot be distinguished here. That does not diminish the strong evidence that Republican party activists were themselves changing and that this was bound to affect party structure, organization, and political strategy quite apart from the consequences of any infusion of new party activists.

Among the Democrats, the more limited amount of net change had divergent sources. The rising assessments of union leaders owed more to replacement than to conversion. On the other hand, the increasing regard for the women's liberation movement and business interests stemmed almost completely from change of heart at the individual level. But the central message among Democrats is their lesser net change overall. If changes in the Republican party were pervasively dynamic, reflecting both conversion and replacement, the Democratic elite, despite the disarray in its search for viable leadership, seemed much less responsive and was apparently moved only by the narrow set of forces surrounding the Carter candidacy.

Candidate Preferences and Political Values

It is appropriate now to take a more systematic look at the role of candidate preferences in structuring the attitudes of the delegates, looking for variations associated with campaign history and preference genealogies.[5] The empirical ordering of the Democratic groups in Table 7.3 seemed to reflect an intuitively reasonable reconstruction of sequences of change in their response to party leadership. One should not attempt to make too much of differences between adjoining groups in this rank ordering. The "wavering liberals" are not sharply more liberal than the "alienated liberals"; McGovernites who moved to Carter in 1976 are not distinctly more liberal than the 1980 Kennedy supporters who had no preference in earlier years; and the difference between the traditionalists who moved to Carter early and late are persistent but not large.

Once this is said, however, the ideological heterogeneity, organized by patterns of candidate preference within the Democratic elite, bears more than passing comment. It is particularly noteworthy to observe the extent to which the ideological base of Carter's

[5]While it does not gainsay the demonstrated associations between candidate preferences and ideological leanings, there is some evidence that the perceived electability of the candidate is a powerful determinant of candidate preference, and that there is a three-cornered relationship between ideological proximity, perceived electability, and candidate preference. See Walter J. Stone, "Party, Ideology, and the Lure of Victory: Iowa Activists in the 1980 Prenomination Campaign," *Western Political Quarterly* 35 (December 1982): 524–38; Walter J. Stone and Alan F. Abramowitz, "Winning May Not Be Everything, But It's More Than We Thought: Presidential Party Activists in 1980," *American Political Science Review* 77 (December 1983): 945–56; and J. Merrill Shanks, Warren E. Miller, Henry E. Brady, and Bradley L. Palmquist, "Viability, Electability, and Presidential 'Preference,' " paper presented at meeting of the Midwest Political Science Association, Chicago, April 1985.

support was sharply bifurcated. Former traditional partisans supporting Carter differed dramatically from the former supporters of George McGovern in the Carter camp. The composition of the 1980 liberal groups was almost as heterogeneous as was that of the Carter supporters, and the differences associated with the 1972 preferences were clearly evident: the McGovern-Udall-Kennedy lineage is distinctively more liberal than that made up of 1980 Kennedy supporters who had started with a Humphrey-Muskie-Jackson preference in 1972.

To provide a systematic appraisal of the differences in the values expressed by the various candidate preference groups, we estimated the contribution of the candidate preference groupings to the overall variance in political attitudes among individual delegates. Consider, for example, attitudes about public policy issues. Given the sharp differences in mean group values reported in Tables 7.3 and 7.4, it is not surprising to discover that a very significant portion of the variation in delegate scores was associated with patterns of preference for presidential candidates (see Table 7.6). Among continuously active Democrats, Eta values associated with the twelve-category grouping of the delegates was a very substantial .46.[6] It was somewhat more surprising to discover that the less elaborate structure of candidate preferences on the Republican side accounted for a comparable proportion of variance in the scores of continuously active Republican delegates, with an Eta of .49.

Carrying this line of inquiry into the full set of attitudinal measures and the distinct elements involved in elite circulation provides further insight into the processes that shape the elites' representations of political values. Despite some variation across our five summary indicators, we see once more in Table 7.6 the presence of generational or cohort effects among the band of continuously active participants. For the Democrats, it is the 1972 cohort that displays coefficients that most sharply reflect value differences associated with particular patterns of candidate preference. The subsequent trend over time is one of consistent decline through the 1976 cohort to the 1980 delegates whose issue preferences and group evaluations were clearly less tied to their patterns of candidate

[6] The Eta statistic is produced by an analysis of variance of grouped data. It measures the relative extent to which intragroup homogeneity and intergroup heterogeneity account for the variance on our various indicators.

Table 7.6

Association of Political Attitudes with Patterns of Candidate Preference Among Campaign Activists, 1972–1980

Democrats

Indices	Continuous Participants by Cohort Year			All Continuous Participants	Disengaged	Mobilized
	1972	1976	1980			
Issue Positions	.54	.44	.38	.46	.57	.39
New Left Groups	.62	.50	.44	.52	.62	.45
Traditional Groups	.30	.35	.24	.31	.33	.35
Moral Groups	.34	.25	.28	.28	.39	.06
Liberal-Conservative Self-Placement	.53	.52	.48	.51	.55	.41

Republicans

Indices	Continuous Participants by Cohort Year			All Continuous Participants	Disengaged	Mobilized
	1972	1976	1980			
Issue Positions	.46	.54	.42	.49	.23	.55
New Left Groups	.32	.44	.40	.38	.17	.48
Traditional Groups	.33	.37	.31	.36	.19	.43
Moral Groups	.49	.56	.50	.51	.45	.58
Liberal-Conservative Self-Placement	.41	.58	.52	.52	.42	.56

Note: Entries are Etas computed from one-way analysis of variance within each party. The larger the entry the greater is the variation by candidate preference.

preference. The cohort differences revealed in Table 7.6 are consistent with the thesis that the cohorts continue to reflect important initial differences in their subsequent roles as campaign activists. Initial differences are reflected in the fact that participants who became delegates in 1980 were less inclined to associate policy preferences with candidate preferences than were those activists who participated in the contentious 1972 convention that nominated George McGovern.

Without exception, Democratic candidate preference groups among the core participants in the 1980 cohort were less polarized than were the counterpart groups in the 1972 cohort. A detailed inspection of the individual attitudes (which form the basis of the various indices in Table 7.6) associated with the unique patterns of candidate preference indicates that diminished polarization was present, in general, at both ends of the candidate-preference continuum. In the 1980 cohort, traditionalists who had moved to Carter, whether early or late, reflected an average of an 18-percentage-point discrepancy from the conservative positions occupied by their counterparts from 1972. With the exception of the "consistent liberals," who are the most extreme liberal group in both years, the various liberal candidate support groups in 1980 participated in the depolarization to almost the same extent as did the traditionalists by reflecting an average of 16 points less support for the liberal positions held by their members in the 1972 cohort. These inter-cohort differences were not, however, a simple or mechanical regression toward the mean. The "consistent liberals" did not contribute to the depolarization. On indicator after indicator they defined the boundary on the left for the party in both years with virtually no difference between the cohorts. Indeed, on the question of abortion, the 1980 cadre representing the left was even more liberal than the 1972 cadre, and only on the questions of defense and detente did they depart from the otherwise universal pattern by showing less support for the liberal position than had been demonstrated by their 1972 counterparts.

For Republicans, it was the experience of the Ford-Reagan contest in 1976 that sharpened the connections between political values and candidates. By a visible margin the members of that 1976 cohort reflect a candidate-oriented structuring of their positions that is more pervasive than in either of the other cohorts.

Turning to the full core of continuously active participants in each party, we note in Table 7.6 a remarkable similarity between the parties on three of the measures of the relevance of candidate preferences for delegates' ideological positions. Quite predictably, however, patterns of candidate preference are more clearly linked to assessments of New Left groups among Democrats than among Republicans. And the same singular role of the moral groups as divisive symbols within the Republican party is once more apparent in the sharper alignment of moral group evaluations and Republican candidate preferences.

An important contrast between the parties becomes evident in the characterization of the disengaged. Except for the scores on the moral groups, attitudes of disengaged Democrats were clearly more candidate related than were those of their Republican counterparts. This again reflects the differences in the recent history of the two parties. The candidate-related polarization of values among Democrats was sharpest in 1972 and appears among the disengaged, who come disproportionately from the 1972 cohort. Not so for Republicans where disengagement in 1976 and 1980 produced low-water marks for candidate-related expressions of political values in three of the five domains.

The two sets of newly mobilized delegates present almost a mirror image of the disengaged. Newly mobilized Republicans went into the 1980 campaign quite certain about the connection between their ideological values and their preferences for party leadership. They matched the 1976 veterans of the Ford-Reagan confrontation in the clarity with which their 1980 positions were aligned with preferred candidates. For the Democrats, on the other hand, the mobilization of 1980 extended the previously noted blurring of candidate-oriented disagreements within successive cohorts. On two of the five summary measures the mobilized Democrats revealed less candidate orientation in their scores than the least structured of the cohorts—the 1980 cohort—and thus, except in their assessments of traditional groups, accentuated the drift in the Democratic party *away* from issues and group assessments structured by party leadership positions.

The net result in both parties was for circulation to accentuate trends reflected in the successive cohorts of continuously active campaigners. As of 1980, policy positions and group evaluations held by Republican campaign elites were more clearly organized to fit differences among their patterns of presidential candidate preference than they had been in previous years. The restructuring of candidate preferences between 1972 and 1980 was also a sorting out of ideological orientations. At the same time, the Democrats had moved in the opposite direction and the candidate-related differences of 1972 had been softened and blurred by 1980. It is appropriate to emphasize that even among 1980 Democrats or 1972 Republicans the decision to support one candidate rather than another is, year-by-year and over time, highly correlated with the delegates' own policy preferences and their own evaluations of societal groups that have acquired symbolic if not direct political meaning for governmental policy choices. But given the ubiquitousness of these relationships, the divergent changes within each of the two parties bear additional comment.

The literature on the American party system in the 1970s and early 1980s reported the Democratic party in great disarray because of the party's loss of control over the presidential selection process.[7] With a quite different evidentiary base, the Republican party was increasingly portrayed as growing ever stronger as the Democratic party weakened.[8] Given these developments, we could have expected the precise reverse of the patterns we have just observed. A recent history of capricious selection of candidates should diminish central tendencies within a party elite and accentuate candidate-inspired divergence over time. Instead of this being true for the Democrats, the end of the Carter era found the ideological positions of Democratic delegates *less* often a reflection of their recent decisions on candidate preference. In counterpoint, the invigoration of the Republican party, including larger roles for national committees and campaign organizations, should have produced a lesser, not a greater, impact of unique candidate preference patterns on elite values. Yet the trend was in the other direction. It may be, of course, that the 1980 Democratic situation reflects a swift reaction *against* the antiparty spirit of 1972 and 1976, while the Republican elites have not yet come to terms with the reality of

[7] Austin Ranney, "The Political Parties: Reform and Decline," in Anthony King, ed., *The New American Political System* (Washington, DC: American Enterprise Institute, 1978); Nelson W. Polsby and Aaron Wildavsky, *Presidential Election* (New York: Scribner, 1980).
[8] James L. Gibson, Cornelius P. Cotter, John F. Bibley, and Robert J. Huckshorn, "Assessing Organizational Party Strength," *American Journal of Political Science* 27 (May 1983): 192–222.

a newly united party. One suspects, however, that we are only beginning to understand the interplay among party, policy, and candidate concerns of the modern-day presidential campaign elite.

The National Move to the Right

The net consequence of the complex set of interrelated changes we have described throughout this chapter was, for both the Democratic and the Republican elites, a visible drift to the right between 1972 and 1980. But if the ultimate change in political attitudes was similar in the two parties, the mechanisms that produced the parallel changes were very different. First, there were no significant differences across the three cohorts of continuing Democratic participants, while the pattern of cohort differences among Republicans was that of an unbroken shift to the right. Indeed, there was not only no evidence of an overall drift to the right among continuously active Democrats, but whatever minor variations are apparent from an examination of individual items suggest a limited *increase* in liberal responses to the issues of the 1980 elections. The 1980 campaign cohort was more in favor of reducing unemployment than of curbing inflation; a marginally greater degree of support for ERA was, however, offset by a slightly more conservative attitude toward abortion; and marginally more positive reactions to union leaders constituted the only other indication of a trend across the three cohorts. Nevertheless, when all of the individual indicators are summed within each of the three sets of Democratic core participants, the resulting indices do not reveal any substantial deviation of any one of the three cohorts. This is, of course, sharply different from the persistent indication of cohort differences that capture a period of change in the Republican elite, a period that culminated in a distinctively more conservative set of core participants coming out of the 1980 cohort.

A second difference between the parties rests on the absence of any substantial contribution to change among the Democrats as a result of delegates' withdrawal from active participation in the presidential campaign. Despite the fact that the disengaged were a large part of the total 1972–1980 Democratic campaign elite, their withdrawal from presidential politics had only a trace impact on the change of attitudinal dispositions among Democratic activists across the eight years. (At this point it should be kept in mind that our earlier concern with the analysis of the attitudes of the disengaged was not centered on them so much because of their conservative postures as because they *did not*, as a group, reflect the strong liberal orientation that we might have inferred from the disproportionate contribution of liberal candidate supporters to their total number.) Their disengagement did not produce any substantial accentuation of the liberal posture that was predominant among continuing participants. This was in clear contrast to the fact that diminished support for moderate leaders in the Republican party *was* accompanied by the demobilization of a visibly more liberal set of delegates from Republican campaign activities in 1980 who thereby accelerated the Republican elite swing to the right.

The third interparty difference relates to the attitudes of the mobilized. While the newly mobilized in the 1980 cohort of Republican activists were, somewhat surprisingly, slightly less conservative than the core participants in that strongly pro-Reagan cohort, the newly mobilized members of the Democratic campaign elite were uniformly and very substantially more conservative than the core participants. On every individual item the scores for the mobilized among the Democrats show less liberal and more conservative support. The magnitude is well represented by one key indicator, the balance of ideological predispositions measured with the self-defined location on the liberal-conservative continuum. The mobilized were less liberal or more conservative than the core by a full 21 percentage points. These differences were of sufficient magnitude to produce a drift to the right in the Democratic campaign activists between 1972 and 1980.

If the disengagement of liberal candidate supporters in the Democratic elite had produced the same decline in liberal ideological support as did the demobilization of moderate supporters in the Republican party, the overall movement among Democrats of course would have been much greater. By the same token, had the disengaged constituted a proportionately larger component of the Republican elite, their disaffection would have meant an even larger shift in Republican attitudes. As it was, both national party elites moved modestly to the right. The limited magnitude of those moves is not in keeping with the conventional wisdom of the mid-1980s. It is true that George McGovern, a symbol of radical left leadership, was replaced by a centrist Jimmy Carter in the Democratic party; and a moderate Jerry Ford was succeeded by Ronald Reagan who at least symbolized the ultimate triumph of the Republican right. It is also true that the supporters of each of these candidates reflected ideological colorations quite in keeping with the attributed ideologies of their leaders. It is not true, for all of the reasons we have just reviewed, that the transitions in party leadership were accompanied by any sea changes in the ideological locations of the party elites. In large part, of course, this was a product of the continuing participation of the core of activists who, although less than visible in most accounts of presidential campaigns, constitute a dominant and a conserving force in both parties.

PART III

Systemic Consequences

CHAPTER 8

The Dynamics of Interparty Conflict

In large measure our previous chapters have been restricted to an examination of within-party analysis at the level of political elites. Differences between the parties have been treated in passing and primarily in terms of different dynamics at work within each party between 1972 and 1980. It was sufficient to observe, in chapters 6 and 7 especially, that party elites stand some distance from each other with respect to attitudes on policy preferences. In this chapter we will focus on the nature of the fundamental and often vast differences between the parties, differences which belie a popular image of the parties as constituting a choice between Tweedledee and Tweedledum. At the same time we will see that the parties are in a dynamic relationship with each other and that the processes of elite circulation can work to widen (or shrink) the ideological distance between the parties. Indeed, a theme of the present chapter will be the widening gulf between the parties during the 1970s.

The element of party in the electorate has been conspicuously absent from our presentation thus far. Ultimately, of course, the fortunes of party leaders rest in the hands of mass publics. This alone dictates an interest in parties at the mass as well as elite levels. Quite apart from the electoral connection, however, there are other questions. One is the degree to which the political cultures of party elites and followers differ. More specifically, to what extent are the cleavages that we observe at the elite levels reproduced at the mass level? A second, related question is the degree to which party elites reflect the ideological leanings of their followers. Viewing convention delegates in their roles as "representatives" of their rank and file, to what extent do they exaggerate, diminish, or accurately reflect the preferences of the party in the electorate? A third question arises in conjunction with the first two: How does the changing composition of party elites affect the comparison of the two political cultures and the congruence of mass-elite preferences? These topics are taken up in chapters 9 and 10.

It might seem axiomatic that there are and should be deep and widespread differences between the parties. After all, what most distinguishes political parties from other politically relevant groups is their unique, pivotal, and long-lived role in the nomination and electoral process. If elections involve choice, then it should follow that party cadres and elites would hold differing views about political alternatives. Yet there is considerable controversy about how polarized the parties should be, whether they should be truly parties of advocacy or parties of intermediation, parties resolutely pursuing coherent, divergent policies and programs, or parties of moderation and compromise, reconciling different interests in the polity.[1]

A first order of business is to set in place the graphic contrasts between the opinion cultures of Republicans and Democrats. We begin with various individual indicators and simple yet compelling expressions of these differences. Subsequently, we move on to take advantage of our multiple indicators by using the cumulative indices introduced in earlier chapters. We shall also use some famil-

---

[1] "Party responsibility" and "party reform" are the relevant catchwords, although neither is unambiguous. The classic work promoting strong advocacy parties remains that of E. E. Schattschneider, *Party Government* (New York: Holt, Rinehart, & Winston, 1948). The ensuing literature is vast. Well-grounded discussions with particular points of view include Nelson W. Polsby and Aaron Wildavsky, *Presidential Elections*, 6th ed. (New York: Scribner, 1984), chaps. 5 and 6; and David E. Price, *Bringing Back the Parties* (Washington, D.C.: Congressional Quarterly, 1984), chap. 4.

iar summarizing statistics. To illustrate the contrasting climates of opinion we will first use the full complement of delegates to all three conventions, giving equal weight to the delegates from each convention year. Other cohorts or combinations from our array of data could be used; some would show greater party differences, some less. In fact, we will play upon this variation in later portions of this chapter. At the outset it is sufficient to use the entire set of delegates to portray differences among partisan elites.

Issue Differences

For many observers of the political scene the presence of issue differences is the prime criterion of whether parties pursue significantly different public policies and offer meaningful alternatives to the electorate. This is particularly true of latter-day reformers who put policy considerations above all others. We will contrast the party elites on seven specific issues and on the general liberal-versus-conservative self-classification. The latter question and those dealing with busing, detente, inflation, and defense spending utilized the seven-point-scale format whereas the abortion, ERA amendment, and environmental protection questions offered specific alternative policy options. To make the presentation of interparty issue differences consistent with each other and with other measures to be employed, we have transposed the issue responses into a 0–100 range and have also ordered the direction so that higher scores mean more conservative attitudes.

Shown in Figure 8.1 are the net differences in mean scores between Democrats and Republicans, the hypothetical range being 0 (no difference) to 100 (maximum difference). Since the Republicans always have the higher mean scores, the differences in means represent the extent of the Republicans' greater conservatism. By any standard the interparty issue differences are large, ranging from the massive contrast on the Equal Rights Amendment to the diminished but still substantial variation on the abortion controversy. On all but this issue, at least one quarter of the maximum interparty difference possible was realized. It is not so much that the parties differ in a relative sense that is impressive, for that is to be expected. Rather, it is the large absolute differences in terms of what

Figure 8.1

Interparty Differences on Issue Positions Among Convention Delegates, 1972–1980

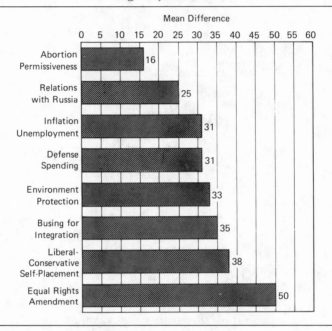

Note: Entries represent the Republican mean scores minus the Democratic mean scores. The larger the difference the more conservative Republicans are compared with Democrats.

are widely recognized by elites as conservative and liberal positions.[2]

[2] Our findings are in accord with a number of previous findings, dating back to the 1956 convention delegates: Herbert McClosky, Paul J. Hoffman, and Rosemary O'Hara, "Issue Conflict and Consensus Among Party Leaders and Followers," *American Political Science Review* 54 (June 1960): 406–27. An example of more recent findings among delegates to 1980 state conventions can be found in Walter J. Stone and Alan I. Abramowitz, "Winning May Not Be Everything, But It's More Than We Thought: Presidential Party Activists in 1980," *American Political Science Review* 77 (December 1983): 945–56. Interparty contrasts also appeared in a 1972 national study of county chairs. See Robert S. Montjoy, William S. Shaffer, and Ronald E. Weber, "Policy Preferences Party Elites and Masses: Conflict or Consensus?" *American Politics Quarterly* 8 (July 1980): 319–43. Especially sharp differences appeared in a 1981 study of California party elites, as reported in Walter Dean Burnham, *The Crisis in American Politics* (Oxford: Oxford University Press, 1982), pp. 297–99.

In terms of specific issues, it is perhaps not surprising that the largest difference between parties emerges with respect to the Equal Rights Amendment. This issue was fresh in the minds of the delegates following the historic rejection of the position by the GOP at its 1980 Detroit convention. In retrospect, this difference was prophetic given ensuing developments over the next four years and the emergence of the "gender gap." As for the other issues, those dealing with busing, pollution, defense, and inflation all tap various fissures in the liberal-conservative fault line that divides the two parties. For example, the emphasis on inflation by Republicans and on unemployment by Democrats has long formed a fundamental policy difference as the parties struggle with each other in the policy-making process. Similarly, the controversy about defense spending is closely tied to classic interparty struggles (guns or butter?) both in the social welfare area and in the way the parties view the international conflict system and the severity and nature of the Communist threat.[3]

Group Evaluations

As witnessed by both political rhetoric and political action, an essential component of American politics is that of group interests. Whether the groups be organized or unorganized, latent or manifest, general purpose or highly specialized, much of allocative politics revolves around the question of group benefits.[4] The degree to which these diverse group interests are channeled into the party system is another indicator of diverse opinion cultures.[5]

[3] This is not to deny a long-term decline in interparty differences in some respects. For example, voting disagreements between the parties in the House of Representatives dropped considerably during the twentieth century—although they seemed to have rebounded somewhat during the 1970s. See, for example, David Brady, Joseph Cooper, and Patricia Hurley, "The Decline of Party in the House of Representatives, 1887–1968," *Legislative Studies Quarterly* 4 (August 1979): 381–407.
[4] Our use of the term "allocative politics" borrows from David Easton and Jack Dennis, *Children in the Political System* (New York: McGraw-Hill, 1969), chap. 2, and is to be distinguished from the systemic or system persistence politics of a more consensual sort.
[5] The proliferation of political action committees, the emergence of new group interests, and the decline of old ones form a vital element in the changing nature of the two major parties and of the party system more generally. For an argumentative interpretation focusing on the socioeconomic aspects of these changes with respect to the parties, see Thomas Byrne Edsall, *The New Politics of Inequality* (New York: Norton, 1984).

In the course of completing the study questionnaire in 1981, the delegates were asked to evaluate thirteen groups on a feeling thermometer. These ratings were introduced in chapter 7. When they are averaged within each of the respective party cohorts, they provide striking evidence of party polarization at the elite levels. For convenience all scores have been transformed, as necessary, to run in a liberal to conservative direction. Figure 8.2 portrays the interparty differences in these ratings in terms of the Republicans' mean score minus that of the Democrats. The higher the score, the greater is the difference between the parties and the more conservative the Republicans compared with the Democrats.

The contrasts between the parties are dramatic. Not surprisingly, the gulf is widest on the delegates' evaluation of their two respective parties, trailed only slightly by the difference accorded the ideological-tag companions of the two parties, conservatives and liberals. Beyond these intuitively expected, though nonetheless striking, contrasts stand those associated with various groups and interests whose names are not synonymous with the parties themselves. Even the smallest of these contrasts, that applying to evaluations of Blacks, produces a difference that virtually equals the standard deviation of the ratings for Blacks generated by Republican and Democrats combined.

Of course any results running contrary to those expected would arouse suspicion. Republicans are "supposed" to be more aligned with groups widely perceived as being conservative and Democrats are likewise supposed to be more aligned with ostensibly liberal groups. Our results simply bear out these expectations with more clarity than is often recognized when discussing the nature of American political parties.

In addition the basic data demonstrate more than simple differential affinity; they also demonstrate differential antipathy. Using 50° on the feeling thermometer as the midpoint of positive-negative affect, it turns out that Republicans granted only one presumptively liberal group a mark of 50° or higher, and that group is the broad population grouping of Blacks. All of the patently liberal groups were rated below 50° on the average, often far below that midway point. For their part, the Democrats accorded no conservative group a mark above 50°, whereas all liberal groups except that of Gay Rights were scored above 50°.

This element of differential rejection and antipathy, when

Figure 8.2

**Interparty Differences on Group Evaluations Among
Convention Delegates, 1972–1980**

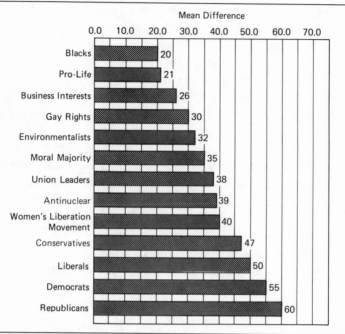

Note: Entries represent the Republican mean scores minus the Democratic mean
scores.

coupled with the element of differential approval, not only produces the extreme differences between the parties in terms of
group evaluations, but it also implies a marked polarization of attitudes toward groups going well beyond varying degrees of favor-
ableness. In this sense the opinion cultures of the two elites are
truly antagonistic.

Evaluations of Candidates

If party elites align themselves in policy preferences and on
group evaluations on a party basis, they should do so to an even
greater extent with respect to partisan figures. The feeling thermometer used to assess reactions to the various groups was also

used to gauge the delegates' evaluations of ten leading partisan personalities of the 1980s. Figure 8.3 presents the results in terms of the differences in mean approval ratings assigned to each personality, including the now almost forgotten third-party candidates, John Anderson and Patrick Lucey. Again, all scores have been adjusted to run in a liberal to conservative direction.

There are two important aspects to the resulting interparty contrasts. First is the sheer magnitude of the differences. With the understandable exception of the Anderson and Lucey candidacies, the elites diverge drastically in their evaluations. The opposite could hardly be expected. What is more convincing with respect to the theme of opinion cultures is the emergent polarization. Republicans ranked all of their own party members (save the renegade Anderson) above 50°. Such partisan generosity was extended even, by a small margin, to their disgraced ex-president. Correspondingly, they ranked all Democrats well below the half-way mark. Not to be outdone, the Democrats placed all of their people (except for the expatriate Lucey) on the positive side of 50° and all Republicans on the negative side. Thus, neither party gives any quarter—the white hats and the black hats are clearly identified but they must be exchanged according to who is doing the judging.

Although the major message lies in these profound interparty contrasts, another observation can be made in passing. By the time of the 1981 study, the Democrats had rather quickly abandoned Carter as their standard-bearer. Indeed, his mean rating of 62° was only fractionally ahead of that accorded Ted Kennedy, who had offered a late challenge to him in 1980. It was Carter's running mate and nominal party head, Walter Mondale, who had already captured the affection, if not the allegiance, of the 1980 delegates. This was reflected in the mean rating of 78° accorded him by his fellow Democrats.

Does this mean that the Democrats are particularly punitive and fairweather friends? Probably not, because the Republicans on their part gave their victorious Reagan an astonishingly high rating of 88°, while placing the short-term President Ford at 67°, fairly close to Carter's placement among Democrats. Aside from demonstrating "what have you done for me lately" effects, these evaluations are important in another sense. They suggest again the powerful place of presidential incumbents and candidates in shaping the nature of party and campaign elites in a prospective sense. Al-

Figure 8.3

**Interparty Differences on Candidate Evaluations Among
Convention Delegates, 1972–1980**

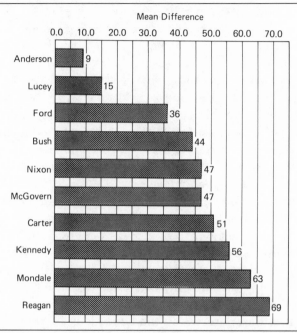

Note: Entries represent the Republican mean scores minus the Democratic mean scores.

though the Democrats would surely have welcomed a second Carter administration, once he was defeated and had declared his noninterest in a prominent future party role, his place as head of the party was grasped by a competitor obviously willing to challenge for party leadership in the role of a presidential aspirant.

Summarizing Interparty Differences

At this point we shall introduce a second summary statistic to supplement the "difference of means" which we have been using to depict similarities and differences between the two parties. The familiar Pearson's r, product-moment correlation, will be used in this chapter and the next two chapters to show the association be-

tween generic group differences and the various indicators of political opinion cultures. In this chapter the groups being compared
will be Democratic and Republican delegates; in the next two
chapters we will concentrate on *intra*party comparisons of delegates with their partisan followers in the electorate. In both instances the groups can be thought of as the "independent" variable,
with Democrats scored 0 and Republicans scored as 1 in the present chapter, or with mass partisans (party identifiers) scored as 0
and elites (delegates) scored as 1 in the following two chapters. The
"dependent" variables, in turn, are provided by our indices. As
differentiation on the independent variable is increasingly associated with differences on the dependent variable, the coeffiecient
becomes greater than zero. And as the sets defined by the independent variable are more and more alike with regard to the dependent
variable the coefficient approaches zero.

We will supplement the measures of differences in party
means with the correlation coefficients for two reasons: (1) in order
to standardize the comparison of a variety of group differences with
a very sensitive measure and, (2) to take advantage of the fact that
one useful statistical property of the coefficient is that, when
squared, it shows the amount of variance than can be attributed to
presumptively causal agents such as party or party status.

As a further summarizing step we will also now drop the individual items used thus far and use summary indices employed in
previous chapters.[6] Table 8.1 presents both the mean scores for the
Democratic and Republican delegates on six measures, including
liberal-conservative self-placement, and the correlations associated
with the differences between the parties. Although all of the interparty differences are very large, they do vary in magnitude. Candidate evaluations and the traditional left-right group evaluations
provide the most vivid interparty contrasts. This is due most directly to the inherently partisan nature of all the stimuli in the
candidate evaluation index and the presence of long-established

[6]The candidate evaluation index has not been used previously. This additive index
was formed following a factor analysis (see Appendix Table F.1) that showed two
strong dimensions in the thermometer rating of ten former or present candidates for
the presidency or vice-presidency. The index used here averages the ratings given
to Ford, Bush, Nixon, McGovern, Carter, Ted Kennedy, Mondale, and Reagan and is
adjusted so that scores of 0 equal very liberal attitudes and scores of 100 equal very
conservative ones.

Table 8.1

Interparty Differences on Six Measures of Ideology Among Convention Delegates, 1972–1980

	Mean Scores		Correlation (r)
	Democrats	Republicans	
Moral Left-Right			
Group Index	17	46	.48
New Left			
Group Index	37	72	.65
Left-Right			
Issue-Index	37	72	.65
Liberal-Conservative			
Self-Placement	34	72	.67
Traditional Left-Right			
Group Index	29	76	.85
Democratic-Republican			
Candidate Index	28	79	.89

Notes: The higher the mean score the more conservative is the political ideology. The larger the correlation the greater is the association between party and ideology, that is, the larger the ideological differences between parties.

partisan objects, including the parties themselves, in the traditional group evaluation index. Despite the large size of all of these overall correlations, we will have occasion to see substantial departures among various elite categories.

Three other indices have accompanying interparty correlations in the vicinity of .66, strong differences indicating that party affiliation alone accounts for well over 40 percent of the variance in the index scores. There is a striking similarity in the differences accompanying self-classification on a liberal to conservative continuum and the left-right issue index. Whereas the former measure is self-consciously subjective in nature, the latter is based on preferences about concrete public policy issues. The similarity augurs well for our ability to locate the delegates in ideological space. It is interesting to note that interparty polarization in evaluations of groups associated with social issues of the 1970s is every bit as sharp as are differences in the other two measures in this set. Finally the weakest, though still marked, partisan difference lies in the evaluations of moral issue groups. Here the incursion of such individual characteristics as education, gender, race, and religion undercuts the pervasive impact of party. On balance, the indices provide us with succinct, discriminating indicators of the contrastors opinion climates found between party elites.[7]

The large absolute differences among these party elites provide another reason for arguing that they are parts of distinctive political cultures. This is mirrored in a comparison with interparty contrasts at the level of the mass public. If mass politics were equally conflicted, it would weaken the case for arguing the uniqueness of political activists, but it would strengthen the sense that American politics is powerfully influenced by the interplay of the two cultures.

For three of the measures of elite culture, we have completely comparable data from the mass electorate from the 1980 National Election Study. The muting of elite differences in the general voting public is reflected in the fact that the mass-based correlation analogous to the delegates' interparty difference on the issue index was .25 (against .65 for the delegates); on self-placement it was .40 (against .67); and mass differentiation in the candidate index hit .59 (against .89). For a fourth measure based on the subset of groups described below, the mass coefficient was .41, against a robust .74 for the delegates. Interparty contrasts were much more exaggerated among our representatives of the party elites, but they were also clearly indexed at the level of rank-and-file citizens.

Replacement, Conversion, and Party Distance

If we use only the results flowing from the analysis of the delegates embraced by our design, it is abundantly clear that the opinion cultures of party elites are radically different with respect to what we have called allocative politics. Much of the ground covered is familiar in the sense that is replicates the general outlines of past studies showing that party elites exist in a world of

---

[7] Compared with other elites, convention delegates appear to be at least as different, by party, as are county chairs and a combination of state chairs and national committee members. See John S. Jackson III, Barbara Leavitt Brown, and David Bositis, "Herbert McClosky and Friends Revisited: 1980 Democratic and Republican Elites Compared to the Mass Public," *American Politics Quarterly* 10 (April 1982): 158–180.

sharp ideological divisions. What has been lacking up to this point is any sense of whether the polarization shown among the delegates as a whole disguises a variety of subgroup patterns. Nor do we have much sense of the role played by the circulation and conversion of elites in any such patterns.

More generally, we may ask whether our study of convention delegates can address a central question of American party politics, namely, under what conditions do the parties move toward or away from each other? Are the parties becoming more polarized and extremist as some latter-day proponents of the politics of moderation warn, or are they becoming more ideologically similar to each other, as advocates of a strong, responsible two-party system fear?[8] In more prosaic terms, has the ascendancy of Reagan Republicanism helped sharpen the cleavage lines at the top of the two parties? Of course our delegate respondents provide only one vantage point on these questions and the time span is limited. Nevertheless, we can make some reasonably strong speculations about the dynamics of interparty cleavages during the 1970s and the implications for the 1980s. To do so we will take a number of different tacks, all of which yield similar conclusions.

Within the framework of our design, one of the most telling pieces of evidence that could be advanced lies in the interparty comparisons between the delegates of 1972 and 1980. Thanks to the precursor of the 1981 data collection, we have data available from the 1972 delegates *as reported in 1972*. And the more recent inquiry enables us to characterize the 1980 delegates as of their reports in early 1981. To the extent that the partisan dispositions serve as markers for interparty conflict, shifts in their ideological distance over time will suggest whether the parties are becoming more distinctive. At a bare minimum, we would have to find an increase in interparty conflict in order to argue that an increase in polarization has occurred.

In analyzing the dynamics of cross-party conflict we can actually draw on three sets of observations involving the 1972 and 1980 delegates. Most pointedly, we can contrast the 1972 delegates as of

[8]Leon Epstein, "The Scholarly Commitment to Parties," in Ada W. Finifter, ed., *Political Science: The State of the Discipline* (Washington, DC: American Political Science Association, 1983); and Evron Kirkpatrick, "Toward a More Responsible Two-Party System: Polticial Science, Policy Science or Pseudo Science?" *American Political Science Review* 65 (December 1971): 965–90.

time 1 (1972) and the 1980 delegates as of time 2 (1981). However, we also have a third set of observations—the 1972 delegates as of time 2. The beauty of the latter observations is that they permit us to judge whether there has been conversion as well as, or even instead of, replacement at work over the eight-year period. As we have already seen to some extent, the dual presence of these initial 1972 and subsequent 1981 observations provides us with invaluable ammunition in interpreting the results from the analyses of other cohorts and campaign elite categories.

Ideally, there would be a large number of strictly comparable measures in both of the studies upon which we are drawing. Owing to the pursuit of other objectives, the number of such questions in the realm of political preferences and evaluations is actually rather small; they are found primarily in the "feeling thermometer" evaluations accorded eight of the sociopolitical groups which were utilized in the last chapter. Many other *similar* questions were asked at both points in time, but the hazard of making cross-time comparisons based on no more than "similar" indicators is that the observed differences may be artifacts of instrumentation rather than "true" differences.[9]

Turning now to the interparty differences uncovered by this approach, we show in Figure 8.4 the results for the eight groups that were evaluated at both points in time. Here we rely entirely on product-moment correlations to summarize the contrasts between the parties, again scoring Democrats 0 and Republicans 1, and arranging all of the group ratings to run in a liberal (low) to conservative (high) direction. Consequently, the higher the correlation the greater are the differences between Republicans and Democrats in the three sets of observations. The signs of the correlations were all positive; that is, Republicans always had the more conservative scores.

The groups that are evaluated range across the political spectrum, they vary enormously in terms of their inclusivity, and they include demographic groupings, organized interests, and ideological labels. Such diversity makes the results even more compelling,

[9] For an ingenious attempt to overcome the problem of different measures in looking at *intra*party differences across time among convention delegates, see John R. Petrocik and Dwaine Marvick, "Explaining Party Elite Transformation: Institutional Changes and Insurgent Politics," *Western Political Quarterly* 36 (September 1983): 345–63.

Figure 8.4

Interparty Contrasts on Group Evaluations Across Cohorts and Over Time

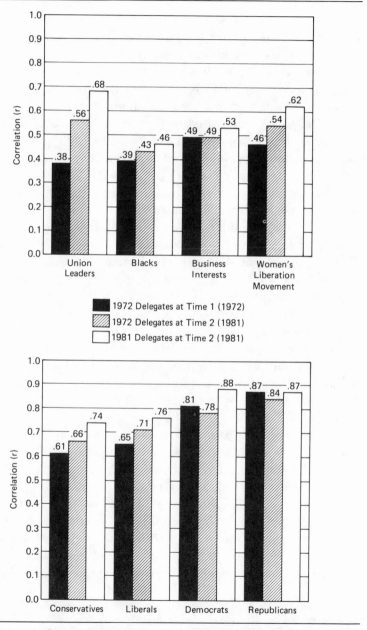

Note: Entries are the correlations (r) between party and the ratings accorded each group; the larger the coefficients the greater the differences between parties.

for they all point toward a decided enlargement of partisan cleavage during the 1970s. This expansion is highlighted in the comparison of the two sets of delegates in their respective delegate years. The increases in polarization range from the truly dramatic in the case of union leaders, liberals, conservatives, and the women's liberation movement to the predictably modest or nonexistent changes in the case of Democrats and Republicans. In the latter instances, "ceiling effects" limit further polarization inasmuch as the parties were already highly differentiated in 1972.

These are impressive shifts, all the more so because the 1972 contrasts had been widely hailed as abnormally vivid owing to the liberal McGovern forces having captured the Democratic convention. An appreciation of the rise in interparty conflict is perhaps best depicted in terms of the variance in group evaluations expressed by party in the two years. For example, the variance accounted for by party in the evaluations of "conservatives" rose from 37 to 55 percent, and the party-based variance in evaluations of the women's liberation movement increased from 21 to 38 percent. Because of the limited party differences in 1972, party-based variance in attitudes toward union leaders shot from 14 to 46 percent. Party elites always diverge in their opinion cultures but the gap opened up between 1972 and 1980 was truly remarkable.[10]

Armed only with these two sets of observations we might be inclined to say that elite replacement was primarily responsible for the change, especially since almost 40 percent of the 1980 Democrats and 30 percent of the 1980 Republicans had not participated at all in the 1972 campaign. We might also be inclined to view the increase as a "one-time" function of the Reaganites' domination of the 1980 Republican convention, while marveling at the notion that his candidacy evoked more partisan polarization than had McGovern's in 1972. Although replacement—especially via the differential appeal of various candidacies—undoubtedly figures in the widening gulf between the parties, it appears that more sweeping forces were driving these deep wedges between the parties.

Such an inference can be drawn by comparing the interparty

[10] A 1969–1978 study of local party activists in the Los Angeles area revealed increasing ideological distance over time. See Dwaine Marvick, "Party Activists in Los Angeles, 1963–1978: How Well-Matched Rivals Shape Electoral Options," in Moshe M. Czudnowski, ed., *Political Elites and Social Change* (DeKalb: Northern Illinois University Press, 1983).

contrasts afforded by the time 1 responses of the 1972 delegates with the time 2 responses of these same individuals. The middle bars in Figure 8.4 portray the time 2 results. For five of the groups there was an over-time increase in interparty differences among the 1972 delegates, ranging from a small increase on Blacks to a very substantial increase on union leaders.[11] That is, the same sets of Republican and Democratic party elites grew further apart during this period, in some instances spectacularly so. Thus, regardless of whether it was the Republicans or Democrats who shifted relatively more along the ideological, liberal-conservative spectrum, the net polarity increased as a function of individual-level changes in political opinion.

In general, something less than half of the difference in party variance between that exhibited by 1972 delegates in 1972 and that found among 1980 delegates in 1981 was reflected in individual-level changes within the 1972 delegates over the same period of time. Even without knowing how much 1980 delegates changed in the same eight-year interval, the evidence of acutely increased polarization among 1972 delegates strongly suggests that the changing context of presidential politics not only resulted in the selection of more highly polarized delegates in 1980, but accentuated partisan differences even further among the delegates who had "produced" the McGovern-Nixon contest.

Concealed in these increments of expanding party distance among the 1972 delegates are further critical differences associated with the circulation of delegates into and out of the ranks of active campaign participants. It will be recalled that members of the 1972 delegate cohort can be divided according to whether they were continuously active over the period or whether they became disengaged following the 1972 campaign. This division generates rather sharp differences in the magnitudes of the interparty cleavage emerging from evaluations of the eight groups as of time 2 (Table 8.2).

The comparison of changes in party differences among core activists with changes in party differences among the disengaged clearly identifies the continuously active delegates as contributing the lion's share to the increase in party conflict over the decade.

[11] The small dip in interparty contrasts with respect to the evaluation of Democrats and Republicans appears to be a function of the disengaged members of the 1972 cohort losing a bit of their partisan fervor by 1981. See Table 8.2.

Table 8.2

**Relationship Between Party and Political Attitudes in 1972
and 1981, According to Campaign Histories of 1972 Delegates**

	Disengaged after 1972		Active in 1972 and in 1980	
	Interparty Differences		Interparty Differences	
Groups	1972	1981	1972	1981
Blacks	.35	.34	.40	.47
Union Leaders	.24	.46	.44	.62
Women's Liberation Movement	.42	.44	.46	.58
Business Interests	.49	.44	.49	.49
Conservatives	.51	.57	.64	.68
Liberals	.58	.63	.67	.74
Democrats	.77	.68	.82	.82
Republicans	.86	.78	.86	.86

Note: Entries are correlations (r) between group evaluations and party. The data
base is the 1972–1981 panel.

Only with respect to the ratings of union leaders was there a substantial increase in party distance among the disengaged. Smaller
increases in party differences in evaluations of liberals and conservatives were matched by actual reductions in party differences in
their evaluations of business interests, Democrats, and Republicans. In fact, the disengaged in 1981 were less conflicted than the
cohort as a whole in 1972 with respect to several of the group
evaluations, and they were more conflicted (.46 to .39) only with
regard to union leaders. Not so for the continuously active. Their
interparty tensions as of 1981 exceeded by a moderate to large
margin their 1972 partisan differences on five of the eight groups
and declined on none of them. Hence the conversion or individual-
level changes leading to heightened party conflict occurred predominantly among those party elites who stayed the course, who
remained active combatants.

   Overall, then, two processes helped produce the step-like pattern of Figure 8.4. Clearly the parties diverged to begin with, at the
first step, in 1972. Even assuming no turnover in elite personnel
during the ensuing years, they would have separated somewhat

more, a divergence attributable to individual-level change or conversion among the 1972 delegates and captured as the second step. Indeed, going only by the evidence at hand—and making some heroic assumptions about generalizing from the 1972 cohorts— it appears that individual-level dynamics contributed disproportionately to the growing cleavage. This is so because the cross-time increases associated with the continuously active 1972 cohorts are almost as large as the differences between the 1972 cohorts at time 1 and the 1980 cohorts at time 2. It is the latter group, made up entirely of different people than the 1972 cohort, that provides support for the turnover thesis and produces the third step in the progression displayed in Figure 8.4. Much of what follows below builds on and is fortified by this progression and the implicit processes by which it was generated.

Intercohort Differences and Party Distance

As we noted earlier, the inferences to be drawn from these results are conditioned by being limited to one type of indicator and, of course, to the particular set of elites at our disposal. A first expansion of the analysis of changes in interparty differences between 1972 and 1980 consists of shifting to the larger base of comparable data available from the 1981 study. We expand our range in two ways. First, we have a greater variety of indicators by which to gauge the dynamics of change in opinion culture differences. Their availability supplies a check against the inferences based strictly on the thermometer ratings of eight groups. Second, we also now have available the 1976 delegate cohort, an important addition if we wish to test the thesis of gradual rather than abrupt change over the decade, or of more generalized change versus the apparent and possibly specious change engendered by one-time "blips" and deviations.

Counterbalancing these plusses is one large negative: the 1972 and 1976 delegates are supplying impressions and attitudes as of early 1981, far removed from the time and setting in which they were delegates in their respective years. There could obviously be substantial discrepancies between their earlier views and those expressed in 1981. Certainly the widening gap between just portrayed within the 1972 panel depends upon change over time. Con-

sequently, any demonstrated cross-cohort differences in polarization in 1981 almost surely *understate* the rate of growth of
ideological distance between the two parties during this period.[12]

In looking at the results for the three cohorts as of the 1981
soundings, we shall again employ the five summary indices as well
as the liberal-conservative self-placement measure. We shall also
continue to use product-moment correlations to summarize the relationships. Without exception the results show a wider gap between the parties across succeeding cohorts (Figure 8.5). As anticipated, the results are not quite so striking as those that begin with
the 1972 respondents' time 1 responses. Nevertheless there is a
sizable difference between the partisan cleavage represented in
1981 by the 1972 party cohorts and that found within the 1980
cohorts. And significantly, the 1976 cohorts fall neatly in between,
much as a model of gradual change would predict.

Of special interest are the intercohort differences on the moral
group index. It will be recalled that this index is based on ratings of
two groups, pro-lifers and the moral majority, groups that enjoyed
little currency in 1972. The successive increases in party differences across the cohorts strongly suggest that the morality dimension has been a key force in pushing newer members of the party
elites toward the extremes. However, even the more traditional
menu—represented by the other group evaluation measures, the
issue index, and ideological self-placement—yields signs of a widening rift associated with the 1976 and 1980 additions to the party
elites. Once more it is worth noting that, at the ranges represented
by the sizes of these correlations, even modest increases in the
coefficients produce noticeable gains in terms of the variance in
attitudes explained by party alone. Thus, the variance accounted
for by party on the issue index moves from 38 percent (r = .52)
among the 1972 delegates to 50 percent (r = .71) among the 1980
delegates.

[12]This analysis includes within each cohort *all* members of the two parties for that
particular year—including convention repeaters. The reasoning is that we wish to
compare the two parties as a whole for each year in order to capture the contrasts of
the parties as presented to the electorate and, in a sense, to each other. As it turns
out, there is little difference in the results generated by this method versus our more
common one of employing only "first-time" convention goers as the base for each
year.

Figure 8.5

**Ideological Differences Between Parties for Three
Convention Cohorts**

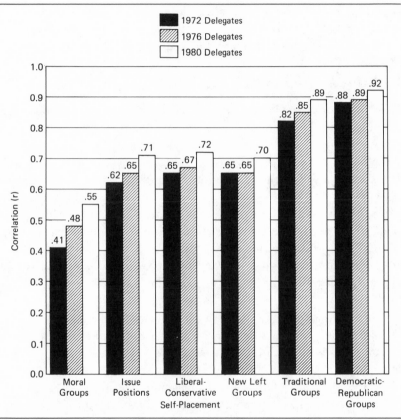

Note: Entries are the correlations (r) between party and scores on the various measures.

The interpretation of a growing distance over time can be challenged by what might be called a recency effect, for there is indeed a correspondence between the recency of convention attendance and interparty distance. Here the 1972 observations and the subsequent panel observations emerge as crucial, because they are not subject to the recency phenomenon. Were that the sole explanation there should have been no difference in interparty divisiveness between the 1972 and 1980 cohorts as observed in their respective years of convention going. Nor should the 1972 delegate panel have increased its divisiveness over time, because only a handful of those panel members attended the most recent (1980) convention. If we bear in mind that the analysis in this section relies in part on attitudinal reports well past the optimal time of observation, and that it takes no account of presidential campaign activity levels, the results comport well with a model of a decided but continuous enlargement of party distance during the 1970s.[13]

Ebbing and Flowing with the Campaign Activists

A further extension of our inquiry into the direction and source of interparty conflict over time consists of utilizing the circulation categories used with much frequency in previous chapters. Although the problem of noncontemporaneous observations is not overcome by this approach, it does have the compensating advantage of drawing on the participation histories of all three cohorts. Thus, we can pair off a variety of key participant categories across the two parties in order to determine the nature, timing, and composition of party conflict in subsets of this elite group. One big advantage of this approach is that it enables us to assess the role of commitment to the party and its candidates over an extended period of time.

Our expectation is that interparty divisions will be greatest among those partisan groupings with the most intense and long-lived histories as presidential campaigners. In the instant case this means those delegates who had been active in at least *both* the 1972 and 1980 campaigns, the great majority of them having been involved in the 1976 contest. Beyond endurance, and intensity effects, however, we would also expect to see conversion and turnover effects; in particular we would expect to see a greater polarization among the more recent delegate recruits than among the disengaged former activists—if our previous observations are any guide. For present purposes, then, we have grouped the campaign elites into five groups: (1) the disengaged delegates, those not active in the 1980 campaign; (2) the mobilized, those activated after 1972; and the continuously active delegates who (first) attended

[13] Although straightforward comparisons with our own work or earlier studies of convention delegates are not possible, another study of 1980 delegates yielded massive differences between the parties on a number of issues. Jackson, Brown, and Bositis, "Herbert McClosky and Friends Revisited: 1980 Democratic and Republican Elites Compared to the Mass Public," *American Politics Quarterly* 10 (April 1982): 158–180.

(3) the 1972 convention; (4) the 1976 convention; or (5) the 1980 convention.

The results are presented again in the form of correlations between party and each of the six indicators of political opinion culture (Figure 8.6). Although the partisan differences vary across measures, the overall pattern has uniformity and a pleasing, monotonic structure. Interparty differences now appear to be highly contingent upon circulation as well as individual change. Several findings speak to this generalization.

The least amount of interparty tension occurs among the so-called disengaged, those who had participated in the campaign of 1972 but were inactive as campaign elites in 1980. One might refer to the differences between these two subsets of the party elites as reflecting the politics of moderation. It is a moderation borne of the earlier observations that disengagement within the Republican party was marked by the withdrawal of moderate Republicans, while the disengaged Democrats were marginally more conservative than counterparts who remained active. We shall return later to a provocative question about partisan conflict among the disengaged, namely, whether lesser partisan conflict characterized these political actors before as well as after their disengagement.

The second category of campaign elites to be considered offers a rather striking contrast to that of the disengaged. Those 1976 and 1980 delegates who were mobilized into the campaign elite of 1980 show a much stronger pattern of interparty friction. Especially compelling is the large shift with respect to opinions on contemporary issues. While the disengaged of the two parties scarcely constituted birds of a feather, they resembled each other far more than did the newly mobilized. To the extent that policy differences constitute the cardinal criterion of party differentiation, the replacement process worked in grand style.

As interparty heat was tempered by the withdrawal of less intense advocates of the party's opinion culture, it was raised by the arrival of new entrants. This exchange could have occurred as a result of attitudinal shifts on the part of one or both parties. In the present case it comes about as the joint function of different sources of change in each party.[14] We noted in chapter 5 that disengaged

---

[14] Dynamic treatments of party (as distinct from elective) elites remain relatively rare. Using longitudinal data of a nonpanel nature, Eldersveld demonstrates the consequences of turnover and replacement processes for intraparty and interparty

Figure 8.6

Ideological Differences Between Parties According to Circulation Patterns, 1972–1980

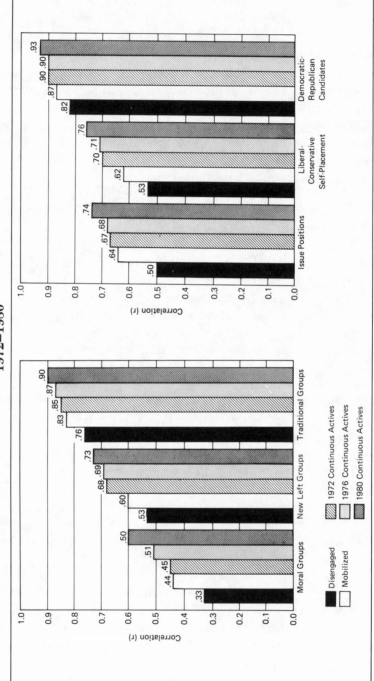

Note: Entries are the correlations (r) between party and scores on the various measures; the larger the coefficient the larger the differences between parties.

Democrats were not significantly different from the continuing paticipants on any of our scales, but that the mobilized were visibly more conservative than either of the other groups. Among Republicans it was the disengaged who were distinctive (more liberal and therefore more like Democrats) while the continuing core and the mobilized closely resembled each other. If the pairs of similar groups within each party are used as the base lines for interpretation (core and disengaged among Democrats, core and mobilized among Republicans), it then follows that disengaged Republicans differed more from their party norm than mobilized Democrats differed from the Democratic norm. Both deviations were in a direction that made the deviant groups more like the other party, and therefore minimized rather than accentuated interparty differences. But the disengaged Republicans were the more deviant of the two aberrant groups; consequently our present analysis finds smaller party differences between the disengaged than between the newly mobilized.

In a sense, the mobilized provide the complement to the disengaged. Although there is no "hidden hand" at work producing these adjustments between dropouts and new entrants, there would seem to be something about the nature of interparty dynamics such that the replacement process ensures that wide party differences remain intact. We shall return to this theme in the concluding chapter.

Finally, let us deal with the continuously active delegates during the 1972–1980 period, recalling that activity here is defined in terms of presidential campaigning and that those delegates who happened to serve in more than one convention are allotted to the year of their first service. The key feature here is that campaign activity is essentially held constant, with the delegate cohort being the variable property. Thus, any differences across cohorts should not be a function of campaigning efforts per se nor of the recency of these efforts.

With these conditions in mind, we now can determine if our expectations about intercohort differences are met. The general answer to that question is positive, though the particulars vary con-

---

differences among local German party elites. Samuel Eldersveld, "Changes in Elite Composition and the Survival of Party Systems: The German Case," in Moshe Czudnowski, ed., *Does Who Govern Matter?* (Dekalb: Northern Illinois Press, 1982). See also Marvick, "Party Activists in Los Angeles, 1963–1978."

siderably. Without question, 1980 Republican and Democratic continuous participants differed from each other more than did their 1972 counterparts. The 1976 cohorts, as predicted by a model of gradual change, fall between the earlier and later cohorts.[15] These findings are wholly of a piece with those already reported. They give added credence to the argument that the circulation of campaign elites acted to increase party differences during the 1970s.

It might be contended that even though campaign activity is being held constant, the freshness of the 1980 cohort's convention and convention aftermath experiences would exaggerate interparty contrasts. That is possible, but our earlier analysis of the 1972 delegates and the 1972–1981 panel respondents argues against that explanation. Moreover, based on that analysis, it seems likely that the 1972 and 1976 cohort differences reported here *overstate* the inferred interparty differences as of 1972 and 1976. That is, period effects were doubtless acting to sharpen interparty differences across all cohorts, with the net impact being—if anything—a flattening of intercohort differences compared with their original differences.

We return now to a puzzle referred to earlier. Interparty conflict is demonstrably less among the disengaged cohorts, but it is not clear what sequence of changes produced that outcome. Did the moderate tendencies of the disengaged result in their becoming discouraged, less motivated, and even excluded by elites nearer the center of gravity within each party? Or is it the case that once having become disengaged, the pull of ideological forces faltered because the reinforcement effects accompanying campaign and other political exertions were absent?

As it turns out the study design provides us with two handy tests of alternative formulations—albeit we have implicitly assumed the existence of only one in much of our discussion. The first, much weaker, test consists of comparing the disengaged of 1972 with the continuously active from that cohort (the first and

[15] Again, the absence of a comparable, contemporaneous 1976 study of both conventions hampers our ability to generalize about interparty contrasts associated with those particular cohorts. This is a limitation that applies not only to our own study, but to the general area. The exception here is the work by Sullivan and associates, most of which has dealt with each party separately and which rests on a fairly small data base. One report with a direct comparison of Republicans and Democrats is Robert T. Nakamura and Denis G. Sullivan, "A Critical Analysis of the Neo-Conservative Critique of Presidential Nomination Reforms," a paper presented at the annual meeting of the American Political Science Association, Washington, DC, 1981.

third bars in Figure 8.6). Clearly the continuously active partisan elites disagreed with each other far more than did the disengaged from the same convention cohort. It strains the imagination to think that these very sizable differences could have sprung up entirely in the interim between the early 1970s and the early 1980s.

A stronger test relying on a feature inherent in our study design reaches the same conclusion. Here we reintroduce the 1972–1981 panel respondents and draw on soundings made of them in 1972. If the hypothesis that the disengaged were already less intensely conflicted *before* they became disengaged is to be supported, the association between party and opinion cultures should be less for them in 1972 than it is for those who did not subsequently disengage (that is, the continuously active).

As evidence we return to the correlations for the eight group evaluations that were used earlier (Table 8.2). For additional evidence we can also turn to opinions about four political issues of the early 1970s and a self-classification of political ideology, all measured only in 1972. Table 8.3 presents a set of clear-cut findings: In 1972 those elites destined to become disengaged later on were already less severely at partisan odds than those destined to become hard-core campaign activists. The pattern holds with great consistency for all but two of the eight groups being evaluated (business interests and Republicans). On the other six group assessments, those delegates who were going to drop out after 1972 were visibly less polarized than were those who were to continue as campaign activists. Similar results hold with respect to four policy questions asked in 1972 and the ideological self-classification used in that year (but not repeated in 1981). Although the waning fortunes of their preferred leaders may well have been responsible for their ultimate disengagement, it would seem that those who were to drop out of presidential campaign politics by 1980 were less intent on the partisan struggle even in 1972.[16]

Establishing the existence of limited interparty conflict among the disengaged is crucial to an understanding of the consequences of push-pull forces at work in the two parties. The key fact is that

[16]This inspection of 1972 data pertaining to the eight group evaluations strengthens the earlier suggestion that individual-level change could have been more important than the circulation of campaign personnel in the development of the interparty cleavages of 1980. Overall the 1980 cohorts of Democrats and Republicans differed somewhat more in their 1981 appraisal of the eight groups than did Democrats and Republicans within the continuously active core of 1972 delegates, but not by a large

Table 8.3

**Relationship Between Party and Political Attitudes in 1972,
According to Campaign Histories of 1972 Delegates**

	Disengaged after 1972	Active in 1972 and in 1980
Group Evaluations		
Blacks	.35	.40
Union Leaders	.24	.44
Women's Liberation Movement	.42	.46
Business Interests	.49	.49
Conservatives	.51	.64
Liberals	.58	.67
Democrats	.77	.82
Republicans	.86	.86
Issues		
Handling Inflation	.20	.32
Fighting Crime	.51	.64
Vietnam War	.58	.63
Busing School Children	.55	.63
Ideological Self-placement	.62	.70

Note: Entries are correlations (r) between attitudes and party. The data base is the 1972–1981 panel.

partisan conflict was least among those who dropped out of our presidential campaign elite in the 1972–1980 period. As a consequence the ideological juxtaposition of the two parties became sharper than it would have otherwise. Thus, one source of increasing polarization during the decade was personnel turnover, with the more polarized recruits replacing the less polarized dropouts. The second source derived from individual level change among the continuously active delegates, especially the Republicans. Both sources had the same effect, and their combined effect produced a dramatic increase in the differentiation of partisan poltical cultures between 1972 and 1980.

margin. Indeed, comparing the measures of party differences among the 1972 core in 1972 with those for the full 1980 cohort in 1981, we found that the average increase in the interparty correlation was .095, while the increase as a result of across-time change *within* the 1972 core averaged .06. In short, individual-level change *within* the 1972 core of continuously active delegates was about two thirds as great as the total difference between that core in 1972 and the 1980 cohorts in 1981.

Chapter 9

Linkages Between Party Elites
and Party Followers

The previous chapter set in place the contrasting opinion cultures of party elites and the impact of circulation and conversion processes in maintaining and modifying interparty cleavages. But if party elites are supposed to exist in an adversarial state vis-à-vis each other, they are also expected to establish a more harmonious relationship vis-à-vis their respective rank-and-file followers. A key normative feature of modern democratic representation theory is that representatives reflect the preferences and demands of those being represented. Of course other, sometimes conflicting, norms are attached to the representation role.[1] Thus, acting on behalf of the represented may involve going against their expressed preferences.

However, Pitkin reflects the prevailing consensus of popular democratic theorists when she contends that ". . . political repre-

---

[1] The literature is large. For a discussion of various conceptions of the representational role, see Heinz Eulau, John Wahlke et al., *The Politics of Representation* (Beverly Hills, CA: Sage, 1978); J. Roland Pennock, "Political Representation: An Overview," in J. Roland Pennock and John W. Chapman, eds., *Representation* (Atherton, 1968); and Paul Peterson, "Forms of Representation: Participation of the Poor in Community Action Programs," *American Political Science Review* 64 (June 1970): 491–507.

sentation is, in fact, representative, particularly in the sense of 'acting for,' and . . . this must be understood at the public level. The representative system must look after the public interest and be responsive to public opinion, except insofar as non-responsiveness can be justified in terms of public interest."[2] To a great extent interests and preferences or opinions are equated in the prevailing view of representation as reflecting the subjective interests of principals (citizens) who cannot act on behalf of themselves but, rather, must depend on a system of representation.

When thinking about political representation, we most often focus on the linkage between officeholders and their constituents. However, the political system contains any number of fiduciary relationships, including those involving interest group leaders and their followers and public administrators and their clientele. American political parties, like other organizations, have both a leadership structure and, though informal rather than formal, a membership structure. Given the presence of popular elections as the foundation of modern democratic governments and the central place of parties in the electoral process, we find it especially appropriate to analyze our party delegates qua leaders from the viewpoint of the representation process.

The classic moment of representation within the American party system comes during the quadrennial national conventions. Although these representative assemblies meet for only a short time, the preparation period is long and the actual convention events are highly visible and closely monitored. Moreover, the decisions taken bear not only on external electoral fortunes but also on party organization and leadership composition. Convention delegates are a direct link to the party base. Perhaps more significantly, they are prime activists in the party and group interest systems. They provide a window on the world of political activists. Thus, an examiniaton of linkage between our delegate-respondents and the various constituencies represented by them will inform us about the process of popular representation within a key institution of popular government.

As with most systems of representation, there is no single configuration within the party system that defines the link between representatives and the represented, the elite and the mass. Rather

[2] Hannah F. Pitkin, *The Concept of Representation* (Berkeley: University of California Press, 1967), p. 224.

there are a number of such linkages, several of which we shall be able to explore. At the broadest level, the delegates assembled at the major party conventions may be said to represent the general public as a whole, just as Congress in some sense provides collective representation to the nation as a whole.[3] However, given the procedures by which the delegates are selected and the functions they serve, we must make an immediate division along party lines. The division at the elite level is self-evident, while that at the mass public level is more problematic. In the absence of widespread official membership at the mass level, subjective affiliation in the form of party identification is the customary device for allocating the citizenry into the two major party camps. Although party identification today is not quite the stable commodity it was once thought to be, it still ranks as one of the most persistent of all orienting devices in the hands of ordinary citizens.[4] One important linkage, then, is that between the delegates and rank-and-file identifiers of the two respective parties.

Party elites and partisan followers as a whole comprise large, rather undifferentiated pairings. A further fundamental division among delegates, except in highly consensual years, is provided by candidate support groups. The preceding section of this book revealed dramatic differences among intraparty delegate groups with contrasting genealogies of candidate preferences. It is likely the case that these groups see themselves as standing in for rank-and-file supporters of their candidates. And it is undoubtedly true that rank-and-file supporters—especially primary and caucus participants—expect their delegates to act on their behalf. Pairings thus can be constructed based on the candidate preferences of delegates.[5] This is a further way in which party elements can be disaggregated so that mass-elite congruence can be assessed.

[3] This is similar to the reasoning put forth by Robert Weissberg in "Collective vs. Dyadic Representation in Congress," *American Political Science Review* 72 (June 1978): 535–47.

[4] Philip E. Converse and Gregory B. Markus, "Plus Ça Change . . . : The New CPS Election Study Panel," *American Political Science Review* 73 (March 1979): 32–49; and M. Kent Jennings and Gregory B. Markus, "Partisan Orientations Over the Long Haul: Results from the Three-Wave Political Socialization Panel Study," *American Political Science Review* 78 (December 1984): 1000–18.

[5] Ideally, identifiers would be divided according to their preferences. However, in addition to the near impossibility of constructing preference histories of identifiers, it is also the case that existing, accessible data sets have typically not contained intraparty preference orders for even a single election year.

There are still other approaches through which the congruence between party elites and followers can be assessed. One approach might be according to the concept of issue publics, wherein one would ask whether segments of the mass public with particularly strong interests and preferences are "adequately" represented among these high-level party activists. Another approach would be to isolate sociopolitical groups in the populace—for example, racial minorities, age strata, income and education groups, and the like— and then determine the degree to which their preferences are echoed by delegates. Because delegations are constituted along state-specific lines, another approach would be to look at delegates and followers of the same party from specific states.

Given the focus of our study, however, we are most interested in those characteristics of the delegates most central to the presidential selection and campaign processes. Moreover, our interest is concentrated on the dynamics of the selection process. To this end we will take advantage of the design features of our inquiry that permit us to assess the impact of elite circulation on mass-elite congruence of political attitudes. Consequently we will incorporate and build on measures and results carried over from the preceding chapters dealing with intraparty change and with intraparty cleavages among campaign participants.

Mass public data will be drawn from the National Election Studies (NES) carried out by the Center for Political Studies (CPS), at the University of Michigan. While the data from the 1980 study will carry the brunt of the analysis, data from the 1972 study will also be introduced as appropriate. Comparisons between elites and masses will be drawn in the same three areas—issue orientations, group evaluations, and candidate evaluations—emphasized in previous chapters. In virtually all instances the measures are based on responses to identical stimuli presented to the elite and public samples, and similar procedures were used in constructing the summary indices. The issue and the candidate measures are the same ones used in the preceding chapter comparing elites with each other.[6]

[6]This is so despite the fact that the factor analysis applied to the mass public's handling of the issue items failed to generate a meaningful single factor in the same way as was true for the delegates. Part of the difficulty here lies with the large and varying amounts of missing data among the mass public respondents as well as the presence of less attitudinal constraint. Our decision to construct an additive scale in

However, because the 1980 CPS election study does not include as many groups for evaluation as does our delegate study, the three group indices used in the previous chapter in the examination of interparty disagreements cannot be employed here. Instead, a single summary index must be used, one based on ratings applied to eight groups: business interests (big business in the election study), conservatives, liberals, women's liberation movement, Blacks, environmentalists, moral majority, and union leaders (labor unions in the election study). Although the factor analyses associated with the inclusion of these eight groups yielded somewhat different structures for the elite and mass public samples, they were sufficiently close to justify using the same scoring procedures on both populations. This consisted of summing the ratings assigned each group, all set to run in a liberal to conservative direction, and then dividing by the number of groups rated (eight). A final summary measure that is present in both studies is that of self-placement on the liberalism-conservatism scale. Because of the somewhat ambiguous meaning that can be assigned to mass public responses to this measure, we shall use it sparingly.

Parties in the Aggregate

Our first approach to the question of elite representation of rank-and-file preferences is to deal strictly with gross classifications by party. Data from the 1980 National Election Study provide the basis for the mass public findings. Although we will at a later point employ the full range of delegate data, the first basis for comparison will be only the 1980 delegate cohorts. This decision follows from the desire to facilitate comparisons with previous studies of other

---

the same fashion as was done for the delegates was dictated by four considerations: (1) our unwillingness to work with an unwieldly set of individual items; (2) the group criterion validation supplied by the delegates themselves, wherein the parties and factions within the delegates sorted themselves out along the liberal-conservative continuum in accordance with self-perceptions and widely applied perceptions by political observers; (3) the post-hoc discovery that the index behaved the way it "should" behave within the confines of mass public sample; and, (4) the absence of alternative data reduction methods that were demonstrably better. On the latter point, see the rationale for a similar though more judgmental scoring scheme in Paul Allen Beck and M. Kent Jennings, "Political Periods and Political Participation," *American Political Science Review* 73 (September 1979): 737–50.

convention-year pairings of delegates and party adherents, as well as from the adjacency of the mass and elite data collection in late 1980 and early 1981, respectively.

In examining the proximity between delegates and identifiers it would be possible to restrict attention to the four primary aggregations: Democratic and Republican elites and Democratic and Republican identifiers. However, it is generally true that the intensity of commitment to party distinguishes the attitudes and behaviors of identifiers in the electorate. Other things being equal, the more intense the attachment, the more faithful will be the electoral behavior and the higher the participation level.[7]

Our initial foray, consequently, consists of partitioning the electorate not just into Democratic and Republican identifiers but into the traditional seven groups running from strong Democrats to strong Republicans. In addition, the elites will be divided into the six groups introduced in chapter 3, ranging from strongly attached Democratic delegates to strongly devoted Republican delegates.[8] For observers accustomed to thinking in terms of the traditional seven-point party identification scale, the addition of the six delegate categories may be thought of as extending the range on each end of the scale. Implicit in this extension is the expectation that the connection between intensity and ideological orientations will

[7] When we take as a point of departure the traditional seven-point party identification scale, this is very much the case with respect to the strong partisans within each party. Although "pure" Independents typically vote at the lowest rate and with the most directional inconsistency, the ordering of weak identifiers and Independent "leaners" is not invariant across time. There is a burning controversy about the meaning, dimensions, and varied consequences of party identification. Two lucid overviews are Herbert Asher, "Voting Behavior Research in the 1980s," in Ada W. Finifter, ed., *Political Science: The State of the Discipline* (Washington, DC: American Political Science Association, 1983), esp. pp. 354–60; and Paul Allen Beck, "Context, Choice, and Consequence: Beaten and Unbeaten Paths Toward a Science of Electoral Behavior," a paper presented at the annual meeting of the American Political Science Association, Chicago, 1983.

[8] Party identification in the mass public was tapped in the customary way. "Generally speaking, do you usually think of yourself as a Republican, a Democratic, an Independent, or what?" Those respondents initially selecting Republican or Democrat were then asked: "Would you call yourself a strong [party name] or a not very strong [party name]?" This yields four categories. Those replying "Independent" (or volunteering other or no preference) were asked: "Do you think of yourself as closer to the Republican or Democratic party?" Those picking one of the parties were classified as Independent leaners, thus yielding two more categories. Those not selecting a party constituted the residual seventh group of Independents. "Apoliticals" have been dropped from this analysis.

Figure 9.1

Summary Candidate Evaluations Among 1980 Delegates and Identifiers, by Party Attachment

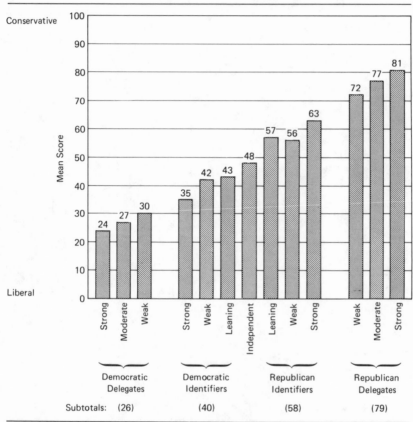

Note: Entries are the mean scores on the eight-candidate evaluation index.

apply to delegates, thereby stretching out the ideological distance to be embraced by the concept of party identification. Altogether, thirteen categories of partisanship are present.

Figures 9.1 through 9.3 contain the results of this ordering within our two populations as they apply to the issue index, the group evaluation index, and the candidate evaluation index. In addition to the mean scores for each of the thirteen categories we have also calculated four subtotals for each party's larger set of delegates and identifiers, which are shown at the bottom of the bar charts.

Figure 9.2

**Summary Group Evaluations Among 1980 Delegates
and Identifiers, by Party Attachment**

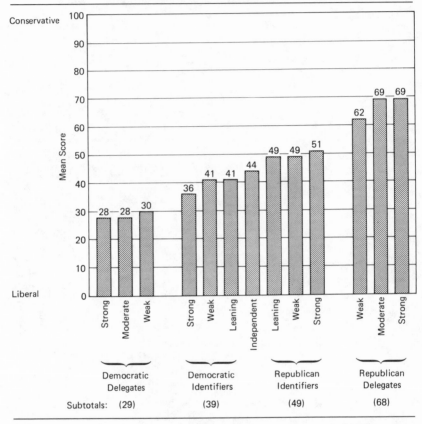

Note: Entries are the mean scores on the eight-group evaluation index.

Several points can be made about the distributions. The first is that although partisan differentiation as gauged by candidate evaluations may not constitute a particularly stiff test (one would expect partisans to differ rather sharply in assessing the leaders of the two parties) the ordering of differences across our thirteen partisan groups is, in fact, remarkably clear. With such a baseline for judging, the orderings on the group evaluation and issue indices are especially noteworthy. They not only exhibit the same basic pattern, but the magnitudes of differences separating the thirteen partisan groups are highly comparable to the differences in partisan

Figure 9.3

Summary Issue Orientations Among 1980 Delegates and Identifiers, by Party Attachment

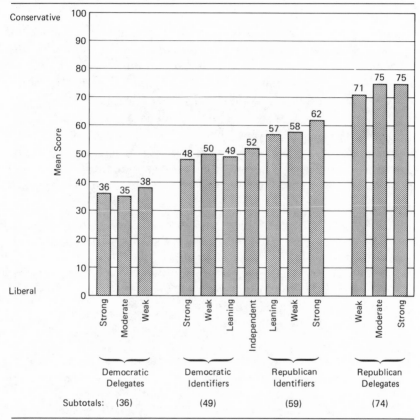

Note: Entries are the mean scores on the transformed seven-point issue index.

candidate assessments. Ideological persuasion is closely tied to party. Party-ideology associations and party-group linkages reveal themselves by the fact that, on average, Republicans of any status are more conservative in their issue and group preferences than are their counterpart Democrats. These differences tend to narrow toward the center of the spectrum, but they are pervasive.

A second point is simply to restate in slightly different form than in the preceding chapter the extraordinary distance separating the party elites. Intense rank-and-file partisans are separated by 14 to 28 points on the three indices, whereas intense elites differ by margins ranging from 39 to 57 points.[9] The corollary is that party status makes for a large difference in political outlook. By status we simply mean whether one is a member of the party mass base— here defined by inclusion in the National Election Study survey— or a member of the elite—here defined by having been a delegate to the 1980 convention. Within our analytic assemblage of both party masses and elites, rank-and-file party identifiers nestle within the confines of the ideological limits set by the delegates. Regardless of level of intensity, no rank-and-file stratum matches the least committed stratum of party delegates in reflecting modal party positions—though this is only one of several plausible configurations within a party.[10] Since delegates are committed activists, it would be surprising if they did not exceed their "constituents" in terms of ideological zeal. Nevertheless, the role of elites in defining the parameters of preference structures, and hence to some extent the context of opinion representation, should not be minimized.

A third and final point has to do with the effect of degree of party attachment. Its impact is variable, though in general the effects are to emphasize the connection between party and beliefs. Intensity within status boundaries accounts for the least difference with respect to the issue index. Indeed, among Democrats neither delegates nor identifiers are distinguished by intensity of partisan support.

Group evaluations are more sensitive to intensity effects and candidate evaluations are even more so. How one feels about the party's electoral representatives is bound to affect and to reflect one's intensity of commitment. Ultimately, these personalities come in large part to stand for the party. If degree of party attach-

[9] Similar findings are reported in Herbert McClosky, Paul J. Hoffman, and Rosemary O'Hara, "Issue Conflict and Consensus among Party Leaders and Followers," *American Political Science Review* 54 (June 1960): 406–27; Robert S. Mountjoy, William R. Shaffer, and Ronald E. Weber, "Policy Preferences of Party Elites and Masses: Conflict or Consensus?" *American Politics Quarterly* 8 (July 1980): 329–43; and John S. Jackson III, Barbara Leavitt, and David Bositis, "Herbert McClosky and Friends Revisited: 1980 Democratic and Republican Party Elites Compared to the Mass Public," *American Politics Quarterly* 10 (April 1982): 158–79.

[10] Analysts of American parties have grown accustomed to this particular configuration, wherein leaders are more extremist than followers. A provocative discussion of several other possibilities is contained in John D. May, "Opinion Structure of Political Parties: The Special Law of Curvilinear Disparity," *Political Studies* 21 (June 1973): 135–51.

ment is to make a difference in any of the three attitudinal domains covered by our indices, it should surely do so for candidate evaluation. The long, stepladder sweep shown in Figure 9.1 affirms the argument that the sense of party identification, with its dual components of direction and intensity, helps bridge the worlds of elites and masses, particularly where evaluations of party leadership are concerned.

Although we shall not have much further occasion to use the differentiation according to degree of attachment, the contribution it makes to our understanding of mass-elite linkages should be borne in mind. An especially relevant point is the close proximity between strong partisan identifiers and weakly attached delegates. Strong partisans tend to be the most participative in the electoral arena. Their generally greater ideological congruence with the party elites bodes well for the prescription that elites should be especially responsive to and attentive to the most committed and industrious members of the party base.

While the mean scores on the ideological measures tell us much about the ideological ordering of party elites and masses, they tell us only imperfectly about the proximity between delegate leaders and citizen followers. Subtracting the mean scores of leaders from followers provides one very summary approximation, but the intuitive meaning of such differences is not always clear nor is the comparison of differences straightforward. A more informative and yet highly standardized way to present group differences takes the form of the Pearsonian correlation coefficients we introduced in the last chapter.[11] The correlation coefficient in the present instance may be thought of as representing the difference (or dis-

---

[11] As will become evident, our usage of the correlation coefficient departs in important ways from that normally associated with representational studies. It shares one characteristic, however, which is its reliance on *relative* association or similarity between the attitudes of representatives and of those being represented. Absolute differences are "standardized away" in this approach, a point made forcefully by Christopher Achen in "Measuring Representation," *American Journal of Political Science* 22 (August 1978): 475–510. Achen proposes two additional measures which take into account distance scores and variance scores among districts being represented. For our purposes the correlation coefficient is especially preferable because we are not examining the congruence between particular sets of delegate-voter pairs. For a lucid discussion of alternative approaches to assessing representation and a generally ringing defense of correlation and regression coefficients, see Philip E. Converse and Roy Pierce, *Political Representation in France* (Cambridge, MA: Harvard University Press, 1986), chap. 16.

tance) between each of the two components in a pairing of mass and elite opinions. In this case the "independent" variable becomes political status or rank, with masses being coded as low (0) and elites coded as high (1); and the dependent variables are the three indices of group, issue, and candidate preferences, all coded from liberal (low) to conservative (high).

Correlations were thus computed, for each party separately, between party status on the one hand and the three sets of attitudes on the other. The larger the coefficient the *more difference* political status makes and the greater is the ideological distance between elites and masses. In terms of representation terminology, the larger the correlation the less the elites resemble the rank and file and, therefore, the *less* representative the elites are of the rank and file. Correspondingly, the lower the correlation the greater is the similarity and the higher the congruence of opinion. Ignoring the sign of the correlation, the range would be from 0.0 to 1.0. A correlation of 0 would mean that delegates are perfectly representative of the identifiers. A hypothetical correlation of 1.0 would mean the largest possible dissimilarity between the delegates and the rank and file.

Because all three attitudinal measures are directional, the sign of each coefficient has substantive meaning and indicates whether the elite group is more or less conservative (or liberal) than the rank-and-file group with which it is being compared. However, with only a few exceptions the signs are always positive for Republicans and negative for Democrats. That is, the Republican elites we shall work with are nearly always more conservative than the rank and file at our disposal and the Democratic elites are ordinarily more liberal than their rank and file. Consequently, we shall ignore the signs *unless* the relationships depart from these regularities.[12]

---

[12] It should be emphasized that the usual interpretation of correlation coefficients as used in representation studies does not apply to our usage. In those studies the higher correlations are associated with greater covariation between elites and mass attitudes, whereas we are examining covariations between status and attitudes, not between attitudes. Our focus on status, mass-elite, or Democratic-Republican differences is simply the mirror image of a focus on attitudes. With our usage we examine the direct effect of status differences and infer the associated level of attitudinal consequence. The seminal work on dyadic analysis using the correlation coefficient in the more conventional style is Warren E. Miller and Donald E. Stokes, "Constituency Influence in Congress," *American Political Science Review* 57 (March 1963): 45–56.

For convenience we will now return to the four larger aggregations of partisan elites and identifiers. Doing so means ignoring
some of the nuances achieved by taking into account the intensity
of attachment. A general rule of thumb to keep in mind is that the
stronger the attachment among the rank and file the closer is the
proximity to the delegates.

Based on the mean scores alone, we know that the correlation
between party status and political attitudes will be well above 0, for
in an absolute sense many of the differences in means were very
substantial. Table 9.1 presents the relevant correlations. Consider
first each of the two party elites and their respective identifiers
within the electorate (columns 1 and 2). Without doubt the Democratic elites were more in tune with their followers in 1980 than
were the Republicans with theirs. That is, party status created
larger differences between mass and elite in the Republican party
than in the Democratic party and, conversely, the two Democratic
strata were closer together and less different from each other.

A partial exception to the generalization about comparative
intraparty differences rests in the single measure reflecting self-
placement on the liberal-conservative scale. Here the two Republican groups are marginally more like each other than are the two
Democratic groups. However, nearly two fifths of the identifiers
were not able to locate themselves on the scale, thereby lowering
the comparability of the results with those from the other measures.
Perhaps the best way of putting the finding is to say that among
respondents sensitive to ideological labels, the two Republican
strata stood a bit closer to each other in their self-categorizations
as liberals or conservatives than did the Democratic strata. It is
also worth noting that when we use this measure that excludes the
less articulate members of the mass electorate, both party pairs
are much closer to each other than they are on the other three
measures.

As has been amply documented elsewhere, and as we shall
subsequently observe, there is nothing invariant about the greater
Democratic harmony. Whereas McClosky et al. noted the same
configuration among 1956 convention delegates, Kirkpatrick found
quite opposite patterns in the 1972 soundings.[13] Clearly such varia-

[13] Jeane Kirkpatrick, "Representation in the American National Conventions: The
Case of 1972," *British Journal of Political Science* 5 (July 1975): 265–322; and
McClosky, Hoffman, and O'Hara, "Issue Conflict and Consensus among Party Lead-
ers and Followers," *American Political Science Review* 54 (June 1960): 406–27.

Table 9.1

Differences Between Convention Delegates and Identifiers, by Partisan Combinations

	(1) Democratic Democratic	(2) Republican Republican	(3) Democratic Republican	(4) Republican Democratic
Delegates: Identifiers:				
Issue Index	.29	.38	.43	.57
Group Evaluation Index	.32	.53	.51	.73
Candidate Evaluation Index	.48	.65	.76	.87
Liberal Conservative Self-Placement	.25	.20	.53	.56

Note: Entries are product-moment correlations (r) and indicate the relationship between party status (identifiers versus delegates) and attitude. The larger the coefficient the greater is the difference between delegates and identifiers.

tions reflect in part the ascent and decline of particular wings of the parties, and especially of particular candidacies. But documenting these variations serves to highlight the dynamics of leader-follower correspondence and may lead to an understanding of how party organizations change with the infusion of new participants while retaining much of their old flavor.

The final two columns in Table 9.1 contain the cross-party combinations, which match one party's elites with the other's rank and file. As expected, each elite is closer to its own rank and file than it is to the opposite one. This is shown by comparing columns 1 and 3 with each other and columns 2 and 4 with each other. These results follow from what we have observed earlier in the liberal-consevative ranking of our four aggregations.

However, a different kind of insight into contemporary intraparty differences is provided by comparing the intraparty matching with the interparty measures of elite-mass differences. Comparisons of columns 1 and 4 with 2 and 3 show the proximity of identifiers to their own versus opposite party delegates. While Democratic rank and file are consistently much closer to their own leaders than to Republican elites, Republican identifiers were at least as close to Democratic delegates as they were to their own Republican delegates with respect to the group evaluation index, and they were almost equidistant from both sets of delegates on the issue and candidate measures. This is an early indication that interparty comparisions in 1980 reveal dramatically different results than were evident in 1972.[14] The year of the Reagan insurgency was not only marked by a relative lack of rapport between the Republican delegates and their rank-and-file supporters, but the "estranged" Democratic elite of 1972 had been replaced by a set of Democratic delegates in 1980 more in tune with their own Democratic identifiers and also one which stood about as close to the Republican base as did the Republican elite.

A similar point emerges if we replace party identifiers with voters. Given the strong correlation between party identification and the vote in 1980, the substitution does not make a large difference. Nevertheless, it makes the point that Reagan's impressive

---

[14] In that year the Democratic rank and file was closer to the Republican elite, whereas in 1956 the Republican rank and file had been closer to the Democratic elite.

Table 9.2

Ideological Positions of Voters and Convention Delegates, 1980

	Issue Index	Group Evaluation Index	Candidate Index
Reagan Voters	59	50	59
Carter Voters	46	38	37
Republican Delegates	74	68	79
Democratic Delegates	36	29	26
Difference Between Reagan Voters and Republican Delegates	15	18	20
Difference Between Carter Voters and Democratic Delegates	10	9	11

Note: The higher the score the more conservative the attitude.

victory occurred despite the fact that his cadre of voters were not as ideologically similar to the Republican elite that nominated him as were the Carter voters to their Democratic elite. Table 9.2 shows the mean scores of Reagan and Carter voters on the three summary indexes and compares them with the counterpart scores for the 1980 Republican and Democratic delegates. Reagan voters were closer to Republican than Democratic delegates just as Carter voters were consistently closer to Democratic than Republican delegates. However, the gaps were larger in the GOP. And Carter voters were considerably further away from Republican delegates than were Reagan voters from Democratic delegates (comparing the difference between rows 1 and 4 with the difference between rows 2 and 3).

What are the implications if a party's leadership finds itself rather seriously at odds with its own rank and file? If electoral results constitute the criteria, the verdict of recent years is mixed. Clearly the Democrats in 1972 seemed to suffer visibly because the liberals had distanced themselves so far from their party base's center of gravity. Much the same apparently applied to the Republicans in the 1964 debacle. On the other hand, Reagan's smashing victory of 1980 and Eisenhower's triumph in 1956 belie the notion that a wide gulf portends disaster. Much more is involved in winning elections than ideological proximity between particular elite cohorts and mass public followers.

It has been demonstrated in a number of places that the crucial element in the 1980 election outcome was not the candidates' positions on contemporary issues so much as the perceived qualities of the candidates, especially the past performance of the incumbent and the perceived competencies of both candidates.[15] Our results add to this image by demonstrating that ideological congruence between high-level Republican activists and Reagan voters was by no means great enough to constitute a necessary condition for a GOP victory. By the same token, the relatively closer proximity of Democratic elites to Republican as well as Democratic masses scarcely assured Carter of sufficient electoral support for reelection.

These short-term electoral outcomes notwithstanding, there is likely to be some consequence of sharp dissonance between a party's leaders and their base of mass support. Indeed the resurrection of the Democratic party and the changes in leadership we have described following the 1972 disaster occurred precisely because it was recognized that a gulf had developed between leaders, including delegates, and followers. Much the same might be said of the post-1964 shift by the leadership of the Republican party. As we have seen, delegates tend to remain active for some time in presidential politics. Extraordinarily attractive candidates such as Eisenhower or Reagan may be able to overcome a noticeable gap, but in the long run a party "out of touch" with its constituents seems destined for difficulty.

The Impact of Circulation on Proximity

Thus far in this chapter we have confined our treatment of delegates to the full membership of the 1980 cohorts. Doing so meant that no comparisons could be made among the three dele-

---

[15] Gregory B. Markus, "Political Attitudes during an Election Year: A Report on the NES Panel Study," *American Political Science Review* 76 (September 1982): 538–60; William Schneider, "The November 4 Vote for President: What Did It Mean?" in Austin Ranney, ed., *The American Elections of 1980* (Washington DC: American Enterprise Institute, 1981); and several chapters in Gerald M. Pomper, *The Elections of 1980* (Chatham, NJ: Chatham House, 1981). For somewhat different interpretations, see John H. Kessel, *Presidential Campaign Politics*, 2nd ed. (Homewood, IL: Dorsey Press, 1984), chap. 8; and Warren E. Miller and J. Merrill Shanks, "Policy Directions and Presidential Leadership: Alternative Interpretations of the 1980 Presidential Election," *British Journal of Political Science* 12 (July 1982): 299–356.

gate cohorts, nor between 1980 delegates who had long been active in presidential campaign politics and those who were just recently mobilized. Based on our earlier findings we might well expect these latter two subgroups to differ in terms of their concordance with rank-and-file adherents. Taking only the 1980 cohorts into account also has meant that the linkages formed through other cohorts which composed part of the full set of presidential campaign activists have not been considered. Again it seems likely, based on our earlier discussion, that the mass-elite congruence achieved by continuously active delegates from earlier cohorts would differ from that of those no longer active in presidential politics. Finally, we have ignored the special qualities that may be attached to the continuously active members of each convention cohort.

A first approach assessing the impact of circulation simply adds the 1972 and 1976 cohorts to the analysis. Here the question is how the two earlier convention cohorts compare with those of 1980 in terms of congruence with the 1980 electorate. In the previous chapters we established the presence of a series of intercohort differences within each party, especially in the GOP. Given that, we should expect variations in mass-elite congruence as we move across cohorts. In the interest of brevity and focus, we present only the findings associated with the left-right issue index, shown in Table 9.3.

Variations in congruence do exist across cohorts, but the pattern differs between the two parties. Within the Republican party in 1981, the 1972 delegates were clearly closer to their 1980 Republican rank and file, and to the electorate as a whole, than were succeeding cohorts. Another way of putting this is to say that a 1980 GOP convention composed of 1972 delegates (holding their 1981 issue preferences) would have been decidedly more like the 1980 mass public than was the actual 1980 assemblage. Indeed, the Republican pattern is one of increasing discrepancy with the addition of each new cohort, assuming that no change has occurred among the pre-1980 cohorts. That model is not altogether accurate, as shall be demonstrated presently.

Turning to the Democratic side, we see that the patterning discloses the uniqueness of the 1976 cohort. On balance, linkage patterns among the Democrats are slightly less varied than among the Republicans. But as the least liberal gathering of the three

Table 9.3

Differences in Issue Preferences of Activists and Identifiers, as of 1981, by Convention Cohort

	Cohort		
Issue Distance	1972	1976	1980
Republican Delegates and Republican Identifiers	.29	.38	.41
Republican Delegates and Total Mass Public	.38	.45	.47
Democratic Delegates and Democratic Identifiers	.30	.23	.31
Democratic Delegates and Total Mass Public	.38	.31	.39

Note: The larger the coefficient (r) the greater the difference.

cohorts under examination here, it is not surprising to see the 1976 Democratic cohort's closer proximity to both rank-and-file Democrats and to the electorate as a whole in 1981.[16] As we shall see shortly, the presence of traditional Democrats and Carter devotees contributed heavily to the 1976 results. By 1980 the Democrats had reverted to a convention whose ideological composition on average resembled quite remarkably that of 1972 (at least as assessed in 1981).

The gross comparisons across cohorts are suggestive, but they speak only indirectly to the question of the impact of circulation on leader-follower congruence. A more dynamic approach takes advantage of the campaign histories of the delegates. As we think of representation in dynamic terms, and of presidential campaign activists in more general terms than provided by a specific convention cohort, attention properly turns to all three cohorts and to distinctions made according to campaign participation. For the 1972–1980 period, both the 1972 and 1980 cohorts are again neatly differ-

[16] Additional evidence that the 1976 Democratic delegates were more in tune with their rank and file is presented in the [Democratic] Commission on Presidential Nominations and Party Structure, "Openness, Participation, and Party Building: Reforms for a Stronger Democratic Party," Democratic National Committee, Washington, DC, 1978; and John S. Jackson III, Jesse C. Brown, and Barbara L. Brown, "Recruitment, Representation, and Political Values: The 1976 Democratic National Convention Delegates," *American Politics Quarterly* 6 (April 1978): 187–212.

entiated into the continuously active versus the disengaged in 1972 and the continuously active and the recently mobilized in 1980. These four groups form the basis for a first informative set of comparisons.

Let us consider first the 1972 delegates according to whether they had withdrawn from presidential politics or had been continuously active since 1972. Figure 9.4 and Table 9.4 present the mean scores for each group and the correlations for the pairings based on the elite and identifier combinations. For the sake of parsimony as well as substantive interest we report only the correlations attending the Democratic-Democratic and Republican-Republican pairings.

Figure 9.4 shows the mean scores for the continuously active and the disengaged of each party as well as those for the identifiers in the 1980 national election study. Without exception, the pattern described is one of increasing conservatism moving from left to right across the chart. More relevant for present considerations is the fact that the disengaged within each party were closer to their party followers in 1980 than were those who had been active over the whole period. This disparity becomes more sharply defined by the correlations presented in Table 9.4. In interpreting these correlation coefficients, it should be recalled that lower values mean less distance (greater similarity) between party elites and followers.

There might seem to be something perverse about this outcome from the viewpoint of representation though not of ideological advocacy. Why do the parties lose the activists who would be more in tune with the attitudes of the parties' followers a few years down the road? To some extent the answer lies in the ideological thrust taken by the two parties over time. This is especially so for the Republicans. As shown already, the Republican dropouts are decidedly less conservative than the continuously active 1972 delegates who, in turn, are less conservative than the 1976 and 1980 cohorts who came to dominate the Republican party elite. This strong net flow toward conservatism among the elites was not matched by a comparable shift at the grassroots level, as we shall document shortly. Hence the relatively greater congruence between the disengaged elite and the 1980 Republican identifiers.

The Democratic case parallels that of the Republicans because the ideological flow within the party had the same consequences for our analysis as in the Republican example. On each of our three

Figure 9.4

**Attitudes of 1972 Delegates and 1980 Identifiers,
by Circulation Patterns**

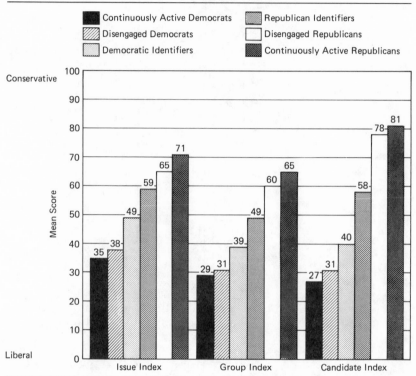

indices, the disengaged Democratic elite was slightly closer to the Democratic masses than were the continuous participants among the 1972 delegates. In general the differences in proximity are not as great among the Democrats as among the Republicans. Still, had those disengaged Democrats of 1972 remained active, the overall correspondence of the 1972 cohort with rank-and-file supporters would have been closer than it actually was in 1981 because, as in the Republican case, the continuing participants were further removed in the extremity of their ideological location.

The 1980 cohorts provide the other vantage point for viewing the consequence of circulation for mass-elite congruence. Here the comparison involves those 1980 delegates who had been active

Table 9.4

Differences Between 1972 Delegates and Their Party Identifiers, by Circulation Patterns

	Continuously Active Democrats	Disengaged Democrats	Disengaged Republicans	Continuously Active Republicans
	(r)	(r)	(r)	(r)
Issue Index	.33	.27	.14	.33
Group Index	.35	.30	.35	.52
Candidate Index	.43	.31	.53	.69

Note: The larger the coefficient the greater the difference between delegates and identifiers.

since 1972 versus those who, in terms of our time frame, were recent inductees. Figure 9.5 and Table 9.5 display the comparisons for each party, including mean scores for the groups and the accompanying correlations. Within each party the pattern is the same: The recently mobilized were less distant from the party base than were the persistent activists. This is a reassuring finding from one perspective. As party elites are replenished with new recruits they should, under classic theories which emphasize the desirability of representation, help achieve closer rapport with their party's rank and file. The recently mobilized would not necessarily reflect changes in mass population parameters, but the odds are in that direction for one major reason. Since they have not been caught up in presidential politics for as long a time, the newly mobilized are

Figure 9.5

**Attitudes of 1980 Delegates and 1980 Identifiers,
by Circulation Patterns**

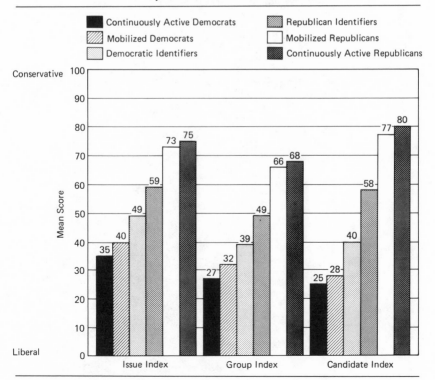

Table 9.5

Differences Between 1980 Delegates and Their Party Identifiers, by Circulation Patterns

	Continuously Active Democrats	Mobilized Democrats	Mobilized Republicans	Continuously Active Republicans
	(r)	(r)	(r)	(r)
Issue Index	.36	.24	.34	.42
Group Index	.42	.26	.50	.61
Candidate Index	.54	.39	.53	.66

Note: The larger the coefficient the greater the difference between delegates and identifiers.

less likely to carry the ideological baggage associated with earlier time periods.

Something of the opposite may well occur in the ranks of the long-time activists. Although we have demonstrated some conversion effects among activists where candidate preferences are concerned, there is also a tendency for the continuously active to retain particular attributes associated with the circumstances in which they actually first became delegates. Over time this could tend to draw them further away from mass publics, assuming that the latter are changing in the direction suggested by the greater proximity of the newly mobilized. By contrast, the newly mobilized presumably reflect a bit more the nature of the times. They are not as hardened or time-bound in this sense, though if our findings are any guide, that will be the eventual fate of those who go on to remain a part of the presidential elite. Of course, if at the same time the positions of the rank and file *are* changing, the consequences for the mass-elite fit will depend on the direction of that change. If the rank and file had themselves moved closer to the positions of the continuously active, the relative differences in correlations—or mean scores— which make the disengaged *and* the mobilized seem more like them would have been moderated. If rank-and-file movement was to increase the distance from the core actives, the result might have accentuated the advantage in proximity held by the disengaged/mobilized.

While both parties exhibited the same patterning as of 1981, it was much sharper among the Democrats than the Republicans. It is part of the larger tapestry that shows that the GOP elite became increasingly conservative during the 1970s. Even though the newly mobilized are not as conservative as the continuously active 1980 delegates, in Figure 9.5 they appear some distance away from their rank and file. The new Democratic activists are much closer than their continuously active colleagues to the mass public; and they are certainly closer to their constituency than are the new Republican elites to theirs.

A comparison of Figures 9.4 and 9.5 renders a striking picture of how circulation within the two parties, especially the Democratic, helped maintain leader-follower proximity. The loss in proximity created by the disengagement of old activists was in some measure restored by the mobilization of new ones. Since there are roughly equal proportions of disengaged and mobilized in the 1972–1980 span, the image of replenishment is an accurate one.

Again, however, there are significant interparty differences. Among the Democrats the newly mobilized, compared with the disengaged, were actually closer to the rank and file on the three summary measures, and closer on six of the seven specific issues (not shown). By contrast, the newly mobilized Republicans were more *distant* from the 1980 rank and file than were the disengaged on the three summary measures and on three of the seven specific issues. On balance, the replacement process of presidential campaign activists had the net effect of bringing the Democratic elite more in line with its base while driving the GOP elite further out of line with the Republican mass base. The contrasting effects of replacement in the two parties might have been greater had there been more turnover of personnel. Given the observed distribution of mean scores, the larger the *amount* of replacement the greater is the impact. In the present case the impact was greater among Democrats because the replacement figure is about 18 percent for them compared with about 12 percent for the Republicans. Representation of mass public preferences is thus sensitive to the volume of turnover as well as the ideological mix among those involved in the replacement process.

A Closer Look at Changes in Republican Mass-Elite Proximity

The decline in proximity between Republican elites and identifiers during the 1970s can be depicted in another, somewhat more striking fashion. It will be recalled from the previous chapters that the 1972 delegates who responded in 1981 form a two-wave panel. In the analysis of interparty conflict we made use of the fact that delegates and identifiers in both 1972 and 1980 (1981 for the delegates) appraised eight sociopolitical groupings on the feeling thermometer. Those placements now provide a set of measures that can be used to explore the relative contributions of conversion and replacement to the inferred changes in elite-mass proximity. Our present analysis consists of examining the correlations between delegates and identifiers for three pairings: (1) 1972 delegates and 1972 identifiers as of 1972; (2) 1972 delegates and 1980 identifiers as of 1981; and (3) 1980 delegates and 1980 identifiers as of 1981. Changes in linkage stemming from both cohort succession and individual-level movements can be traced with these three pairings in hand.

Before interpreting the results a key point must be made. Any differences to be observed across these three combinations could be attributed only in part to over-time changes on the part of rank-and-file Republicans. Mean scores on five of the group ratings had altered no more than 3°. Of the three registering shifts larger than this the direction was liberal in the case of evaluations of the womens' liberation movement (42 to 49), and conservative in the other two instances—evaluation of liberals going from 47 to 42 and of Democrats from 57 to 52. Using our correlation coefficient as a measure of similarity, the interyear (1972–1980) correlations for Republican identifiers averaged less than .06, indicating virtually identical distributions of scores in the two years for both pairs of identifiers.[17]

Standing in vivid contrast to this aggregate stability is the difference between Republican delegates in 1972 and in 1980. Those attending the 1980 convention had universally more conservative ratings than did their 1972 predecessors. Moreover, these increases were on the average over 3° on the feeling thermometer with respect to six of the eight groups and over 10° with respect to four of the groups (conservatives, liberals, union leaders, and business interests). Consequently, adjustments that occurred in the proximity of the elites and masses were much more a function of differences among the delegates than within the rank and file.[18]

The results of our analysis of the over-time proximity between Republican strata are not entirely unequivocal, but the thrust is clear enough (Table 9.6). Two major points emerge. First, a com-

[17] In this equation, year becomes the independent variable and attitudes the dependent variable. A low correlation means that year makes for little difference in attitudes.

[18] There is also little evidence to suggest that the increase of presidential primaries affected the changing relationships among the Republicans, or among the Democrats, for that matter. See Barbara G. Farah, M. Kent Jennings, and Warren E. Miller, "Convention Delegates: Reform and the Representation of Party Elites, 1972–1980," a paper presented at the Conference on Presidential Activities, College of William and Mary, 1981.

Table 9.6

Differences Between Republican Delegates and Identifiers Across Cohorts and Over Time

	1972 Delegates and 1972 Identifiers, as of 1972	1972 Delegates and 1980 Identifiers, as of 1981	1980 Delegates and 1980 Identifiers, as of 1981
	(r)	(r)	(r)
Conservatives	.01	.02	.16
Business Interests	.09	.29	.33
Blacks	.09	.18	.11
Women's Liberation Movement	.24	.37	.43
Union Leaders	.31	.46	.48
Liberals	.38	.48	.51
Republicans	.36	.46	.48
Democrats	.58	.55	.53

Note: Entries are the correlations (r) between delegate and rank-and-file scores; the larger the coefficient the greater the difference between delegates and identifiers.

parison of columns 1 and 3 demonstrates the total effect of all the processes of change within the Republican party. Six of the eight correlations are substantially higher for the 1980 pairings than for the 1972 pairings. In these six instances, therefore, distance increased considerably. Essentially no change occurred with respect to similarity on the evaluations of Blacks, occasioned in large part by the tendency of both types of respondents to give Blacks a score of 50° on the feeling thermometer. The one comparison marked by greater *convergence*—evaluations of Democrats—involves only a slight gain in proximity. On balance, the delegate selection process and the candidacies associated with it yielded up a set of Republican delegates in 1980 that was further removed from its constituency than the 1972 set had been.

However, there are strong grounds for believing that this distancing might have occurred even in the absence of turnover. This second point is evident from the data in column 2 containing the figures for the 1972 delegates, as of 1981, paired with the same 1980 Republican identifiers involved in our first comparison. An examination of columns 1 and 2 reveals, in five of the six cases involving growing differences, that changes among the 1972 delegates had to have been at work. Party status made more of a difference in attitudes in 1980 than in 1972, holding constant the identity of the delegates (the 1972 cohort) and comparing them to mass party identifiers who had virtually identical scores in the two years. Only in the case of evaluations of conservatives was there no decrease in proximity by 1980 because of change on the part of the 1972 delegates.

As time passed, then, the 1972 delegates tended to draw away from their party base. If the delegates of 1972 had been reassembled as the convention body of 1980, they would have been virtually as distant from their 1980 base of rank-and-file identifiers as were the actual 1980 delegates (comparing columns 2 and 3).[19] Assuming that our panel respondents reflect adequately the universe of 1972 delegates, we have again witnessed the effects of individual-level change. Individual members of the party's elite became more conservative over time, which abetted the drift within the party. Coupled with modest replacement effects appar-

[19] They would have been slightly more distant with respect to ratings of Blacks and Democrats.

ent in the comparison of columns 2 and 3 in Table 9.6, these conversion effects created a growing schism between elite and masses.

The intracacies of the dynamic processes of change within the GOP deserve yet closer scrutiny, for the conversion effects did not fall equally across the circulation strata of the party. Again we take advantage of our multiple points of observation and the delegates' campaign histories to depict the origins of changing congruence or representation. For the sake of brevity we will summarize the results by forming a cumulative index based on scores assigned to only six of the groups listed in Table 9.6. Ratings for Republicans and Democrats are omitted because they are literally self-other ratings and far less responsive to changing times and personnel than most of the other groups in the list.

The results of analyses using the circulation components provide a striking panorama of within-party variations that is consistent with all we have learned thus far. Two features stand out. First, as adumbrated by previous results, there is a noticeable distinction between the 1972 Republican delegates who remained active and those who dropped out. In 1972 those who were to become disengaged were extraordinarily closer to the 1972 rank and file Republicans than were those destined to be continuously active (coefficients of .36 to .55). This difference between disengaged and active persists in 1981, when the contemporaneous (that is, 1981) scores of the same subsets of delegates are compared with 1980 identifiers (.49 to .63). What has been added to our earlier knowledge is that the disengaged *started out* as more sympathetic with the rank and file and continued to be so. Analysis based on measures available only in 1972 confirm this greater proximity between the ultimately disengaged and the 1972 identifiers. If anything, the contrasts are sharper using these other indicators.

At the same time, while the greater proximity of the disengaged persisted over time, they, too, shared in a movement away from the party base. By 1980 both the disengaged and the continuously active had increased the distance between themselves and the Republican followers. Because Republican supporters changed very little in the aggregate, it is apparent that even the disengaged became more conservative over time. Conversion applied to them as well as to the core activists within the presidential elite.

The same analysis applied to the newly mobilized rounds out the picture and supplies a third point. As was demonstrated in

Figure 9.5, on all three dimensions the newly mobilized Republican delegates of 1981 were actually, and somewhat surprisingly, closer to the Republican laity than were 1980 delegates who had been presidential campaign activists across the entire 1972–1980 period. (Using our six-group index the coefficients were .63 and .68, respectively.) In this respect the activity patterns of the 1980 delegates follow those of the 1972 delegates. Regardless of vintage, the chronic activists are the most removed from the mass followers, though it should be noted that in none of these instances are the differences large. What emerges as more striking here, especially because we are employing the same measure throughout time and across both elite and mass samples, is the wide range and systematic decrease in congruence within the Republican party. At one end stand the 1972 delegates who dropped out of presidential politics (with a disagreement coefficient of .36 in 1972); at the other stand the persistent, and predominantly conservative, 1980 delegates (with a disagreement coefficient of .68 in 1981).

The growing distance between Republican elites and the party base is not without its ironies. We have already noted its electoral success in the face of this widening rift. A second irony has to do with party as organization. As noted at several points, the GOP has strenuously resisted mandated reform in its nomination procedures in general and in the composition of state delegations in particular. It has, in fact, devoted relatively little attention to the question of composition, concentrating instead on strengthening the party's internal organization and striving to overcome its numerical disadvantage in the electorate. Meanwhile, the Democrats have devoted enormous energies to the question of representation; in many ways this has been the quintessential question for them. These reforms in representation were largely blamed for the "unrepresentative" character of the 1972 convention and continuing strains between leaders and followers within the party, a charge with which we do not wholly agree but one which has obvious merit. What is ironic, however, is that the Republicans arrived at a point by 1980 when their elite cadres were seriously out of tune with their followers in the *almost total absence* of mandated reform in delegate selection procedures. Rules do make a difference, but it is quite clear that additional forces, such as ideology, candidate coalitions, mobilization, and strategies—and perhaps chance—contribute heavily to the nature of mass-elite relationships accompanying the nomination process.

CHAPTER 10

Candidate Preferences, Circulation, and Mass-Elite Linkages

The question of political representation by campaign activists is perhaps most focused when attention is turned to the various candidate support groups, for candidates become the focal point around which much of the preconvention and postconvention activities form. Well beyond the convention period, and even the election year, the parties are often characterized in terms of particular factions made up of leaders and followers identified with a single candidate or with a succession of candidates having similar pedigrees. Given the centrality of candidate groups that we have observed in earlier chapters, it is important to see how closely their preferences correspond to those of the mass public, and how the waxing and waning of various candidacy groupings has affected the proximity between leaders and followers within the party.

In addition to the three indices used previously, we now reintroduce self-placement on the liberal-conservative scale. The reason for doing so is that candidates and candidate support groups are so frequently tagged and summarized by labels representing steps along the liberal-conservative continuum. Politicians and pundits apply these labels to candidates and these tags are frequently picked up by the mass public. However, it should be recalled that upwards of two fifths of the electorate cannot locate themselves on this scale. Therefore, the accompanying results, though compatible with those based on the other measure, are less generalizable.[1]

We turn first to the 1980 delegates and their preferences for the 1980 nominations, following which we take up the full set of delegates at our disposal. The structure of the 1980 preferences is rather simple in each party. On the Republican side, the basic dichotomy was between the Reaganites and those supporting Bush and fellow moderates. On the Democratic side, the division was between Carter supporters and those backing the late-blossoming Kennedy candidacy.

The two eventual nominees represented the more conservative wings of their respective parties and, correspondingly, their delegate supporters held more conservative views than did those delegates who supported the more liberal candidates. Because we know that the rank and file within each party holds more moderate views than do the elites, the congruence between the candidate preference groups and the rank and file varies in a predictable fashion. Among Republicans the Bush supporters were less distant than Reagan supporters from Republican identifiers; among Democrats the Carter delegates were closer than the Kennedy supporters to the Democratic rank and file. While these orderings are predictable, the magnitudes and differences involved are much less obvious.

Figure 10.1 presents the data in terms of the mean scores for the candidate support groups and the partisan identifiers in the mass public. Table 10.1 shows the distances between strata within each party in terms of correlations. (Again, higher correlations mean *greater* distances and less faithful representation by elites of identifiers' views.)

The bar charts clearly reveal the ideological sweep in 1981, running from Kennedy supporters on one end to Reagan advocates on the other. The progression is nicely monotonic across the spectrum and shows the vast ideological differences within and across the components of the party system. Moreover, the general contours of the results are the same for each of the four summary measures employed, though the Republicans exhibit more internal variation than do the Democrats.

[1] To facilitate comparison, the scores on the seven-point scale have, as before, been converted to a scale having a 0–100 range.

Figure 10.1

Attitudes of 1980 Delegates and Identifiers, by Candidate Preference

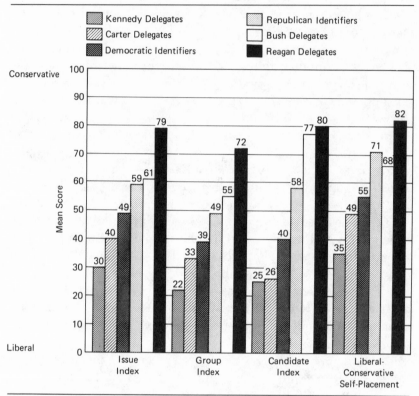

These internal variations are captured more systematically by the correlations for the partisan pairings. Taken as a whole, the results are described by a U curve, with the Reagan and Kennedy delegates forming the points of the U and being most distant from the rank and file, while the Carter and Bush delegates form the arc and are the most proximate to the party identifiers. Here it becomes even clearer just how sharp the difference was in the proximities of the moderate (Bush) and conservative (Reagan) delegates to the Republican party constituency. The former were universally closer to the rank and file, though this was not true of all the individual issues making up the issue index.[2] So close were

---

[2] Indeed, Reagan delegates were somewhat closer to the party balance on such "hot" emotional issues as ERA and spending for defense.

Table 10.1

**Differences Between Delegates and Their Party Identifiers,
by Candidate Preference**

	Kennedy Delegates	Carter Delegates	Bush Delegates	Reagan Delegates
	(r)	(r)	(r)	(r)
Issue Index	.46	.23	.06	.53
Group Index	.58	.22	.21	.71
Candidate Index	.55	.50	.58	.70
Liberal-Conservative				
Self-Placement	.48	.14	−.16	.37

Notes: The larger the coefficient the greater the difference between delegates and identifiers.

Minus sign means negative correlation; delegates are more liberal than identifiers.

they that the distance between moderate delegates and identifiers does not even achieve statistical significance (at the .05 level) for the issue and the group evaluation indices. Although it is problematic whether a Bush nomination would have secured a Republican electoral victory, a convention dominated by moderates instead of conservatives would have been far more representative of the lay partisans' views on issues, groups, and personalities. And, of course, it would have been far closer to the views of the Democratic identifiers. As it was, however, the moderates comprised only a fourth of the combined Bush-Reagan preferences at the convention.

Contrasts within the Democratic ranks are less striking. True, Carterites always stood closer to Democratic identifiers than did Kennedy backers. But in no instance were these contrasts as pronounced as in the Republican case. Ironically, the Democrats, long noted for intraparty strife, nevertheless managed to organize their 1980 convention and energies around two candidates whose candidate support groups stood closer to their mass partisans than did those attached to the Republican victor, Ronald Reagan. Even had the losing Kennedy supporters—who constituted two fifths of the combined Kennedy-Carter backers—dominated the conventions, the Democratic delegates as a whole would still have been more akin to their followers than the Reaganites were to theirs. In both parties the more liberal candidate lost the nomination but the outcome for "representativeness" differed. For the Democrats the result was greater congruence between the winning coalition and party followers whereas for the Republicans the result was greater distance between the winners and party followers.

Candidate Preference Genealogies and Elite-Mass Congruence

We have just observed that rank-and-file partisans achieved differential representation among 1980 delegates according to which faction of which party was being considered. Just as activity levels among the delegates have a dynamic property, so, too, do the candidate preference groupings. To some degree this dynamic element is inevitable, even given the relatively brief historical era covered by our inquiry. During the course of the three presidential races at hand, a number of candidacies attracted varying amounts of attention and following at both the public and elite levels. Some delegates were consistent in their support of candidates who occupied certain ideological locations within their parties, others moved around more, and still others were essentially one-candidate devotees. Chapter 7 introduced the rather diverse ideological orientations across these groups. These candidate support patterns can now be employed to explore in more dynamic fashion the question of political representation between elites and their followers.

Our procedure consists of taking the major preference patterns within each party, casting aside a small percentage of cases that do not fit easily into the major groupings, and examining the correspondence between these groups and the 1980 rank-and-file party identifiers. One way of viewing this procedure is to see it as a partial simulation of what would have happened had any particular constellation of elite activists come to dominate the party. It should be noted that we are not making any assumptions about what the attitudes of the delegate support groups might have been at the time when one or more of the candidacies being supported was in full bloom. Rather, the focus is on ideology as of 1981, at a point proximate to the survey of the mass public in the fall of 1980. Our concern here is simply this question: How close were the various support groups to rank-and-file partisans as of 1980? What sets of delegates qua political leaders would have best reflected the sentiments of party identifiers had they been in the ascendancy within the party?

We turn first to the somewhat simpler structure offered up by the Republicans. For present purposes the preference genealogies have been grouped into three primary patterns: (1) the consistent supporters of moderate candidates, essentially the Nixon, Ford, Bush lineage; (2) the delegates with mixed preferences, moving between moderate and conservative candidates, primarily between Ford and Reagan; (3) the consistent supporters of conservative candidates, basically the 1976 and 1980 Reagan backers.

As Figure 10.2 and Table 10.2 show, dramatic contrasts exist among the various preference groups, with correspondingly divergent similarities to the scores of Republican identifiers. With one exception, all of the candidate groupings are more conservative than the party followers on each of the four measures. (Both the mean scores and the sign of the correlation coefficient indicate that those consistent supporters of moderate candidates were less likely than rank-and-file identifiers to proclaim a conservative self-identity.) Aside from the near-unanimity of delegates on the candidate evaluation index, the scores become progressively more conservative as we move from delegates having a consistently moderate genealogy to those having been long-time Reagan backers. Although the consistent moderates are liberal by Republican standards, they are more conservative than party identifiers on all measures except self-placement on the liberal-conservative scale.

Turning to the correlations between the views of identifiers and candidate support groups (Table 10.2), we see striking contrasts. Congruence with respect to political issues and group evaluations varies remarkably according to which set of delegates is being considered. If the backers of moderate candidates had controlled the party, there would have been high similarity (little distance) between leaders and followers. The distance increases somewhat when mixed preferrers are considered and reaches a rather staggering magnitude with consistent Reagan supporters. Considering the fact that it is the latter who were by 1984 firmly entrenched as leaders of the Republican party organization, it is apparent that the leader-follower gap had grown accordingly. Backers of the conservative faction may have brought many qualities to the party, but close similarity to the political attitudes and preferences of the party's rank and file was not among those qualities.

Figure 10.2

Attitudes of All Republican Delegates and 1980 Identifiers, by Candidate Support Histories

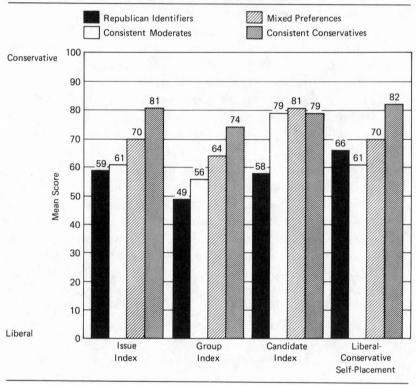

About 5 percent of the Republican delegates expressed a preference for Nixon in 1972 and failed to register any candidate preference during subsequent years. In light of Nixon's fate, it is interesting to note the essentially moderate positions of these Nixonites. They were closer to the party's base than were those backing conservatives and even those moving from the centrist Ford to the conservative Reagan. Indeed, they were closer to the rank and file than any other group with respect to candidate evaluations and indistinguishable (r = .02) from identifiers on the liberal-conservative self-placement scale. Whatever the ex-President's faults might have been they did not include a set of devotees seriously out of step with the party base.

Table 10.2

Differences Between All Republican Delegates and Their 1980 Party Identifiers, by Candidate Support Histories

	Consistent Moderates	Mixed Preferences	Consistent Conservatives
	(r)	(r)	(r)
Issue Index	.08	.32	.58
Group Index	.26	.52	.76
Candidate Index	.64	.69	.70
Liberal-Conservative Self-Placement	− .15	.10	.44

Notes: The larger the coefficient the greater the difference between delegates and identifiers.

Minus sign means negative correlation; delegates are more conservative than identifiers.

As usual, the Democrats present a somewhat more complicated candidate support picture, but one with a patterning that complements that on the Republican side (Figure 10.3 and Table 10.3). Again, it is possible to compress the myriad Democrat preference histories into a few manageable categories that take into account the number of cases and ideological flavor of the support groups without losing or obscuring any vital information. The five groupings used here are as follows: (1) consistent supporters of liberal candidates for the 1972–1980 period; (2) mixed left supporters, those who ultimately supported left-wing candidacies; (3) wavering left supporters, those who moved back and forth between traditional and liberal candidates before supporting Carter in 1980; (4) supporters of traditional candidates who switched to Carter; (5) Carter only supporters and disaffected traditionalists with no 1980 preference.

As with the Republicans, the Democratic mass partisans are always less ideologically extreme than their delegate representative. The correlations presented in Table 10.3 summarize the relationships between candidate factions and the party's rank and file. True to widespread belief, even in 1981 the hard-core left stood at a great distance from the party base. It is as though little had changed since 1972, when delegates of this persuasion were widely, and correctly, perceived as being far removed from everyday Demo-

Figure 10.3

**Attitudes of All Democratic Delegates and 1980 Identifiers,
by Candidate Support Histories**

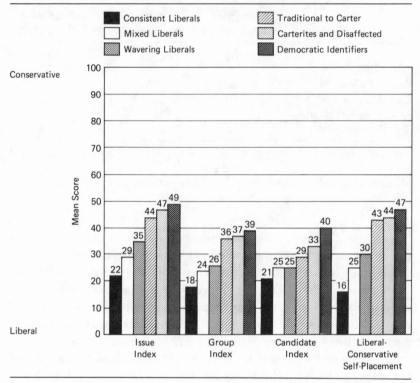

crats. So great is this distance that it approaches that found between
conservative Republicans and the GOP party base. Had the liberal
leaders remained in ascendancy, the 1972 gap between leaders and
led would have been maintained in 1980. As it turned out, new
centers of power developed during the Carter years, all of which
tended to be less distant from the party's constituency. In fact,
those mobilized into the Carter camp were virtually indistinguishable from rank-and-file Democratic identifiers with respect to issue preferences, group evaluations, and location on the liberal-
conservative scale, and they had only a modest gap in the realm of
candidate evaluations.

Table 10.3

Differences Between All Democratic Delegates and Their 1980 Party Identifiers, by Candidate Support Histories

	Consistent Liberals	Mixed Liberals	Wavering Liberals	Traditional to Carter	Carterites and Disaffected
	(r)	(r)	(r)	(r)	(r)
Issue Index	.59	.48	.36	.14	.06
Group Index	.69	.53	.46	.13	.07
Candidate Index	.60	.52	.52	.39	.21
Liberal-Conservative Self-Placement	.58	.47	.38	.10	.06

Note: The larger the coefficient the greater the difference between delegates and identifiers.

The Dual Effects of Circulation Patterns and Candidate Preferences

We saw in chapter 9 that two processes vitally affect the fit between the political attitudes of party elites and the rank-and-file supporters. One depends on the turnover of party personnel. Especially within the Republican party, both the newly mobilized and the disengaged delegates tended to be less distant from the party base. Those delegates who maintained involvement in presidential politics throughout the three presidential races proved to be the most distant from the rank and file. There is sound evidence to indicate, however, that they were more distant to begin with. Moreover, the second process affecting the linkage between the two strata—conversion or change of attitude at the level of individual delegates—appeared to move GOP core activists in a conservative direction and thus somewhat further away from the party base.

Overlaying these two processes—and in fact fueling them—were the evolving patterns of candidate preferences. We have just seen that these support patterns, of both a contemporary (1980) and a longer time interval (1972–1980), were also associated with substantial differences in the degree to which the elites achieved rapport with opinions and attitudes of the party base. In general, the more moderate the candidate preferences within the Republican party, the closer was the alignment with the party identifiers. Conversely, the more conservative the candidate preferences among the Democratic delegates, the closer was the tie with the party's base.

It is now time to consider how preference structures interact with other processes to affect linkages. Given the limitations of the data base, that will be difficult to do with respect to conversion effects, but the same limitation does not apply to circulation effects. Two basic questions can be asked. First, once we control for candidate preference genealogy, how large an impact does circulation continue to have on the proximity of leaders to party rank and file? Second, and alternatively, if we take into account circulation patterns, what is the contribution of candidate preference histories?

To answer these questions we present in Tables 10.4 and 10.5 the discrepancy scores (correlations by party status) according to participation histories within each of the major candidate preference groupings. By examining the results presented in these tables,

Table 10.4

Differences Between All Republican Delegates and 1980 Identifiers, by Circulation Patterns and Candidate Support Histories

	Liberal-Conservative Self-Placement	Issue Index	Group Index	Candidate Index	N
Consistent Moderates					
Continuously Active	−.12	.09	.29	.64	(378)
Disengaged	−.13	−.03	.15	.40	(55)
Mobilized	−.13	.02	.09	.32	(79)
Mixed Preferences					
Continuously Active	.13	.32	.54	.69	(442)
Disengaged	.03	.14	.30	.47	(79)
Mobilized	.13	.25	.40	.45	(91)
Consistent Conservatives					
Continuously Active	.44	.59	.77	.70	(727)
Disengaged	.17	.17	.34	.27	(25)
Mobilized	.36	.36	.66	.50	(176)

Notes: Entries are product-moment correlations (r); the larger the coefficient the greater the difference between delegates and identifiers. N equals the average number for delegate groupings across the four measurers. Ns for the identifiers range from 515 to 795. Minus sign means negative correlation; delegates are more liberal than identifiers.

Table 10.5

Proximity Between All Democratic Delegates and 1980 Identifiers, by Circulation Patterns and Candidate Support Histories

	Liberal-Conservative Self-Placement	Issue Index	Group Index	Candidate Index	N
Consistent Liberals					
Continuously Active	.55	.56	.67	.57	(253)
Disengaged	.41	.42	.48	.39	(71)
Mobilized	.18	.20	.25	.20	(23)
Mixed Liberals					
Continuously Active	.49	.49	.57	.53	(353)
Disengaged	.34	.38	.40	.37	(172)
Mobilized	.22	.23	.29	.25	(78)
Wavering Liberals					
Continuously Active	.37	.36	.47	.53	(425)
Disengaged	.22	.17	.23	.24	(65)
Mobilized	.27	.29	.39	.38	(174)
Traditional to Carter					
Continuously Active	.13	.18	.19	.44	(496)
Disengaged	+.02	+.04	+.11	.02	(40)
Mobilized	.03	.08	.06	.27	(206)
Carterites and Alienated					
Continuously Active	.11	.12	.17	.27	(212)
Disengaged	+.03	+.09	+.09	+.05	(67)
Mobilized	.01	.06	.02	.22	(114)

Notes: Entries are product-moment correlations (r); the larger the coefficient the greater the difference between delegates and identifiers. N equals the average number for delegate groupings across the four measures. Ns for the identifiers range from 377 to 519.
Plus sign means positive correlation; delegates are more conservative than identifiers.

it is possible to assess the dual effects of campaign histories and preferences. Based on our prior analysis of each characteristic, and assuming additive effects, within each cluster of candidate preferences we should find the continuously active to be the least proximate to the party's rank and file. The scores attached to the disengaged and the newly mobilized may be expected to vary by party but should always reflect closer linkage to the party's identifiers. The effect of candidate preference groupings can be gauged by comparing the scores of delegates with the same campaign histories across the various preference groupings. If these scores differ systematically, evidence accumulates for the importance of candidate preferences as a key element in mass-elite linkages.

If we turn first to the simpler structure of the Republican party (Table 10.4), we find that the results provide striking support for the presence of both circulation and preference effects. Continuously active delegates within each candidate support pattern were virtually always the most removed from their party's rank and file. The only clear exceptions to that generalization are with respect to self-placement on the liberal-conservative scale, where participation histories make for no difference among the consistent moderates and only marginally so among those with mixed or conservative preferences. As for policy issues, the differences between the continuously active and the two categories of circulating participants were the greatest among the consistent conservatives, differences occasioned by the extraordinary distance found between the continuously active consistent conservatives and the party's rank and file. But the consistent conservatives merely exaggerate a common tendency. On balance, regardless of preference genealogy, the hard-core activists represented the more conservative segment of each grouping. The consequence was persistently less similarity between the continuously active elites and the masses.

Similarity as a measure of representativeness also varies dramatically according to candidate support groupings. With a couple of exceptions, the pattern is uniform. Holding constant participation history, the distance between delegates and identifiers increases dramatically as one moves from consistent moderates to mixed preferrers and on to consistent conservatives. Because the continuously active compose a disproportionate share of each preference grouping, it is especially important to note their different scores. For example, among the continuously active delegates, the consistent moderates were virtually indistinguishable from the rank and file with respect to issue index scores (r = .09). The gap increases for those with mixed preferences (r = .32), and reaches a high with the consistent conservatives (r = .59). This pattern tends to hold equally well for the disengaged and the mobilized. Thus, among those mobilized after 1976, dissimilarity on the group index increases from .09 to .40 to .66 across the three candidate preference groups.

A similar tendency prevails among the disengaged. However, although both the disengaged and the mobilized delegates were generally more in harmony with the rank and file, that was much less true of the mobilized in the camps of consistent conservatives and those with mixed preferences. Particularly where the consistent conservatives were concerned, the disengaged, not the mobilized, provided the sharpest contrast to the discontinuity between the mass and the core activists. Consequently, given the fact that the disengaged were outnumbered by the mobilized in both of these preference groups, the net effect of the personnel exchange was to decrease the linkage between delegates and followers in both the mixed preference and conservative groups.

Exactly the opposite pattern of differences held among the supporters of moderate Republican candidates. Quite ironically, in the wing of the party that was once dominant in the choice of party leaders, the recruitment processes that would have produced greater representativeness were overwhelmed by the processes of disengagement. Consequently, even though the newly mobilized were more representative of mass preferences, their limited numbers placed a sharp restriction on their contribution to keeping the party elite in touch with its mass base.

An especially intriguing aspect of the Republican dynamics rests in the comparison of the three groups of mobilized delegates. Contrary to popular impressions, the recently mobilized Reaganites were not quite as distant from the party's identifiers as were their continuously active colleagues. Moreover, this recently mobilized Republican elite contains a visible number of consistent moderates. These moderates were quite close to the party's base in an absolute sense. Thus, the Republicans, through 1980 at any rate, continued to attract a cadre of activists who remained very much in ideological touch with the rank and file. From the linkage perspective, however, the problem was, again, one of numbers. As shown by the numbers of cases in Table 10.4, the conservatives outnumber the newly mobilized consistent moderates by more than two to one. Circulation dynamics within the party had the net effect of increasing the gap between activists and followers.

On the Democratic side (Table 10.5), the results are not necessarily more complex despite the greater number of identifiable candidate support groups to be compared. Rather, the general contours are much the same as in the Republican case. Regardless of candidate preference history, the continuously active always stood further away from the rank and file than did the disengaged and the mobilized within the same grouping. If anything, the pattern here is even more regular than it is among the Republicans. Sustained activism, regardless of candidate preference, had the somewhat perverse result of widening the gap between leaders and led.

Similarity between the parties also extends to the persistent ordering of candidate support groupings. The effects are clearest among the continuously active, who compose by far the largest slice of all the delegates. As we read down Table 10.5, a clear monotonic pattern emerges. At one extreme the hard-core activists among consistent liberal supporters are far removed from the ideology of the party base. At the other extreme, the Carterites and disaffected are relatively close to the mass base. The same pattern holds among the disengaged. They stand universally closer to the rank and file than do the continuously active, but their proximity also increases with the movement from support groups on the far left to the center. Clearly, then, the delegates' attachments to various candidates within the party have an effect over and above the delegates' activity patterns.

Because the fluid portion of the activity histories concerns both the disengaged and the mobilized, comparisons between these two categories within preference grouping again warrant special attention. Preference and activity patterns interact with each other in each party and produce parallel variation in the linkage between delegates and identifiers. Among the two most liberal Democratic preference blocs (just as with the most liberal of the Republican groups), the recently mobilized were closer to the rank and file than were the disengaged. If the proportions involved had been the same, the exchange of the disengaged for the mobilized would have resulted in a substantial gain in similarity as old activists on the left moved out and new ones moved in. As it turns out, just as among the Republicans, the disengaged outnumbered the recruits in the left blocs, so the overall result was not as dramatic as it might have been.

The picture within the other three preference groups is remarkably like that witnessed among the more conservative Republican groupings. Among the so-called wavering new liberal supporters the recently mobilized were clearly *less* proximate to the
rank and file than were the disengaged. There is also little question
of the greater propinquity of the disengaged on the candidate
evaluation index among the two most conservative support groupings. Although there was essentially no difference in proximity
between the disengaged and the mobilized on the other three measures, the contributions of the newly mobilized in the two most
conservative Democratic groups did not offset the loss of representation stemming from disengagement.

Overall, then the dynamics were a bit more complicated in the
Democratic party, especially with respect to the place of the recently mobilized among the less liberal candidate support groupings. Nevertheless it seems appropriate to note that the dynamics of
personnel circulation produced parallel results. In both parties the
declining factions mobilized activists who were more representative of the parties' mass supporters than were those who disengaged from participation in the campaign elite. Among the Democrats, however, the trade-off in sheer numerical strength prevented
the mobilized from making a significant contribution to elite representation of mass opinions. In the ascendant factions of both parties
the mobilized were either clearly less in tune with party rank and
file or no more representative than the disengaged. In the Republican party the net result was to diminish the representatives of the
elite activists. When coupled with the earlier evidence of individual levels of change in elite attitudes between 1972 and 1980, the
picture is one in which all of the various processes involved in the
transition of leadership in the Republican party have contributed to
a potentially troublesome widening of the gap between the active
elite and the many Republican identifiers. As of 1980 the Republican party was suffering the same absence of elite-mass rapport that
had troubled the Democratic party eight years earlier.

In the Democratic case, however, there was no personable,
attractive leader to command popular votes and thereby obscure
the lack of representativeness in elite attitudes (nor were the Democrats of 1972 blessed with facing an incumbent president who was
widely perceived as being ineffective). The rift between party leaders and their constituents that was created by the liberal Democratic triumph of 1972 led, instead, to a continuing search for new

leadership. That search did produce a nominee, Carter, whose supporters were in much closer rapport with the party's rank and file. But, as we have noted before, rapport between mass and elite certainly does not guarantee electoral support—witness the Carter defeat of 1980—nor does the absence of rapport necessarily spell electoral defeat, as Reagan can now testify.

Both the circulation of campaign activists and the shifting fortunes of their leaders play a role in fixing the relationship between party elites and followers. The personal and structural forces retaining certain individuals in the campaign elite, while pushing others out and pulling still others in, have a great bearing on how well the elites represent the ideological preferences of the party's followers. By the same token, the fortunes and misfortunes of presidential aspirants produce presidential elites that vary tremendously in the degree to which they mirror the preferences of their followers. The sum total of these two processes during the 1970s was to produce a Republican elite more estranged from its rank and file that it had been at the start of the decade, whereas the effect was to leave the Democratic elite at about the same distance from the party base, a substantial distance created by the successful challenge for party leadership in 1972. While the outcomes were thus different for the two parties, our analysis suggests that the processes at work within each party were rather similar.

Perhaps the largest message of this latter phase of our analysis is that the worlds of elite politics and mass politics can be very different worlds, indeed. The liberal forces of the Democratic left may have both apprehended and helped create a national swing to the left between 1968 and 1972. But they overestimated the scope of that swing and the delegates nominated in the name of McGovern were dramatically more liberal than their nominal followers, the Democratic rank and file.[3] Eight years later an equally mild national jog to the right was signaled by, or was the signal for, a rather massive surge of Republican party leadership to the right.[4] Success in the quest for nomination, and then election, produced the dominant set of Reagan supporters among the Republican campaign elite who were as much out of step with their mass supporters as the McGovernites had been with theirs.

[3] Warren E. Miller and Teresa E. Levitin, *Leadership and Change* (Cambridge, MA: Winthrop, 1976).

[4] Warren E. Miller and Merrill J. Shanks, "Policy Directions and Presidential Leadership: Alternative Interpretations of the 1980 Presidential Election," *British Journal of Political Science* 12 (July 1982): 299–356.

CHAPTER 11

A Summing Up

Continuity and Change in Party Elites

Political parties, like most organizations, are made up of both stable and variable elements. Because presidential parties are focused on the selection and election of a presidential candidate they, probably more than most party units, are destined to remain in flux as constitutional constraints and the dynamics of social and economic change produce an ebb and flow in the fortunes of various presidential aspirants. Particularly in a time in which party leadership and possibly the foundations of the party system are in transition, it is difficult to understand and to assess the highlights associated with individual nominating conventions, or even individual elections, when they are examined separately. Descriptions of the parties based on analyses of the composition, proceedings, and outcomes of the 1972 Democratic convention in Miami, or the 1964 Republican conclave in San Francisco, would properly portray the parties in the throes of radical transformation. Conversely, the Democrats nominating Johnson in 1964 or the Republicans acclaiming Nixon in 1972 would suggest the dynamic tranquillity of stable and unified parties. Neither the analyses of the Democratic landslide of 1964 nor the Nixon sweep in 1972 forecast the reversals in party fortunes that occurred in 1968 and 1976. The limitations inherent in such snapshot perspectives lie in the analytic exclusion of history and context. A single convention, and its participants, captures only part of the action and a portion of the actors in what is in reality a much larger array of interconnected scenes in the ongoing drama of presidential politics. A more inclusive analytic definition of the actors and their stage that includes many more campaign activists in an extended time period covering a series of campaigns and elections leads to a more adequate rendering of the continuity and change that occurs among party elites.

A central feature of our analytic strategy was anticipated by the study design. In that design, convention delegates, often taken to represent presidential party elites, were treated as campaign activists (not as decision-makers in the nominating process), and their history of participation in past campaigns became a major factor in our analysis. With the explicit introduction of the temporal dimension it became evident that party elites change in two fundamental ways: circulation and conversion. Most familiarly, elites change by a process of circulation or turnover—the replacement of "old" members with new ones. Some versions of circulation effects emphasize the contraction or expansion of elites. Successful challenges by insurgents, the effects of "normal" competition, voluntary withdrawals, and rule changes are all means by which alterations occur through circulation processes.

Our measures of circulation took advantage of the design and data collection features of the study. Whereas most studies of convention delegates use the single convention cohort and subdivisions thereof as the focal points of their analysis, we took a different tack. On occasion, to be sure, the full cohorts for each convention became the objects of analysis. Our more common strategy, however, consisted of aggregating cohort-specific delegates according to commonalities in their presidential campaign histories from 1972 through 1980. This produced the familiar tripartite division: those delegates who had been active throughout the period, those who had dropped out of presidential politics after 1972, and those who had been mobilized subsequent to the 1972 election. Because each convention does symbolize a unique gathering and configuration of forces, we often also attempted to isolate the unique as we divided the continuously active delegates into the specific cohorts to which they were attached (that is, defined by the first convention attended during this period).

In effect, our division permitted a measure of circulation into and out of two elite party bodies. Not only did this division help meet the goal of providing a nonstatic perspective, but it also served to shift the focus away from delegates qua delegates to concentrate on their roles as presidential campaign activists. Our approach was dictated by a recognition of the fact that attending a convention, though not at all unimportant, is but one act in the life of presidential campaign activists. What happens prior to and subsequent to a given convention, and across a series of presidential elections, defines more completely the composition and nature of presidential party elites.

A signal contribution of the present inquiry is the demonstration that, even in a time of massive change, the large majority of delegates are hard-core, quadrennial campaign participants. They are not one-timers, drawn only by the uniqueness of a given year. These hard-core activists tend to be the most loyal, the most devout, the most party-oriented, and the most at odds with the opposition party. Since the continuously active delegates exemplify many of the core elements of what the party stands for and what it presents to the public, they are in general a conserving force in the evolution of parties.

Nevertheless, parties do change in complexion, although typically at a slower rate than the drama of a particularly emotional presidential year might convey. As Kessell has said in another context, and based on party activists from an earlier era and on a different level than convention delegates: "A presidential party at any time is a residue of its past campaigns. . . . A party is never completely taken over by the new arrivals who come into politics in a given campaign, but it never goes back to being what it was before that campaign either."[1]

Circulation is one prime source of change. A second source of change in political elites, as in the political mass, takes the form of alteration or conversion *within* the individual elite participants themselves. Here the complexion of the elites alters because individual members change their attitudes or behaviors in a given direction and produce a shift in the body as a whole. Longitudinal or

[1] John H. Kessel, *Presidential Parties* (Homewood, IL: Dorsey Press, 1984), pp. 322, 323.

quasi-longitudinal data at the level of individual actions, as distinct
from data pertaining to cohorts as collective wholes, are necessary
for locating these conversion processes. Thanks to our pseudo-
panel data, built up from apparently reliable recollections, as well
as our true panel data from the 1972 cohort, we were able at several
points to ascertain the workings of conversion as well as replacement in assessing change and continuity within these party elites.

Much of the change that we observed, in fact, came about as a
result of individual-level change or, as we called it, conversion.
Most generally the conversion was in accordance with the secular
winds of change sweeping over the party and inspired by events
both internal and external to the party. Hence, a fundamental point:
Party elites can change in outlook and behavior even in the absence
of turnover in personnel. Given the fact that studies of adult citizens have shown the presence of malleability with respect to basic
political orientations, we should perhaps not be surprised that party
activists are not impervious to change, their elitism notwithstanding. Thus, the rightward drift of the Republican party overall could
be expected to occur at the individual level among the continuously active delegates from the 1972 cohort. Similarly, the increased emphasis on party welfare compared with other goals could
be anticipated among the continuously active Democratic delegates from the 1972 cohort, as well as in the concerns of the 1976
and 1980 delegates. By the "laws" of human inertia and conserva-
tion it is undoubtedly more difficult (*ceteris paribus*) to achieve
change through conversion than through replacement. As our results amply demonstrate, though, the place of reorientation among
existing elite members should not be overlooked in studying transitions in leadership.

If persistent, continuous involvement does not preclude alterations among party activists, a parallel holds with respect to the
circulation process. Replacement and turnover do not necessarily
yield political movement. When existing activists are replaced with
look-alikes, then clearly the amount of net change will be negligible.

One could imagine such outcomes in systems with tightly controlled succession rules and practices and in political eras marked
by high consensus. The nature of presidential campaign politics in
the United States tends to work in the other direction. The battles
for within-party control, the candidate-driven politics of national
conventions, and the larger, changing political landscape encour-

age and occasionally force the withdrawal of quite distinctive elements of the party. Their places, in turn, are occupied by recruits often embodying newer forces at work.[2] Illustratively, the newly mobilized among *both* parties in our study tended to be more conservative than their disengaged colleagues, a reflection of broader currents at work in American society. Moreover, we should not view these push-pull forces and what lies behind them as unique to the contemporary period. Even a casual reading of American political party history offers up numerous examples of how organizational battles, competing candidacies, and external events have led to consequential turnover patterns among party elites.

In addition to affecting the internal composition of the parties, the circulation process has external consequences as well. During the period of this study, interparty differences among the deactivated delegates, while still substantial, were fewer and lesser than among the continuously active and the recently mobilized. Adherents of strong party differences may applaud this outcome as it purifies the parties, while those favoring a politics of moderation may look less favorably on such outcomes.

A similar set of consequences was observed in the area of linkage between campaign elites and the party base. Disengaged Republicans stood closer to their rank and file than did the consistent actives or (usually) the new additions to the party. By the same token, disengaged Democrats also resembled their party followers more than did their far more numerous continuously active colleagues. Circulation, therefore, generated external consequences of some moment in addition to the within-party effects. Beyond these effects, circulation patterns, when combined with candidate preference patterns, worked to produce varying results, sometimes accelerating net party shifts and sometimes retarding them.

Interparty Similarities and the Party System

Yet another consequence of our basic study design is that our analyses of continuity and change in the presidential party elites treat both parties rather even-handedly. The natural result is a dis-

[2] The contrast with the frequent fate of the congressional parties is marked. Seniority rules combine with turnover to mark the nature of change. Presidential party is not constrained in this fashion. We thank John Kessel for bringing this point to our attention.

cussion that has a dual emphasis on interparty comparisons and intraparty dynamics. This seems particularly instructive and helpful at a time in which it is tempting to dwell on those occurrences that are more or less unique to each party. Our analyses have, indeed, reaffirmed the rather singular impact of presidential selection reforms on the Democratic party, as well as the unique experience of a political triumph for a modern-day ideological movement within the Republican party. Nevertheless, we have also observed many instances of parallel development within the two parties.

In particular, this has meant that we could determine where similar processes were at work within each party, where there are certain apparently inherent properties of political parties that drive them to similar developments and configurations although the particulars vary considerably. The presence of observations on both parties also enabled us to assess their reactions to a changing national political environment common to both parties. Knowing if and how one party behaves in response to a changing environment acquires much more meaning when laid alongside the simultaneous development within the opposition party. Finally, having comparable data on both parties over time has made it possible to study their positions relative to each other in the combative sense. Parties exist in a dynamic, adversarial relationship with each other. The face they present to each other and to the electorate for which they are competing is conditioned, in part, by the appearance of the other party. Thus, a shift in the ideological makeup of one party assumes a different meaning, depending upon whether the opposite party is moving in the same, or a different, direction.

Although we have not taken the concept of the two-party system as an organizing rubric for our analysis, we have noted much evidence that there is, indeed, a structure of interrelated parts that seems to reflect systemic attributes. This is true in the extent to which the parties are alike in their responses to party leadership, alike in their elites' convergence on the desirability of instrumental goals, and alike in the extent to which processes of conversion and replacement make similar contributions to change over time within both parties.

The symmetry of our interest in the two major parties also laid the foundation for strong conclusions about the pervasiveness of ideological differences between the two parties—differences sustained by the parallel processes in each party governing the circulation of party elites. The same parallelism emphasized the comparability of intraparty schisms. Not only is each party rent by ideological conflict, but both pairs of factions disagree as to the importance of party qua party and ideology as represented by public policy alternatives.

At the same time, the uniformity of our research operation regarding each party places each elite's dominant preferences in contrast with those of the other party. Thus, we can see the extent to which Republicans are more inclined than Democrats to affirm the centrality of partisan concerns in the nomination process *and* the extent to which the very question of centrality is a matter of sharper controversy among Democratic factions than between the major Republican factions. In like manner we can note that while the Democratic elite was more likely than the Republican elite to emphasize the centrality of policy positions in the nominating process, the two sets of party elites were equally sharply divided internally over the same questions.

At a different time and under different circumstances the many parallelisms and symmetries that made the party elites resemble each other in so many ways in the period from 1972 to 1980 may not have existed. If so, it seems all the more remarkable that our sense of interparty similarities is borne of the epoch in which party reform and the transitions in party leadership were being treated so very differently by the two parties.

Factions, Coalitions, and Intraparty Tensions

Another analytic strategy facilitated by our overall approach lay in our emphasis on candidate-preference groupings and the effects of the interaction between patterns of candidate preference and the tripartite division of campaign activity patterns. Paying attention to candidate-preference groups is not, of course, a novelty in the study of presidential elites. What is unique is the capacity to construct preference genealogies across a series of presidential elections. The longer view afforded by three elections enable us to chronicle the rise and fall of several candidacies, and the lineage associated with these movements, within this group of party activists. It also enables us to link fundamental and long-term coalitions within each party to such phenomena as political ideology, goal orientations and motivations, and the representation of rank-and-file preferences.

James MacGregor Burns has said:

> If the fundamental party conflict is that between parties contending for power, also significant and often more illuminating are the conflicts *within* parties. Any party of size is an aggregate of group interests embracing all the conflict endemic to groups. . . . As a widely based organization the party is rent also by competing regional interests and by parochial elements rebelling against centrist direction. As a staging area for present and future leaders the party attracts the politically ambitious; as an organization girded for perpetual battle it attracts the combative; as a visibly power-seeking enterprise it attracts both the pragmatic and the ideological, both the moderate and the extremist. Along the lines of such conflicts power within the party is channeled and distributed, creating transactional structures of political leadership.[3]

Both the Republican and Democratic parties have provided sterling evidence of intraparty divisions in the post–World War II period. A struggle between moderates and conservatives, overlaid with regional and style considerations, has characterized the Republican party throughout the entire period. The Democrats' internal divisions following the long Roosevelt reign were perhaps more episodic and less structured until the 1968 nomination campaign. That campaign ushered in an era of conflict, angst, and mandated reform seldom equaled in American political history.

Our results do little to undermine the contention that the schisms within parties—while not as great as those across parties—are deep, pervasive, and less easily handled than the more institutionalized conflict across party lines. The jumping-off point for our analysis of intraparty conflict was the recognition that, especially in the modern era, candidate-preference groupings come to represent coalitions and factions within the parties and that these factions, while stable in many respects, are also susceptible to challenge and change.[4]

Partly because of the fortunes of recent presidential elections

---

[3] James MacGregor Burns, *Leadership* (New York: Harper & Row, 1978), p. 311.
[4] The most cogent contemporary analysis of party factionalism and party reform is presented by Austin Ranney in *Curing the Mischiefs of Faction* (Berkeley: University of California Press, 1975).

and partly because it is essentially a more homogeneous party, the coalitional structures of the Republican party were simpler than those of the Democratic party. At most we could identify six distinctive genealogies within the GOP, a number which was fairly easily reduced to three or two without great loss of information. If the Democratic party was not a party in disarray, it was at least a many-splendored thing from the late 1960s through most of the 1970s. Democratic activists displayed a great variety of candidate-preference patterns, with twelve of the patterns having enough adherents to warrant at least initial analysis. It also proved more difficult to reduce these diverse genealogies into a more manageable number for purpose of analysis, but such reductions fortunately proved to be workable in terms of identifying a basic liberal-moderate split within the party.

It will be remembered, however, that we did not dwell on Jimmy Carter's role in shaping or reshaping Democratic factions. His candidacy, both in 1976 and in 1980, was treated largely as an alternative choice that intruded on the basic liberal-moderate split among the Democratic elite. In retrospect it seems likely that his presence was even more disruptive for the Democrats' redefinition of party and party leadership than it was for our analysis scheme. We could use his candidacy as an analytic foil with which to identify a continuing intraparty conflict, with Kennedy as the symbolic leader on the left. In larger fact, Carter was a major intrusion on the Democratic attempt to redefine the party and reestablish the meaning of the enduring party factions. In his outsider's appeal to the electorate he was explicitly anti party-establishment; in his conduct of the presidency he turned Lyndon Johnson's vow to be a president of all the people into a demonstration of an unremitting lack of regard for or understanding of his own party.

Carter and his personal followers were not representative of a party faction as McGovern had been. Carter did not represent a "movement" or a cause—only an alternative to apparent losers. It may be that subsequent investigation will disclose that Carterites—as with McGovernites before them—have been "socialized" into the role of party elites and, as with the 1972 cohort members who have remained active, have adapted to the norms of the party. Unless that is unmistakably and powerfully the case, the 1976 experiment with a true outsider may have done little for the cause of Democratic party reform, and even less for the redefinition of party image and the reaffirmation of party legitimacy.

In general, however, candidate support groups differed widely in terms of issue orientations and group evaluations, our main measures of political ideology. The coalitions we observed were not simply the result of certain candidates exuding great personal charm, or of party or interest group leaders playing the role of power brokers. Rather, the groupings stand for basic divisions of thought about matters of public policy and the political process. Like-minded campaign activists, mainly through a process of self-selection, gather around attractive candidates who ostensibly share their ideological views.

Interestingly enough, intraparty variation among the stable core of Republican participants was fully as sharp as among their Democratic counterparts, even though the GOP coalition configurations were less numerous and less complicated. However, a key difference between the parties was that the ideological differences were much more substantial among the disengaged Democrats than among comparable Republicans, this in large part because the Republican dropouts during the 1970s were concentrated among the moderates, whereas the Democrats lost participants throughout a wide spectrum of candidate coalitions. It is also the case that as time passed the links between candidate factions and ideological orientations became less evident within the Democratic party, while tending to increase within the Republican party. To some extent, then, the parties switched positions from the beginning of the decade to the end. The ascendancy of Reaganism in the GOP seems to have woven the tighter connection between candidate coalition and ideology in much the same way that the New Left challenges of 1968 and 1972 produced the same results in the Democratic party during an earlier era.

Mass-Elite Linkages

One of the most important consequences of shifting coalitional strength within the parties lies in the area of political representation. Because the campaign supporters associated with different candidates also tend to line up behind different issue positions, the ideological fit between campaign activists (delegates) and rank-and-file partisans tends to vary with the ascendancy of one coalition or another. Rather curious results can occur in the process. When McGovern lost so decisively in 1972, the sharp discrepancy between the Democratic delegates and Democratic followers was widely cited as indicative of how distant the dominant elite and its candidate were from their party base and, by inference, how such a distance must translate into defeat at the polls. However, our results for 1980 reveal that the 1980 GOP delegates were, on average, even further removed from their party base than were the Democratic delegates from theirs. Yet Reagan won in smashing style.

Short-term electoral success obviously depends on much more than the ideological distance between party elites and party rank and file. And subsequently it may be that a party's followers will catch up with its leaders, as is obviously the hope of the ascendant Republican conservative coalition. It may also be that a winning nomination coalition has to move back toward its party base, as happened to some extent with the liberal Democrats of 1972.

None of these considerations should obscure the fact that the likelihood of adequate representation of rank-and-file preferences by campaign activists depends very much on long-term coalition strength as composed of the candidate support groupings. To the extent that conventions and campaign elites perform a representative function—and it is widely believed that they do, or at least should do so—the role of factional strength is absolutely crucial. Illustratively, even though Republican followers' issue orientations were not necessarily well served by the winning coalition of 1980, a substantial part of the 1980 campaign elite was composed of more moderately inclined participants who did, in fact, come closer to giving their followers "attitudinal" representation. These more moderate activists must have contributed, in a variety of ways, to giving the campaign a different tone than it would otherwise have had, especially in the states and localities. We are now acutely aware that a campaign elite, and hence the basis of representation, extends well beyond the set composed of the winning elite at the most recent convention and beyond the confines of any single convention.

At the same time we have only begun to understand the tightening and loosening of the bonds between political representatives and the represented. In 1972 the McGovern campaign apparently overestimated the extent of the national drift to the left. Nevertheless, despite the accompanying landslide victory for their opponents and subsequent indications on many fronts of a national reaction and swing to the right, the members of the 1972 McGovern cohort who remained active in Democratic presidential politics in 1980 also remained unrepentant and apparently uninstructed as to the errors of their ways, staunchly liberal in their policy commitments in the latter year. At that same time the Reaganites of the Republican party won the nomination and the election, even though they were even more removed from the ideological center of their electoral support than the McGovernites had been from theirs. And, although our data do not follow events after 1980, it appears that the Republican right held fast to their beliefs, as had the McGovernites before them, albeit with less pressure to change, given the public evidence in the election returns indicating that their presumed mandate of 1980 was indeed renewed in 1984. At the very least, the repeated evidence of the lack of elite rapport with a mass electoral base reveals a certain looseness or weakness in the institutional linkage that is supposed to ensure representation of mass demands through the workings of the competitive two-party system. At best the electoral success of the Reagan administration provides a unique opportunity for a future study of the consequences of their concerted effort to exercise leadership in reshaping national mass-policy preferences.

More generally, even an eight-year time span now seems too brief for the mapping of the dynamics of mass-elite linkages through national party politics. The period of our study was a period of volatile and almost cataclysmic change for the party elites. As of the 1980 election it was not clear that changes of even remotely comparable magnitude had taken place in the electorate at large. And it was certainly not clear what was cause and what was effect for those changes that did seem imminent if not actual. At least it was not as clear to the academic student of politics as to many observers who are themselves as deeply committed as are the principal participants.

The worlds of political action (and political reporting) are sustained by convictions (or myths) concerning the effects of political decisions and political acts; the world of political research is sustained in fair part by the challenge of testing many of those convictions and demonstrating their errors. Every effect may have a cause; but it often turns out that the cause is not that heralded by the politicians, and many actions intended to be causes do not have their predicted effects at all. In earlier arguments we demonstrated that changes in representation between 1972 and 1980 seemed not to be the product of change at the mass level, but only on the part of the elites. The evidence was fragmentary and left the specification of conditions that maximize or minimize, increase or decrease representation to some unspecified future. From our other and related programs of research we carry an impression that mass preferences and behavior change with almost glacial slowness over time, and seldom at the pace implied by much elite rhetoric. We do believe that political leadership can influence and shape mass attitudes and preferences but we also believe that specific acts of leadership are often inaccurately appraised because of elite misperceptions of what is thought to be mass response.[5]

We would now move beyond the guess that, in the short run, the different degrees to which the various party factions "represent" the values and interests of their party's followers are more the consequences of accidental fits or misfits of ideological convictions than they are the product of leaders' anticipatory reactions or their powers as political persuaders. We would also hazard the observation that we need to know more about the ways in which conversion and circulation of elite personnel produce *intended* change in the representational relationship as the process of presidential selection determines party as well as national political leadership. Jimmy Carter may not have contributed much to the redefinition of the nature of the Democratic party, but the relative conservatism of his supporters in the party elite enhanced elite representation of the voices of rank-and-file Democrats. Institutions intended to produce representational rapport between elites and masses clearly cannot guarantee the outcome, but our analysis at least suggests an approach with which to study the process.

Whither the Parties

A nagging, persistent concern of observers of the American political scene for some time has been the apparent atrophying of political parties, and of the party system in general. As Leon Epstein points out, political scientists who study parties tend to have a positive bias in favor of healthy political parties as the key inter-

[5] Philip E. Converse, Aage R. Clausen, and Warren E. Miller, "Electoral Myth and Reality: The 1964 Election," *American Political Science Review* 59 (June 1965): 321–36.

mediary between mass publics and elites. "There may be some quarrel with the adequacy of the intellectual case that political scientists expound in behalf of parties in a democratic society, but there should be no doubt about its widespread scholarly acceptance."[6] And with respect to electoral politics in particular: "Even while acknowledging an association of independent voting and high educational levels and thus a modernity about party switching and split-ticket ballots, political scientists rarely see virtues in weaker electoral parties."[7] Finally, with more of an organizational perspective: "The relative *ineffectiveness* [emphasis in the original] of contemporary American parties is now our field's principal concern."[8]

Never seen as strong in the classical responsible parties mold reputed to characterize many European democracies, American political parties have recently been described as being in a state of decomposition, decline, decay, disarray, and dealignment. One has to look rather hard for positive terms. The list of culprits and consequences is familiar—lack of partisan loyalties at the mass public level; candidate-centered campaigns; failing discipline in legislative bodies; package-oriented, media-driven politics; the increased use of primaries in the presidential nomination process; the influx of enormous sums of money via political action committees that circumvent the parties; and the decreased visibility of elected officials in some key party settings such as national conventions.

Several antidotes to these symptoms have been more recently advanced. Especially impressive as a counterprognosis is the argument, with evidence, that parties as organizations have improved remarkably at the state level and at the level of the two respective national committees and their allied campaign committees.[9] Al-

[6] Leon D. Epstein, "The Scholarly Commitment to Parties," in Ada W. Finifter, ed., *Political Science: The State of the Discipline* (Washington, DC: American Political Science Association, 1983), p. 131.

[7] Epstein, "The Scholarly Commitment to Parties," p. 141.

[8] Epstein, "The Scholarly Commitment to Parties," p. 146.

[9] See John F. Bibby, "Party Renewal in the National Republican Party," in Gerald M. Pomper, ed., *Party Renewal in America* (New York: Praeger, 1980); Cornelius P. Cotter and John F. Bibby, "Institutional Development of Parties and the Thesis of Party Decline," *Political Science Quarterly* 95 (Spring 1980): 1–27; David E. Price, *Bringing Back the Parties* (Washington, DC: Congressional Quarterly, 1984), pp. 32–46; and Cornelius P. Cotter, James L. Gibson, John F. Bibby, and Robert J. Huckshorn, *Party Organization in American Politics* (New York: Praeger, 1984).

though the Republican party has taken the longest strides toward a more centralized and resource-rich role for the party organization, the Democratic party is also trying to move in that direction. At the mass electoral level, it is apparent that the move away from partisan affiliation and toward independence had already bottomed out several years ago. Moreover, without moving into a longish discussion of what is still an ambiguous outcome, it is apparent that a fundamental shift has been occurring in the base of the two respective parties, accelerated in part by two successful Reagan campaigns for the presidency.[10] These and other developments suggest that the "party" is far from over, although the party of the future will undoubtedly be different in several essentials.

What does our study contribute to this large-scale worry about the fate of American political parties? The answers are multifold and reflect the complexity of presidential party politics and the currents at work during the 1970s and early 1980s. If one takes as an indicator of viable parties the holding of distinctive policy orientations among the activist strata, then surely the parties are in robust health. It has by now become something of a truism to note that American party elites differ rather sharply in an ideological way, especially as reflected in their stands on issues of the day and in their identification with groups and actors aligned with different political priorities. Contrary to the observations of such scholarly observers as Duverger[11] and the attributions often encountered in the mass electorate, party elites in America are remarkably divergent.

Beyond documenting and extending the temporal basis for the cleavages found between party elites, our results add an important new element. Not only did the interparty differences remain intact over the decade, they actually expanded among our band of activists. Polarization thus increased despite the fact that the 1972 Democrats had seemed, at that time, to embody ideological outliers who created an interparty gap of unique proportions. Not so, because by 1980 the distance separating the campaign activists was by all accounts wider than it had been in the early 1970s. The increasing ideological distance was achieved by both circulation and conver-

---

[10] See, for example, various pieces of evidence in "The 1984 Election Results," *Public Opinion* 8 (December-January 1985): 23–42.

[11] Maurice Duverger, *Political Parties* (New York: Wiley, 1954).

sion processes, with much of the shift being fueled by the increasing conservatism of Republican activists. How long this heightened level of interparty contrasts in presidential politics will persist is problematic. Certainly the impression emerging from the 1984 conventions and campaigns suggests no diminution in this gap during the near future.

Another indicator of party saliency and resilience takes the form of the incentives for involvement in politics and the goals to be maximized at the nominating conventions. Here the results suggest party vitality because of the general *similarity,* rather than dissimilarity, between the two parties. It is a similarity that highlights the role of party enhancement as a goal to be achieved in convention politics. Of the various goals which could be sought, divided between those stressing policies on the one hand and party on the other, an emphasis on party clearly emerged as important as, if not more important than, an emphasis on policy. Moreover, the Democratic party—widely suspected of harboring antiparty elements in its midst during the early 1970s—increased its concern about party between 1972 and 1980. Similarly, an interest in party emerged as a prime incentive for personal political involvement, far outweighing the solidary and personal rewards, and standing at least on a par with policy concern as a motivation for involvement.

Finally, subjective attachment to party remains high among the elite activists. Significantly, the Democratic party enjoyed sharp gains across time, as assessed by looking at progressive cohorts. The 1980 cohort very nearly matched the typically high levels of party attachment evinced by Republicans. Indeed, the newly mobilized Democrats were as fully attached to their party as were their GOP counterparts. Moreover, strength of party attachment within each party was related to positive evaluations of party standard-bearers, the quadrennial embodiments of what the party strives to represent. If party were declining as a reference point, then levels of subjective attachment should be declining, as should the relationship between attachment and other indicators of commitment to party. In our view, neither condition prevails.

While the foregoing points attest to the vitality, if not indeed the centrality, of party among these elite actors, some contrary evidence was also uncovered. And this evidence speaks rather directly to the worries which many observers have about the place of candidate organizations and followers in the nomination and electoral processes. This Achilles heel proved most visible with respect to the motivations which seemed to be the foundation of our respondents' campaign endeavors. The relative importance of party, candidate, and issues altered during this period, with candidate emphasis increasing at the expense of party among most major segments of the Republican party. Thus, the party that has traditionally been more geared toward advocacy of party seemed to be succumbing, especially among its newer recruits, to candidate-centered electoral politics.

On the other hand, the net effect of cross-cutting trends within the Democratic party was at least to arrest the further diffusion of issue and candidate emphasis as the prime motivating factors. Of course, the Democrats began the decade with more emphasis on candidates and issues than did the Republicans, in part because of the Nixon incumbency and the radical rule changes set in motion after the 1968 Democratic convention. In a sense the Republicans have been catching up on candidate and issue emphasis, encouraged by the phenomenally attractive candidacies of Reagan and the emergence of "neo-conservatism."

On balance, however, our results run counter to the argument that the significance of parties is declining for those in the midst of presidential politics. Viewed in one light, resurgence or restoration of party might be an apt term. Viewed in another light, reinterpretation of party strength might be more apt, for it is now clear that the parties never disappeared; they merely changed. To be sure, the place of party had apparently reached low ebb among Democrats in the late 1960s and early 1970s. Even those cohorts were much concerned with party and stood light years away from their Republican adversaries. Since then, Democrats have expressed even more concern for party. As for the Republicans, they continue to be a party that values itself as a party. Conjecture is always risky, but it seems at least likely that the attachment to Reaganism can, for those not already committed to party, be transferred into a concern about the party itself. Were this to happen, dealignment would have given way to realignment and a new era of American party politics would have begun.[12]

[12]Warren E. Miller, "Party Identification Re-examined: The Reagan Era," *American Political Science Review* (forthcoming).

APPENDICES

Appendix A
Delegate Attributes

Table A.1

Selected Comparisons of 1972 Delegate Attributes Based on Personal Interviews and Mail Questionnaires (1972)

	Republicans		Democrats	
	Personal Interviews	Mail Questionnaires	Personal Interviews	Mail Questionnaires
Age				
18–30	8%	9%	24%	24%
31–49	50	49	48	47
50+	40	39	27	26
No Answer	2	3	17	3
	100%	100%	100%	100%
Sex				
Male	66%	64%	58%	57%
Female	34	36	42	43
	100%	100%	100%	100%
Ethnic Identification				
White	94%	94%	79%	79%
Nonwhite	6	5	19	20
No Answer	0	0	2	1
	100%	100%	100%	100%

Education				
12 Grades or Less	13%	11%	16%	12%
Some College	28	24	26	23
B.A.	27	20	27	15
Some Graduate School	0	8	0	12
M.A.	8	6	12	13
Ph.D., L.L.B., etc.	23	18	17	18
No Answer	1	13	2	7
	100%	100%	100%	100%
Income				
Under $4,999	2%	1%	5%	4%
$5,000–9,999	3	4	8	10
10,000–14,999	7	11	16	20
15,000–19,999	10	11	18	18
20,000–24,999	15	15	15	13
25,000–29,999	14	10	10	8
30,000–49,999	22	21	13	13
50,000 and Over	22	22	11	10
No Answer, Don't Know	5	5	4	4
	100%	100%	100%	100%
Marital Status				
Single	11%	10%	20%	18%
Married	80	79	75	75
Other	9	11	5	7
	100%	100%	100%	100%

Table A.1 (*continued*)

	Republicans		Democrats	
	Personal Interviews	Mail Questionnaires	Personal Interviews	Mail Questionnaires
Attended Convention Before				
Yes	34%	30%	17%	17%
No	66	66	83	79
No Answer	0	4	0	4
	100%	100%	100%	100%
Method of Selection as Delegate				
Party Primary	29%	29%	36%	40%
State Convention	41	47	30	29
Committee	13	12	15	8
Other	15	10	16	21
No Answer	2	2	3	2
	100%	100%	100%	100%
Candidate Preference at Convention				
Ashbrook	0%	1%		
McCloskey	0	0		
Nixon	98	96		
Other	1	1		
No Answer	1	2		
	100%	100%		

McGovern			50%	56%
Chisholm			3	2
Humphrey			16	13
Kennedy			2	7
Mills			1	0
Wallace			6	4
Jackson			5	5
Muskie			11	9
Other Democrat			3	2
Don't Know, None			0	0
No Answer			3	2
			100%	100%
Unweighted N	(351)	(519)	(985)	(879)

Notes: Because the two instruments contained relatively little overlap in content, it is not possible to make many comparisons on political variables. Columns add to 100% except for rounding error.

259

Appendix B
The 1981 Survey

The fundamental prerequisite for a mail questionnaire study is to have correct names and addresses for the potential respondents. When an up-to-date list is available, meeting this prerequisite is rather simple, which proved to be very much the case with the delegates to the 1980 conventions inasmuch as lists that were less than a year old were available from the two parties. Obtaining current addresses for the 1976 and 1972 delegates proved to be much more problematic. Our efforts included sending postcards to the last known addresses, using the directory assistance services of the telephone system, and contacting state party organizations for lists of party activists and officials.

As a result of the varying levels of difficulty in establishing correct addresses, the delegates were divided into three groups: (a) 8,460 individuals who were identified and presumably correctly located very early in our search; (b) 1,689 delegates who required considerably more investigation before accuracy was assumed; and (c) 1,817 individuals whose locations were by no means verified. Rather than wait until as much verification as possible had been accomplished, it was decided to stage the initial mailing according to the order of address certainty. Additional mailings were also made in an effort to increase the response rate beyond that registered by the first wave of mailing. As a consequence of these twin factors of different groups and multiple mailings, the pattern of questionnaire distribution is rather complex, but can be summarized as follows:

	Wave 1	Wave 2	Wave 3
Group A	January 29–February 5	March 14	April 17
Group B	March 5	April 13	None
Group C	April 27	June 10	None

The staggered distribution meant that a small number of delegates received their initial mailing after some of the other delegates (mainly in the large Group A) had received their second or third mailing. Although this was not a desirable situation, it had two saving graces. First, no monumental political events occurred that would have affected the later respondents in a way that would have made their responses different from those of earlier-reached delegates. This argument applies as well, of course, to those delegates who responded to a follow-up questionnaire rather than the original one. Second, the later-contacted delegates did differ in some ways from those more easily reached. Thus, the aim of representativeness was furthered even though simultaneity of questionnaire distribution was not achieved.

As is usually the case, the biggest share of respondents came as a consequence of the initial mailing. But the subsequent ones also yielded substantial numbers and proved to be well worth the effort. Shown below are the contributions that each wave made to the total for each party cohort and to the two parties combined. These numbers include respondents who were members of multiple cohorts; thus, the sum of the cohort Ns (6,233) is larger than the actual number of respondents (5,453).

	Wave 1	Wave 2	Wave 3	N
1972 Democrats	76%	19%	5%	(879)
1976 Democrats	79	17	4	(1,082)
1980 Democrats	74	18	8	(1,643)
1972 Republicans	72	22	6	(519)
1976 Republicans	81	14	4	(985)
1980 Republicans	68	22	10	(1,126)
All Delegates	75	18	6	(5,453)

Note: Row percentages total to 100 except for rounding errors. Wave information is absent for 24 delegates. A recalculation of these figures based on the allocation of the multiple convention delegates to only one convention disturbs the figures very little.

Table B.1

Selected Comparisons of Delegate Attributes from Three Cohorts as of 1980

	Republicans			Democrats		
	1972	1976	1980	1972	1976	1980
Age						
18–30	3%	3%	5%	5%	7%	12%
31–49	21	31	37	36	43	51
50+	74	63	55	56	46	35
No Answer	3	3	3	2	4	3
	100%	100%	100%	100%	100%	100%
Sex						
Male	61%	65%	68%	55%	60%	47%
Female	39	34	31	44	38	52
No Answer	0	1	1	1	2	1
	100%	100%	100%	100%	100%	100%
Ethnic Identification						
White	93%	95%	93%	83%	85%	82%
Nonwhite	4	3	4	12	11	15
No Answer	3	2	3	5	4	3
	100%	100%	100%	100%	100%	100%
Education						
12 Grades or Less	7%	10%	9%	10%	9%	11%
Some College	27	25	26	17	18	22
B.A.	19	23	22	14	13	15

Some Graduate School	12	10	14	12	13	13
M.A.	9	8	8	17	17	19
Ph.D., L.L.B., etc.	24	22	19	27	26	20
No Answer	3	2	2	4	4	2
	100%	100%	100%	100%	100%	100%
Income						
Under $15,000	2%	2%	2%	4%	3%	5%
$15,000–22,499	3	4	4	7	7	7
22,500–29,999	6	7	8	8	9	11
30,000–37,499	8	10	9	9	11	13
37,500–44,999	6	6	9	10	10	10
45,000–52,499	9	9	10	9	10	8
52,500–59,999	5	7	6	6	5	4
60,000–67,499	4	5	5	6	4	5
67,500–74,999	6	4	4	3	2	3
75,000–99,999	8	7	7	6	5	3
100,000 and over	17	14	13	9	10	8
No Answer	28	25	23	24	23	23
	100%	100%	100%	100%	100%	100%
Marital Status						
Single	4%	6%	8%	9%	10%	16%
Married	80	81	82	72	72	68
Other	13	12	9	17	15	14
No Answer	3	1	2	3	3	2
	100%	100%	100%	100%	100%	100%

Table B.1 (*continued*)

	Republicans			Democrats		
	1972	1976	1980	1972	1976	1980
Attended Convention Before						
Yes	29%	28%	39%	18%	29%	30%
No	71	72	61	82	71	71
No Answer	0	0	0	0	0	0
	100%	100%	100%	100%	100%	100%
Method of Selection as Delegate						
Party Primary	26%	35%	36%	40%	39%	21%
State Convention	61	56	54	53	49	64
Meeting of Delegates	2	2	3	5	5	5
Committee	9	7	7	2	4	3
Add on Delegates	Inap	Inap	Inap	Inap	0	6
No Answer	2	1	1	1	3	1
	100%	100%	100%	100%	100%	100%
Unweighted N	(519)	(985)	(1,126)	(879)	(1,082)	(1,643)

Notes: Attributes are as reported in the 1981 data collection. Columns add to 100% except for rounding error.

Comparisons reveal high similarity between our results and those obtained in other studies. The same is true for the 1972 delegates as of the original data collection in 1972. Even if we allow for some slippage due to the time lapse between their convention year and our data collection time for them, that conclusion also applies to the 1976 delegates. For comparisons, see Warren J. Mitofsky and Martin Plissner, "The Making of the Delegates: 1968–1980," *Public Opinion* 3 (October–November 1980): 37–43.

Appendix C
Comparison of Panel and Nonpanel Respondents

Table C.1

Comparison of Panel and Nonpanel Respondents from the 1972 Survey: Demographic Characteristics

	Democrats		Republicans	
	Panel	Nonpanel	Panel	Nonpanel
Sex				
Male	56%	57%	62%	66%
Female	44	43	38	34
	100%	100%	100%	100%
Race				
White	90%	79%	97%	91%
Nonwhite	10	21	3	9
	100%	100%	100%	100%
Age				
18–30	21%	28%	8%	10%
31–40	24	23	18	20
41–50	29	25	39	30
51–60	20	16	22	22
over 61	7	8	14	18
	100%	100%	100%	100%
Education				
12 years or Less	12%	16%	11%	16%
Some College	25	26	29	27
College Graduate	16	16	23	19
Higher Degrees	47	41	38	38
	100%	100%	100%	100%
Income				
Under $15,000	31%	37%	16%	17%
$15,000–19,999	20	17	13	10
20,000–29,999	23	22	26	28
30,000–49,999	15	12	23	21
Over $50,000	11	11	22	24
	100%	100%	100%	100%
Maximum unweighted N	(775)	(1,339)	(458)	(497)

Note: Missing data have been excluded from the calculation base here, as in Tables C.2–C.4. Columns add to 100% except for rounding error.

Table C.2

Comparison of Panel and Nonpanel Respondents from the 1972 Survey: Career Characteristics

	Democrats		Republicans	
	Panel	Nonpanel	Panel	Nonpanel
Attended Previous Convention				
No	82%	77%	69%	63%
Yes	18	23	31	37
	100%	100%	100%	100%
Party Positions Held				
None	24%	34%	7%	10%
Local	17	15	5	7
County-District	29	19	28	19
State-National	29	32	60	64
	100%	100%	100%	100%
Public Positions Held				
None	72%	74%	65%	62%
Local	15	9	14	13
County-District	3	6	8	10
State-National	9	12	14	14
	100%	100%	100%	100%
Political Ambitiousness				
Low 0	10%	14%	25%	19%
1	13	10	18	21
2	15	16	12	16
3	32	32	25	22
4	17	19	12	15
High 5	12	9	8	8
	100%	100%	100%	100%
Affiliation Need				
Low 0	20%	22%	16%	18%
1	34	36	33	39
2	32	28	24	26
3	10	11	23	12
High 4	5	4	5	4
	100%	100%	100%	100%
Achievement Need				
Low 0	2%	1%	1%	1%
1	10	9	5	5
2	26	26	18	16
3	35	34	41	33
High 4	27	30	34	45
	100%	100%	100%	100%
Maximum unweighted N	(775)	(1,339)	(458)	(497)

Note: Columns add to 100% except for rounding error.

Table C.3

Comparison of Panel and Nonpanel Respondents from the 1972 Survey: Political Attitudes

	Democrats		Republicans	
	Panel	Nonpanel	Panel	Nonpanel
Issues				
Curing Inflation	2.1	2.0	3.0	3.0
School Busing	3.1	3.0	6.1	6.1
Fighting Crime	2.2	2.3	4.7	4.6
Aid to Southeast Asia	2.5	2.4	5.2	5.2
Group Ratings				
Conservatives	28	29	67	66
Liberals	73	72	29	30
Union Leaders	55	57	35	34
Business Interests	37	38	62	62
Democrats	80	80	28	30
Republicans	24	25	84	83
Ideological Self-Classification				
Radical (1) to Reactionary (7)	2.7	2.7	4.6	4.6
Maximum unweighted N	(775)	(1,339)	(458)	(497)

Notes: The seven-point issues scales run from 1 (liberal) to 7 (conservative).

The thermometer ratings run from 0° to 100°; higher scores mean more favorable ratings.

Table C.4

**Comparison of Panel and Nonpanel Respondents from the 1972
Survey: Incentives for Involvement in Politics**

	Democrats		Republicans	
	Panel	Nonpanel	Panel	Nonpanel
Policy-Oriented				
To Support Policies	90	90	79	82
Elect Particular Candidates	97	97	94	96
Partisanship				
Strongly Attached to Party	59	57	90	89
Politics a Way of Life	72	72	80	77
Civic Responsibility	74	75	91	86
Social				
Friends and Family Active	26	29	33	37
Enjoy Social Contacts	57	57	68	68
Fun and Excitement	55	53	64	62
Personal Career				
Make Contacts	9	12	10	14
Political Career	33	37	32	37
Close to Important People	39	48	47	50
Visibility and Recognition	28	32	36	36
Maximum unweighted N	(775)	(1,339)	(458)	(497)

Note: Entries are the proportion who responded "extremely important" or "quite
important."

Appendix D
Patterns of Candidate Preference

Table D.1

Republican Patterns of Candidate Preference, by Cohort, 1976–1980

Preference Patterns	Preference		1972 Cohort	1976 Cohort	1980 Cohort	Total	N (weighted)
	1976	1980					
1. Consistent Moderate	Ford	Moderate	35%	27%	17%	26%	(386)
2. New Moderate	None	Moderate	1		5	2	(32)
3. Former Ford	Ford	None	8	7	1	6	(81)
4. Reagan Moderate	Reagan	Moderate	2	3	1	2	(33)
5. Former Reagan	Reagan	None	2	9	1	4	(54)
6. Ford-Reagan	Ford	Reagan	13	9	15	13	(184)
7. New Reagan	None	Reagan	1		10	4	(56)
8. Consistent Reagan	Reagan	Reagan	22	44	49	39	(571)
9. Former Nixon	None	None	16	0	0	5	(76)
			100%	100%	100%	100%	(1,473)
Unweighted N			(519)	(848)	(852)		

Note: Scores of less than one half of 1% are not reported.

Table D.2

Democratic Patterns of Candidate Preference, by Cohort, 1972–1980

Preference Patterns	Preference			1972 Cohort	1976 Cohort	1980 Cohort	Total	N (weighted)
	1972	1976	1980					
1 Consistent Liberal	Liberal	Liberal	Liberal	16%	12%	10%	12%	(295)
2 Liberal to Carter in 1980	Liberal	Liberal	Carter	6	5	3	5	(114)
3 Alienated Liberal	Liberal	X	None	17	4	1	7	(175)
4 Predominantly Liberal	Liberal	X	Liberal	12	7	12	10	(242)
5 Liberal to Carter in 1976	Liberal	Carter	Carter	6	10	7	8	(181)
6 Recent Liberal	None	X	Liberal	1	2	8	4	(87)
7 Traditional to Liberal	Traditional	X	Liberal	11	13	11	12	(273)
8 Traditional to Carter in 1980	Traditional	Traditional	Carter	11	11	12	11	(259)
9 Carter Only	None	X	Carter		4	14	6	(144)
10 Traditional to Carter in 1976	Traditional	Carter	Carter	6	20	18	15	(351)
11 Alienated Traditional	Traditional	X	None	12	10	3	8	(184)
12 Other				2	2	1	1	(34)
				100%	100%	100%	100%	(2,339)
Unweighted N				(879)	(937)	(1,387)		

Notes: X represents "Other" or None for Waivering Liberal, Liberal or None for Alienated Liberal and Recent Liberal; Traditional or Liberal for Traditional to Liberal, Traditional or None for Alienated Traditional, and "Not Carter" for Carter Only group. Scores of less than one half of 1% are not reported.

"Other" includes all other combinations as well as conservative preferences. As noted in Appendix A, delegates who supported conservative candidates are underrepresented in our study.

Appendix E
Reasons for Political Involvement

Table E.1

Incentives for Involvement in Politics by Party Cohort as of 1980

	Democratic Cohorts			Republican Cohorts		
	1972	1976	1980	1972	1976	1980
Policy Oriented						
To Support Policies	81	79	82	71	81	82
Elect Particular Candidates	97	97	95	95	96	96
Partisanship						
Strongly Attached to Party	68	67	74	80	81	80
Politics a Way of Life	76	81	84	73	78	77
Civic Responsibility	69	72	78	79	78	80
Social						
Friends and Family Active	36	37	41	38	33	30
Enjoy Social Contacts	62	64	72	66	65	67
Fun and Excitement	56	59	67	60	60	63
Personal Career						
Make Contacts	10	13	18	7	7	8
Political Career	25	31	43	23	27	33
Close to Important People	35	39	47	39	38	41
Visibility and Recognition	27	30	38	27	27	29
Maximum unweighted N	(879)	(937)	(1,387)	(519)	(848)	(852)

Notes: The twelve responses were offered for the following question: We are interested in people's reasons for being involved in politics. How important is each of the following reasons for your own participation in politics?

Entries are the proportion who responded "extremely important" or "quite important."

Proportions who responded "extremely important to elect particular candidates" are 61, 57, and 60% for the Democrats and 54, 61, and 63% for the Republicans.

Appendix F
Index Construction

In chapters 5–10 we use a number of summary indices that are based on the additive scoring of constituent items composing the indices. The basic purposes of these indices are to make the data more manageable, to improve the reliability of the indicators, and to uncover and portray the dimensions underlying the concepts that we are dealing with. Our procedure for constructing these indices rested on a heuristic, exploratory utilization of factor analysis.[1] Sets of items were first subjected to a principal components analysis and then the axes were rotated orthogonally (varimax method) so that the resultant factors were constrained to be unrelated to each other. The items loading heavily (usually .45 or higher) on a given factor were used in the construction of the corresponding index. However, the factor loadings themselves were not used. Rather, simple additive indices were formed such that each item had equal weight in the index construction. The controlling logic here is that such cumulative indices have a more straightforward interpretation than do summary indices based on factor loadings and that there is great similarity between a well-grounded cumulative index and its companion factor scale that both utilize the same constituent items.[2]

A classic problem in index construction, to which factor-derived and inspired measures are no exception, is that of possible dissimilarity across distinct populations (and samples) or even sub-populations within a given population.[3] With two parties and three cohorts the present study has at least six identifiable subpopulations that might conceivably have quite different structuring in the dimensions that we are trying to capture with our summary measures. Parallel factor analyses were carried out on each of the six party cohorts, on all Republicans, on all Democrats, and on all delegates combined, using weighted and unweighted data. It

---

[1] See Jae-On Kim and Charles W. Mueller, *Introduction to Factor Analysis* (Beverly Hills, CA: Sage, 1978), for a lucid discussion of basic factor analysis.

[2] For an argument along these lines, see Douglas A. Hibbs, Jr., *Mass Political Violence* (New York: Wiley, 1973), pp. 7–17.

[3] A discussion of the problem and an example of structural similarity among a number of disparate political groups, including political party leaders, is presented in Sidney Verba and Gary R. Owen, *Equality in America* (Cambridge, MA: Harvard University Press, 1985), Appendix C.

would be misleading to say that the same structuring prevailed regardless of which population was being examined. In one instance, that dealing with the relative importance of party and issues in nomination politics (chapter 6), the interparty differences were sufficiently strong to warrant indices based on somewhat different constituent items across the two parties. There were other instances where a purist approach, based only on the results of the factor analytic solutions, would have occasionally led to different ingredients for the indices within each party. This was most notably the case for the left-right issue index, first presented in chapter 7. However, the aesthetic desirability of matching indices across the parties coupled with the analytic utility of the resulting single index (as well as the argument to be made based on the solutions derived from combing the two parties) persuaded us to use the same component items for all of the indices which tapped what we have called elements of political culture or ideology.

Table F.1

Factor Loadings (Varimax) of Candidate Evaluations Used in Constructing the Additive Candidate Index

Candidates	Factor 1 (Democrat- Republican)	Factor 2 (Third Party or Renegade)
Reagan	−.88	.26
Bush	−.85	−.08
Mondale	.81	−.31
Ford	−.80	−.23
Nixon	−.79	.16
Carter	.74	−.13
Ted Kennedy	.69	−.49
McGovern	.67	−.56
Lucey	.13	−.82
Anderson	−.05	−.87

Notes: Factor 1 explains 49% of the total variance in the results and Factor 2 explains 22%.

Boxed items were used to build the corresponding additive indices. Signs refer to the factor analytic results rather than the final scoring.

Table F.2

Factor Loadings (Varimax) of Group Evaluations Used in Constructing Three Additive Indices

Groups	Factor 1 (New Left)	Factor 2 (Traditional)	Factor 3 (Moral)
Blacks	−.78	.22	.02
Environmentalists	−.76	.32	.21
Gay Rights	−.73	.14	.41
Women's Liberation Movement	−.70	.30	.43
Antinuclear	−.70	.36	.21
Liberals	−.67	.57	.27
Republicans	.28	−.86	−.19
Democrats	−.38	.79	.08
Conservatives	.41	−.67	−.43
Business Interests	.14	−.66	.30
Union Leaders	−.56	.60	−.01
Pro-Life	.15	−.12	−.90
Moral Majority	.29	−.47	−.66

Notes: Factor 1 explains 31% of the total variance in the results, Factor 2 explains 27%, and Factor 3 explains 16%.

Boxed items were used to build the corresponding additive indices. Signs refer to the factor analytic results rather than the final index scoring.

Table F.3

Factor Loadings (Varimax) of Issue Positions Used in Constructing the Additive Liberal-Conservative Issue Index

Issues	Factor (Liberal-Conservative)
Busing to Achieve Integration	−.85
Opposition to ERA	.80
Support Strong Environmental Program	−.77
Opposed to Detente with Russians	.75
Emphasize Unemployment over Inflation	−.73
Proabortion	−.52
Decrease Defense Spending	−.06

Notes: This factor explains 48% of the total variance in the results and was the only factor meeting Kaiser's criterion for factor retention.

Boxed items were used to build additive indices. Signs refer to the factor analytic results rather than the final index scoring.

Table F.4

Factor Loadings (Varimax) of Items Used in Constructing
Indices on Importance of Party and Policy
for Convention Decision-Making

	Democrats	
	Factor 1 (Party)	Factor 2 (Policy)
Reward Party Service	.75	−.06
Minimize Role of Party	−.68	.14
Minimize Intraparty Strife	.57	.08
Stand Firm on Issues	−.54	.37
Select Committed Candidate	−.01	.79
Broaden Party Participation	.02	.74
Play Down Issues to Win	.30	−.54

	Republicans		
	Factor 1 (Policy)	Factor 2 (Party)	Factor 3 (Party)
Play Down Issues to Win	.75	.06	.13
Stand Firm on Issues	−.67	.24	−.06
Select Committed Candidate	−.66	.02	.13
Minimize Role of Party	−.11	.80	.20
Reward Party Service	.01	−.77	.24
Broaden Party Participation	−.15	.09	.79
Minimize Intraparty Strife	.37	−.26	.54

Notes: Factor 1 (Democrats) explains 25% of the total variance and Factor 2 explains 23%.

Boxed items were used to build the corresponding additive indices. Signs refer to the factor analytic results rather than the final index scoring.

Factor 1 (Republicans) explains 23% of the total variance, Factor 2 explains 20%, and Factor 3 explains 16%. For reasons discussed in chapter 5, items from Factors 2 and 3 were combined in the additive party index for Republicans.

Index

abortion issue, 142, 163
Abramowitz, Alan I., 91n, 150n, 164n
Achen, Christopher, 199n
activism, voluntary, 8
age groups, campaign elite and differences in, 73–74
allocative politics, 165, 172
Almond, Gabriel, 130n
amateur-professional differences, 90
amateurs, 88
analysis design of study, 29–33
Anderson, John, 11, 41, 168
Asher, Herbert, 194n
attitudes, dimensional organization of, 100–103
Auspity, Josiah L., 69n

Baker, Howard, 41
Banfield, Edward C., 21n
Bayh, Birch, 54
Beck, Paul Allen, 193n, 194n
Bibby, John F., 14n, 68n, 155n, 251n
Blacks: attitudes toward, 142, 166, 167; as campaign elite, 72, 73; representation of, 68
Blumenthal, Sidney, 69n

Bositis, David, 172n, 182n, 198n
Brady, David, 165n
Brady, Henry E., 150n
Brown, Barbara Leavitt, 172n, 182n, 198n, 207n
Brown, Jerry, 54
Brown, Jesse C., 207n
Burnham, W. D., 13n, 164n
Burns, James MacGregor, 245, 245n
Bush, George, 11, 40–41, 121
business interests, 147, 148, 167

Caesar, James, 13n
campaign activity, 114–116; Democratic, 121–128; Republican, 116–121
campaign elites: contribution of cohorts to, 34–38; defined, 21–22, 30; delegate status of, 34; elite character of, 75; interparty conflict among, 183; nonwhites as, 72, 73; party base and, 242; party commitment among, 79–85; as political elite, 75–78; presidential candidates and circulation of, 19, 27–29; representation of women among,

277